T0270662

THE ROAD TO TICONDEROGA

ALSO BY MICHAEL G. LARAMIE

*King William's War: The First Contest for
North America, 1689–1697*

*Queen Anne's War: The Second Contest for
North America, 1702–1713*

*By Wind and Iron: Naval Campaigns in the
Champlain Valley, 1665–1815*

*Gunboats, Muskets, and Torpedoes: Coastal
North Carolina, 1861–1865*

*Gunboats, Muskets, and Torpedoes: Coastal
South Carolina, 1861–1865*

*The European Invasion of North America: Colonial Conflicts
Along the Hudson-Champlain Corridor, 1609–1760*

*Colonial Forts of the Champlain and Hudson Valleys:
Sentinels of Wood and Stone*

MICHAEL G. LARAMIE

THE ROAD
TO
TICONDEROGA

THE CAMPAIGN OF 1758
IN THE
CHAMPLAIN VALLEY

WESTHOLME
Yardley

Westholme Publishing, LLC
904 Edgewood Road
Yardley, Pennsylvania 19067
Visit our Web site at www.westholmepublishing.com

ISBN: 978-1-59416-407-1

Also available as an eBook.

Printed in the United States of America.

*To the Pell Family and those dedicated
to the preservation of Fort Ticonderoga*

CONTENTS

Appendices

Illustrations

PREFACE

W<small>ITH THE EXCEPTION OF THE</small> B<small>ATTLE OF</small> L<small>ONG</small> I<small>SLAND IN</small> 1776, <small>THE</small> Battle of Ticonderoga was the largest engagement in North America until the Civil War began redefining the scope and size of military warfare. The battle itself is of interest for other reasons. Foremost, it is a tale of an unexpected victory and a gamble against the odds that succeeds. Such battles, regardless of the period, are always of interest by pointing out that the impossible is often just an opinion. Ticonderoga certainly captures this element, but it also points to a number of others, such as the power of a dynamic and charismatic leader and the chaos that can ensue when there is no one to take his place, the art of calculated risk, and in particular, the peril in underestimating the ability of your own troops while overestimating the enemy's. It speaks to the fog of war, misinterpreted orders, indecision, and how a series of small mistakes can cascade into a catastrophe under weak leadership or be exploited by a strong one.

However, there is another matter of just as much interest. The Battle of Ticonderoga was one of the most widely recorded engagements of the French and Indian War, particularly among the colonial contingents. These provincial troops, which included six future American generals as well as numerous future officers and soldiers, watched as the powerful British Army was defeated by a vastly outnumbered French force. Such memories do not fade quickly, and as if by fate, the first battle of the American Revolution, Bunker Hill, proved quite similar to Ticonderoga. Stranger still, the American general in command, Israel Putnam, was also at Ticonderoga. So too was General John Stark, who as a colonel of a New Hampshire regiment would play an instrumental part in the battle that day. Stark's old nemesis, Captain James Abercrombie, would find himself at the head of a British regiment and once again involved in another foolish decision from a commander, General Thomas Gage, who would play a questionable role at the Battle of Ticonderoga.

Beyond the entwined fates of many of the British and American participants, as well as the odd tale of Major Duncan Campbell, the story also speaks to the success of the Marquis de Montcalm and his white-coated French regulars. Montcalm was a seasoned field commander who was able to navigate a path of calculated risks that would ultimately place the enemy in just the position he desired. While it is true that the marquis would be aided in this by his opponent's mistakes, it is not a question of whether or not Montcalm was fortunate but how he handled the contingencies and how he was prepared to capitalize when the opportunity presented itself.

There is also the question of how both sides handled the outcome of the campaign. As the deficiencies in the conduct of the operation came to light the British response was somewhat predictable, leading to General James Abercromby's replacement.*The French response to the victory was not as expected, and in fact was so corrosive that they might well have been better served to have simply abandoned both Fort Carillon and Fort St. Frederic and entrenched farther north. The polarization between Governor Vaudreuil and Montcalm over a matter that could have been turned into a unifying event, and the arguments that followed between their two camps, were perhaps personally satisfying to the participants, but the division that grew out of these efforts further weakened an already weak colony. While this rivalry would be calmed, it would resurface and play an important part in the siege of Quebec and the Battle of the Plains of Abraham the following year.

Lastly, this story is also the one that first interested me in the French and Indian War. Many years ago, in late-seventies Waitsfield, Vermont, on a summer day too hot to play baseball I went into the old Joslin Memorial

---

*General James Abercromby's last name is also spelled "Abercrombie" in primary sources, but in order to disambiguate Captain James Abercrombie from General James Abercrombie, I use Abercromby for the latter in this book.

Library near the center of town, the latter of which consisted of nothing more than a cluster of buildings and a covered bridge that spanned the Madd River. I delighted in the cooler atmosphere, and then not wanting to give the impression that I had only come in to get out of the heat, which was true, I began to scan the bookshelves. My eye came to rest on *The Battle for North America* by John Trebbel, which I soon discovered was actually from the works of Francis Parkman. I quickly took to the subject, believing that I had discovered this lost tale, this seldom-discussed thread in history that predated the birth of the country. Surely this was a foundational topic that people should know about, I reflected.

Now, over forty-five years later, with numerous articles on the subject, books on the naval history of the Champlain Valley (*By Wind and Iron*, *King William's War*, and *Queen Anne's War*), and the completion of the draft of *King George's War* before me, I returned to the topic which inspired the start of this journey. I hope you enjoy it.

INTRODUCTION

T HE ANCIENT CASTLE OF INVERAWE STANDS ON AN ELEVATION ALONG
the west bank of the River Awe in the highlands of Scotland. This
stone manor belonged to the Clan Dhonnachie Campbells. From the
establishment of the initial grant in 1330 by David II of Scotland, a
nearly unbroken line of inheritance from father to son led to Captain
Duncan Campbell of the 43rd Highland Regiment. Duncan had in-
herited the castle at the age of twenty-eight when his father died in
1730. The new Laird of Inverawe's affairs seemed of the normal sort
until 1745. The return of Prince Charles Stuart was quickly drawing
lines across the western highlands. The Campbells had sided with the
government, and Duncan was no different, raising a company for the
43rd Highlanders. One of three companies raised, it did not immediately join the regiment but remained in the highlands. One of these
companies, under Sir Patrick Murray, was overrun and captured at the
Battle of Prestonpans later in the year, but Campbell's company seems
to have avoided any major trouble, spending most of the year scouting
in the highlands, oftentimes among the lands of his former friends. It
was on one of these forays that this strange tale begins.[1]

According to one rendition of the story:

Returning from the discharge of this unpleasant duty, [Duncan] was separated from his followers, and, night falling rapidly, he lost his way among the many mountain passes; when, turning sharply into a ravine, he was startled to find himself confronted by a stalwart Highlander, with black hair and piercing eyes. Each grasped his sword, when the stranger accosted him and demanded his errand. Duncan replied that he had lost his way and required a guide: a voice from behind said, "He is alone, else we would not have suffered him to pass." Whereupon the stranger escorted Duncan to an unknown camp in the recesses of the mountains, gave him food to eat, and shared his couch with him. The stranger refused to reveal his name, but it was apparent that he knew who Duncan was and his errand in that part of the Highlands. When day broke the Highlander escorted his guest past the sentinels and set him on the road toward his own home. Inverawe expressed his gratitude in fitting terms, and vowed he would repay the kindness shown him if the opportunity ever afforded. In time he came to know that his benefactor was none other than Donald Campbell, a member of the same clan as that to which he himself belonged. This adventure, which is strikingly similar to that of Fitz James and Rhoderic Dhu, had become well-nigh forgotten, and years afterward, when Inverawe asked for and obtained leave of absence from his military duties, one night, while sitting alone in his castle, he was startled from his reverie by the sound of hasty foot-steps at his door, accompanied by loud and hurried rappings. Answering the summons, he was surprised to find at his door Stewart of Appin, a man for whom he had but little love. In hurried words Stewart told his host that in a feud he had slain a man: that he was pursued: his life was now in danger: he besought Campbell to give him sanctuary, and asked an oath of secrecy. His distress, the extremity of his need and evident terror prevailed. Duncan Campbell gave the required oath and received Stewart of Appin into his castle, where he was secreted in an underground room. Scarcely had Campbell returned from this errand, when a second alarm, louder and more imperative than the first, called him again to his door, where he was confronted by a band of his own clansmen, who told him that at the stepping-stones in the ford of the Deergan his kinsman—Donald Campbell—had been slain by Stewart of Appin: not in open, manly fight, but treacherously and by a blow in the back: the assassin had made his escape; the hue and cry raised and the murderer followed through difficult and obscure passes in the direction of Inverawe. Campbell, sick at heart at the thought of concealing the murderer of one of his own clan who had thus been foully slain, and to whose chivalric generosity he owed his life, yet mindful of the obligations of his oath, gave an evasive answer to the pursuing party and sent them away. That night, after he had retired to his chamber, which is still called the "Ghost Chamber" at Inverawe, in the "dread, vast and middle of the night," he was awakened by a light "like that which never shone on land or sea." It filled the room and he distinctly saw the manly form of Donald Campbell of Lorn—his murdered clansman, his jet-black hair disheveled, his clothing disarranged and soiled with blood. He instantly recognized the apparition as that of his former benefactor. The consciousness that beneath his own roof he now gave shelter to the cowardly murderer filled his soul with remorse and regret. The silence was broken by the ghostly visitor, who said:

"Inverawe, Inverawe; blood has been shed; shield not the murderer" After which the vision disappeared.

When morning broke the memory of the vision of the man and of the voice troubled the mind of Duncan Campbell. He sought Stewart of Appin in his hiding-place, and plainly told him that, while, by reason of his oath, he would not betray him, yet he could no longer shelter him. Stewart reminded him of his promise, and at his entreaty Duncan led him to a secure hiding-place in the solitary mountain passes of Ben Cruachen. But the recollection of the horrors of that night haunted him through his waking hours, and the second night, as he sat before his fire reading, as was his custom before retiring, his hound, his sole companion, trembling in every limb, began to howl in that low, dismal tone which indicates the presence of the sense of terror in the brute creation. Raising his eyes from his book, he again saw the ghostly form of Donald Campbell of Lorn standing before him, radiant in the sheen of the same weird light. There was the same unearthly presence; the black hair, the piercing eyes, the same disheveled dress, the same ghastly blood-stain; the hands were outstretched as if asking for aid. The hound's broken whimpering sank almost into silence, and again the apparition spoke:

"Inverawe, Inverawe; blood has been shed; blood must atone for blood; shield not the murderer." And in a moment the vision, faded in the air and was gone. All that night the sense of horror of the supernatural presence filled the soul of Duncan Campbell, and the recollection of the spoken words lingered long in his memory. In the morning he sought the spot in the mountain wilderness where he had left the murderer, but he was gone. All the second day the memories of the past, the vision, the voice, and the gesture of the apparition harassed his soul, and the third night, weary with watching, he sought his couch, but, as the midnight hour approached, he was again awakened by that undefinable feeling which accompanies the consciousness of the presence of an invisible person. And the third time he saw the vision accompanied with all of the customary demonstrations, but this time the voice was not one of warning, nor was the attitude of the apparition that of supplication, but, on the contrary, the tone and appearance were threatening, and the spoken words were: "Inverawe, Inverawe; blood has been shed; blood must atone for blood. We shall meet again at Ticonderoga."[2]

Campbell would continue to serve with the 43rd, which would officially become known as the 42nd Highlanders, or the "Black Watch," when Oglethorpe's 42nd Regiment was disbanded in 1749. Throughout this time the strange name haunted him. He questioned his comrades, some who had been overseas, but all he received were shrugs or more questions. In time, Campbell would rise to the rank of major, and his tale would become something of an open secret within the Black Watch. For some it became a puzzle to be solved. "Ticonderoga?" a new recruit would respond with a lifted brow. "Never heard of it."[3]

THE FRENCH AND INDIAN WAR IN THE HUDSON AND CHAMPLAIN VALLEYS

U NLIKE THE THREE PREVIOUS FRENCH AND INDIAN WARS, WHICH had been imported from Europe, the last French and Indian War would begin in North America and would be exported to Europe in the form of the Seven Years' War. In May 1754 a young Virginia colonel named George Washington, looking to enforce the colony's land claims, clashed with French forces in the Ohio Valley. Washington would come out on the losing end of this campaign, and after surrendering at Fort Necessity, he was sent back over the Allegany Mountains in early July with word that the Ohio belonged to France. The initial British response to this defeat was to send a small force of regulars under the command of General Edward Braddock to capture the French fort at the junction of the Allegany and Monongahela Rivers and secure British rights to the region. This approach, however, was soon altered. Braddock would attack Fort Duquesne in the spring, and after securing this post, he would advance on the disputed Fort St. Frederic on Lake Champlain before moving against Fort Beausejour in Nova Scotia. The plan was approved by the first minister, Thomas Pelham-Holles, the Duke of Newcastle. Newcastle believed that responding in a limited fashion to what both sides viewed as a colonial matter would not rupture the peace in Europe. Just as importantly, he viewed the intervals between the sequential attacks as key, as they would allow time for the negotiated solution he sought.

This approach might have worked were it not for the scope of the retaliatory effort suddenly expanding when the king's son, the Duke of Cumberland, became involved in the operational planning. Cumberland had been approached to convince the king to release the regiments that would accompany Braddock. This Cumberland did, but allied with Newcastle's political enemies he was able to alter the plan to now include an expedition against the French fort at Niagara, the raising of two thousand-man regiments of colonials to assist Braddock, and more importantly, the expansion of Braddock's orders to now include attacking all four targets simultaneously if possible.[1]

Newcastle, who had been politically outmaneuvered, felt the plan went too far and would trigger a response from France, which even if it did not rupture the peace in Europe would certainly complicate matters in North America. When he read advertisements in the London newspapers recruiting officers for the two regiments being raised in America, he worried that France would respond to British efforts in North America, and when news arrived of a naval buildup at Brest in late February and March 1755, he became convinced that it would.

The first minister was correct. The French ministry had concluded that action was required on their part to protect New France. The breakdown of negotiations in London and Braddock's departure for Virginia in January, with its unknown but suspected intentions, placed the French court in a difficult position. Given the threat posed to Canada, it was agreed that reinforcements would have to be sent, even though doing so would certainly aggravate any chance of reaching a peaceful settlement to the American problem. In the end, caution dictated that the worst should be planned for, and as such, preparations were begun in Brest in February to reinforce New France with six regiments of French regulars. Two regiments, those of Artois and Bourgogne, would be sent to reinforce the naval fortress of Louisbourg on Cape Breton Island, while the regiments of La Reine, Languedoc, Guyenne, and Bearn, under the command of General Jean-Armand Dieskau, the Baron de Dieskau, would be sent to Quebec and deployed within the interior.[2]

Accompanying these reinforcements was the new governor-general, Pierre de Rigaud, the Marquis de Vaudreuil. Unlike the troops traveling

Pierre de Rigaud, the Marquis de Vaudreuil, the last Governor of New France. The Canadian-born Vaudreuil is perhaps best known for his disputes with Montcalm, and because of this, has been much maligned over the years eventually becoming the scapegoat for the fall of New France. Such simple judgements however, are far removed from the truth. Vaudreuil's initial conduct of the conflict, despite the criticism of Montcalm, proved successful, but by 1758 this approach required modification. His failure to accept this change, and put aside his personal feelings towards Montcalm in pursuit of his duty, may be said to be his great failing. (*National Archives of Canada*)

with him Vaudreuil was neither new to the colony nor the position of governor-general. Canadian-born, and the son of a former governor, in 1715 Vaudreuil began his career as a captain of a company of the Free Companies of the Marine in Canadian service. He served with the colonial troops in this position and later as major of all Marine troops of Canada for thirteen years. During this time the future governor learned the art of Indian negotiations, visited the various Canadian outposts, and came to understand firsthand the basics of wilderness warfare by serving on several expeditions. However, it was by observing his father, the governor-general of New France at the time, that the younger Vaudreuil came to appreciate the internal problems of the colony and the threat posed to its borders by the English.

Three years after his father's death in 1725, Vaudreuil and his younger brother Rigaud returned to their family's estate in France. In 1733 the Minister of the Marine appointed Vaudreuil to fill the vacant governorship of Trois-Rivières, third in importance to Montreal and Quebec. Vaudreuil performed admirably in this position for seven years before returning to France upon the death of his mother. This return to France happened to coincide with the retirement of Governor Le Moyne of Louisiana. The Minister of the Marine had been actively searching for a replacement when Vaudreuil appeared before the court. Familiar with the former Trois-Rivières governor, the minister wasted no time in appointing him to succeed Le Moyne. Vaudreuil reached New Orleans in May of 1743 and began his ten-year tenure in a post which he considered a stepping stone to his father's former position. His immediate task was to deal with the pressures of a sprawling, undermanned, undersupplied, and continually threatened corner of New France. His former dealings with the tribes of Canada served him well as he successfully guided the colony through King George's War. Passed over for the governor-generalship of New France several times, Vaudreuil was finally rewarded when the new Minister of the Marine recalled him to France in mid-1752 and directed him to replace the Marquis Duquesne, whose health was known to be failing under the pressures of his office.[3]

There were serious military risks involved in sending Vaudreuil, Dieskau, and their troops to Canada. Normally the movement of such a large number of troops would be conducted by transport vessels, but with indications that the British navy might attempt to intercept the convoy, this was deemed unacceptable. First, these transports would require a large escort to ensure their safety, something that the weak French navy was in no position to do. Second, the slow speed of these vessels would risk the entire convoy by giving the English more time to arrange an intercept. To resolve these problems, it was decided to use French warships to transport the troops. To accommodate this additional load, the armament of these ships would have to be drastically reduced, by as many as fifty guns in some cases. This would make them vulnerable if engaged, but it was hoped that their speed and maneuverability would make such an encounter unlikely. Up to fourteen of France's finest warships would be committed to the task, ships that the struggling French navy could hardly afford to lose, but given the circumstances, there seemed little choice but to take the risk.[4]

If Newcastle still held out hope that Braddock did not possess the force required to attack all four French encroachments at once, thereby resetting the plan to the more conservative sequential attacks, he would be disappointed when Braddock met with the principal colonial governors at Alexandria, Virginia, on April 14, 1755. The general's orders were read to the group and his plan of operations discussed. The general had expected upon his arrival that he might have as many as three thousand colonial

British Expeditions in North America, 1755. (*Author*)

troops in addition to his two regular regiments to deal with the French at
Fort Duquesne, Niagara, Crown Point, and in Nova Scotia. Instead, what
he found were two nearly complete thousand-man American regiments, a
two-thousand-man Massachusetts force ready to unite with Colonel
Charles Lawrence's troops in Nova Scotia, and an additional five thousand
colonials currently being assembled for an attack against Fort St. Frederic
at Crown Point.

The surplus of manpower and the powers granted to him presented
Braddock with the opportunity to attack all of the French encroachments
at once. The Nova Scotia campaign, in its final stages, would move forward.
The general would personally lead the attack on Fort Duquesne with the
44th and 48th Regiments, while Governor William Shirley of Massachusetts, appointed Braddock's second in command, staged a similar effort
against Niagara with the two American regiments from the British position
at Oswego. Given that the Crown Point expedition was to be solely spon-
sored by the northern colonies, the general had no objection to it proceeding, nor to the appointment of William Johnson, recently made the
Commissioner of Indian Affairs for the North Department, as its commanding officer. After all, there was little reason for Braddock to object.
The destruction of the French position at Crown Point had been included
in his orders, and if the colonials wanted to do it without diverting either
troops or funds from his efforts, so much the better. The project was even
beneficial as far as he was concerned. For whether or not it succeeded, combined with the other three expeditions it would stretch French resources
to the breaking point. Thus, what had started as a limited response to an
isolated colonial incident in the Ohio Valley was about to become a four-
pronged assault on the limits of New France and the genesis of the last
French and Indian War in North America and the Seven Years' War in Europe.[5]

When it became clear that the French would attempt to reinforce
Canada, the Newcastle ministry was initially torn over what to do. If these
French reinforcements, far more than the two regiments sent with Braddock, were allowed to reach New France the upcoming North America
campaign would be in jeopardy. On the other hand, if efforts were undertaken to intercept these vessels, particularly in European waters, it might
very well provoke a general war. After ruling out a naval blockade of Brest
and an attack on Quebec, it was decided to intercept the French fleet in
American waters. By doing so there was the possibility that the action
might be viewed in the light of a continuing colonial problem, and open

hostilities hopefully avoided. Given France's recent aggressions in North America, this limited effort could then be defended in the courts of Europe as a just and appropriate response.[6]

Militarily, the approach proved less than successful. The French vessels *Alcide* and *Lys* were captured after a brief fight off the Newfoundland coast, but the bulk of the French fleet slipped past the blockade and reached their Canadian destinations in early June. The action netted the English four companies of the Languedoc and La Reine Regiments, as well as a number of key personnel. The empty *Esperance* was also captured on her return voyage after a three-hour fight with four British ships-of-the-line. The public went wild over the news, but for the Newcastle ministry it was a political disaster. The worse possible scenario had occurred. France had been attacked, but the majority of its reinforcements had safely reached Canada. To all involved it appeared that the peace had now been ruptured in the Old World as well as the New. When the news reached Newcastle he wrote to Philip Yorke, the Earl of Hardwicke, "What we have done is either too little or too much." To the First Lord of the Admiralty George Anson, he was more specific, saying, "Voilà the wars begun!"[7]

With the exception of the Nova Scotia expedition, which quickly captured Fort Beausejour, on Chignecto Neck, the British campaign of 1755 proved a disaster. In early July Braddock's force of British regulars and colonials were routed near the banks of the Monongahela, just a few miles short of Fort Duquesne. The entire artillery train had been captured along with Braddock's papers, which contained all the specifics on the year's military operations. The general himself was also to be counted among the fallen. The defeat of Braddock's column left French forces in the Ohio free to shift to the defense of Fort Niagara. This, coupled with severe logistical issues in transporting men and supplies to Lake Ontario, undermined Shirley's Niagara campaign, which in the end accomplished little more than reinforcing the British position at Oswego.[8]

In the Hudson and Champlain Valleys, which would become a centerpiece of the last French and Indian War, success was declared when General William Johnson and an Anglo-Iroquois force of 3,300 defeated a French preemptive strike near the headwaters of Lake George. Informed by prisoners that the bulk of Johnson's army was at Lake George, French General Jean-Armand Dieskau led a detachment of 1,500 regulars, Canadians, and native allies out of Fort St. Frederic, and following the Lake Champlain-Wood Creek waterways, targeted the recently erected Fort Edward in Johnson's rear. Dieskau reasoned that if he could capture and reduce the stronghold, then Johnson, with his supply lines cut, would have no choice but to retreat and abandon any thoughts of attacking Fort St. Frederic.

In this task Dieskau was thwarted, not by the British but by his own troops. As the need to move quickly was paramount, most of the general's troops were Canadians and native allies. Both of these groups balked at the idea of storming a fort, especially one equipped with cannons. With too few regulars in his detachment to attempt the operation, and unable to convince the rest of his forces to attack, a deal was struck. It was agreed that they would march on Johnson's army at Lake George, and upon defeating it, would return to demolish Fort Edward.[9]

In this Dieskau initially proved successful, ambushing and routing a large detachment sent by Johnson to reinforce Fort Edward. The French general, whose motto was "fortune favors the bold," then chased this disorganized force back to Johnson's main camp on the shores of Lake George. With sword in hand Dieskau ordered a charge, hoping to carry the makeshift fortifications while the retreating troops in front of him disrupted the enemy's lines. After a morning of marching and fighting, however, the general's Canadian and Indian troops were not interested in storming anything. Instead, a duel of musketry took hold for the next few hours, with Johnson's men firing from behind their improvised barricade and the French returning fire from the nearby tree line. Eventually, the French had seen enough and withdrew, leaving a thrice-wounded Dieskau behind to become a prisoner.

Although the losses on both sides were roughly equal, given that Johnson had avoided annihilation and held the field at the end of the day, the Battle of Lake George on September 8, 1755, was declared a British victory. Among Johnson's army there was no such feeling. It was clear that the collection of amateurs had been badly rattled by the French attack and had no real intentions of pressing forward to face an even stronger French force at Fort St. Frederic. Thus, after some posturing against the new French post being erected on the Ticonderoga Peninsula, Johnson settled for the construction of Fort William Henry as the fruits of his victory.[10]

Vaudreuil responded to Dieskau's defeat by sending thirty-two-year-old colonial engineer, Michel Chartier, sieur de Lotbiniere, to erect a fort at Ticonderoga. He was to stop at Fort St. Frederic and consult with Colonel Jean Dejeau de Roquemaure, now in command of Dieskau's detachment, and the fort's commandant, the Chevalier Paul-Louis Dazemard de Lusignan, regarding the resources required for the task. Lotbiniere met with the two men on a late September day. The men exchanged greetings, after

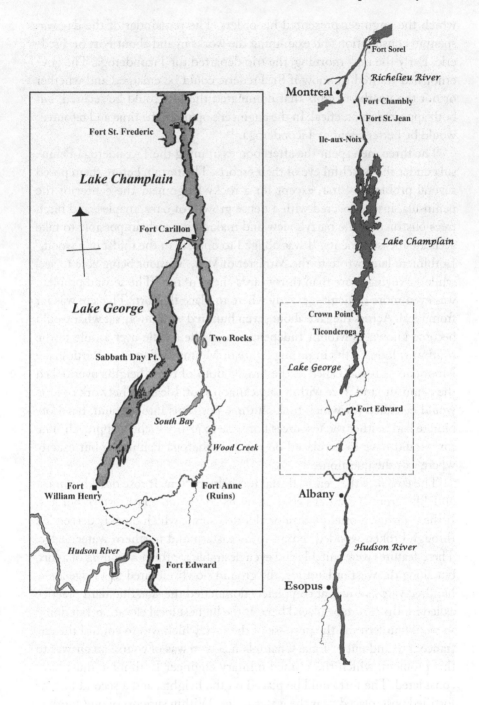

The Champlain Valley and the upper portion of the Hudson Valley. (*Author*)

which the engineer presented his orders. The remainder of the day was spent in consultation and examining the works in and about Fort St. Frederic. Early the next morning, the trio departed for Ticonderoga. The governor had wanted to know if St. Frederic could be enlarged and whether or not the nearby heights that dominated the fort could be secured, but both appeared impractical. In the engineer's opinion, the time and resources would be better spent at Ticonderoga.[11]

The three men spent the afternoon examining the Ticonderoga Peninsula under the watchful eye of their escorts. The terrain before them posed several problems. First, except for a rocky ledge near the center of the peninsula, it was covered with a dense growth of oaks, maples, and birch trees obstructing the party's view and making it nearly impossible to take accurate measurements. "I was obliged to operate in the midst of a wood," Lotbiniere later wrote to the Minister of War, "without being able to see, while surveying more than thirty yards ahead of me." The second problem was even more difficult—exactly where to place the fort? The site was far from ideal. Across the lake about seven hundred yards away sat what would become known as Mount Independence, while a little over a mile to the southwest loomed the imposing figure of Mount Defiance, or Rattlesnake Mountain as it was called at the time.[12] Both of these heights overlooked the peninsula and were within easy cannon shot. Ideally, a network of forts would be called for which took all three positions into account, but Lotbiniere had neither the resources nor time to justify such an approach. The fort would have to be placed on the Ticonderoga Peninsula, but exactly where was the question.

The layout of the peninsula did not help matters. It rose quickly, almost cliff-like, from the water's edge along its south and southeastern borders. It then formed a brief plateau or elevated spine, which quickly descended through broken wooded terrain to its eastern and northern water's edge. These features were suitable and even desirable for the positioning of a fort, but along the west or landside, the ground slowly elevated to a ridge a few hundred yards away that completely dominated the site. Standard practice called for the fort to be placed here, at the highest local elevation, but doing so would undermine the purpose of the fort, which was to control the entrance into and out of Lake Champlain. There was of course an answer to this problem, which the trained military engineer Lotbiniere must have considered. The fort could be placed on the heights, and a second fort, or fortified post, placed near the water's edge. Within support of one another, the pair of strongholds would accomplish both aims and prove stronger

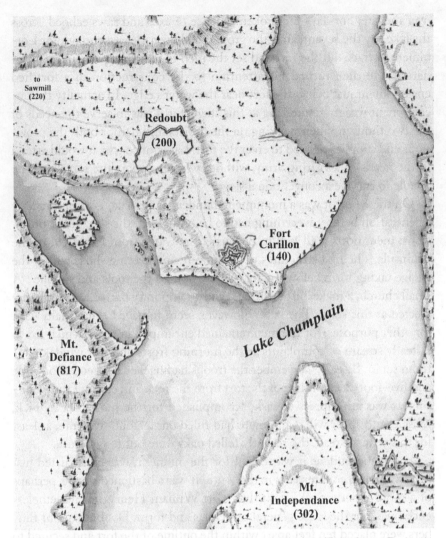

to
Sawmill
(220)

Redoubt

(200)

**Fort
Carillon
(140)**

Mt.
Defiance
(817)

Lake Champlain

**Mt.
Independance
(302)**

A sketch showing the area and elevations (in feet) on and near the Ticonderoga Peninsula.
(*Author*)

than any single fort. But again, he was forced to compromise. The governor
had made it clear that whatever fortifications were decided upon had to go
up this fall, and it would simply take too long to construct a pair of posts.
With some reluctance, the rocky plateau near the water's edge was chosen
as the most suitable site.[13]

On October 14 Roquemaure's army, bolstered by several hundred recently arrived workmen and detachments from Fort St. Frederic, swarmed

over the site. For days the broken cadence of axes and saws echoed across the lake. By the seventeenth the ground had been cleared enough for Lotbiniere to trace out the fort and set the men to work digging out its foundation. He then turned his attention to the construction of a fortified encampment just below the fort near the water's edge. In actuality the encampment was more pressing at this stage, for it was to serve the needs of the two thousand men working on the project and harbor both the provisions and supplies needed to erect the fort. Later, of course, it would attend to the needs of a visiting army, without whose support the fort would be unable to survive a conventional siege.

On the whole it was a monumental undertaking. Like Fort St. Frederic a generation before, everything had to be brought to the site. Tools, provisions, men, horses, all had to be carried by water from Montreal to the peninsula. The first structures to go up were engineering sheds within the village taking form below the fort. These housed the tools and supplies. A small church, a makeshift infirmary, and a temporary barracks or two were erected at this stage. The latter, however, seem to have been initially used for other purposes, for the men remained encamped in tents, which led to a steady stream of complaints as the morning frosts and wet winds of autumn set in. By early November the troops had hacked a fifteen-foot-wide and five-foot-deep outline of the fort from the rock and earth of the peninsula. It was an impressive task, accomplished for the most part by pick, muscle, and sheer will. Lotbiniere had ruled out a stone structure, at least for this year. Instead, the recently felled oaks were put to good use.

Fort Vaudreuil, as it was called for the moment, was constructed just like its English counterparts to the south. It was a bastioned square, perhaps of a more symmetrical layout than Fort William Henry, but nonetheless encompassing the same general principles and form. Double rows of timbers were placed ten feet apart within the outline of the fort and secured to one another at intervals with dovetailed cross members. This hollow box was then filled in with earth, as was the trench at its foundation. By late November the walls had reached seven feet, and a few crude buildings had been added within the compound to serve as barracks and storehouses for the garrison. A number of cannons sent by Vaudreuil had been brought down from Fort St. Fredric and were temporarily mounted along the ramparts and near the fort's gate. To support these works and cover the boat landing, a fortified post, known as Lotbiniere's redoubt, had been raised along the water's edge. At this point it was nothing more than a rude palisade of interlocking logs, but backed by a few small cannons and an alert

Captain Michel Chartier, sieur de Lotbiniere. Born in Quebec, Chartier was commissioned second ensign in the Free Company of the Marines in 1744, and served at the Battle of Grand Pre, Acadia in 1747. Two years later he was promoted to Ensign by Governor Roland-Michel Barrin de La Galissoniere and dispatched on a scientific mission to the upper Great Lakes. The following year Galissoniere obtained an appointment for Chartier in the Royal Engineering Academy. When he returned to Quebec in 1753 Chartier held an engineer's warrant and had been promoted to Lieutenant in the Marines. (*National Archives of Canada*)

garrison it more than served its purpose. This was only the first of several outworks envisioned by Lotbiniere. A palisade about the village was on the list, as was a series of fortified camps along the La Chute River to guard the outlet of Lake George, but time had limited his efforts in the latter area to a few flying camps which were abandoned when the army departed for Montreal on November 28. The architect of Ticonderoga remained until February in hopes of continuing the work with the fort's garrison, but apathy and the weather limited the effort to the completion of the fort's barracks. Realizing that nothing further was to be accomplished, Lotbiniere left for Montreal disheartened, and with the long list of tasks to be completed, but confident that the fort was capable of defending itself.[14]

While the onset of winter and the reluctance of Johnson's force to move on Ticonderoga had allowed Vaudreuil time to erect Fort Vaudreuil, which would soon be renamed Fort Carillon, it was the arrival of Dieskau's replacement, Louis-Joseph de Montcalm-Grozon, the Marquis de Montcalm, along with a significant number of reinforcements in the spring of 1756 that ensured its survival for the next few years.

Montcalm was born into an old and distinguished family on February 28, 1712. He was raised at the family's ancestral estate at Candiac in the typical manner for nobility of the day. His father Louis-Daniel was lieutenant colonel of the Hainaut Regiment and spent long periods away from his son, as did his mother, Marie-Therese, who was pressed to meet the courtly obligations incumbent with her social standing. At the age of six he was placed in the care of a tutor by the name of Dumas. He schooled the young chevalier in Latin, Greek, history, and the science of the day. Dumas frequently expressed misgivings at Louis-Joseph's dedication and feared for his future, but it seemed that the young Montcalm had a much better hold over his abilities than his tutor gave him credit for. And as for his destiny, that was clear. In 1724, at the age of twelve he was commissioned an ensign in his father's regiment. At the time the regiment was stationed near Paris, which allowed Montcalm to expand his education into the realm of spectacles, burgeoning philosophies, and social gatherings of the day, much to the frustration of Dumas, who seemed to have had difficulties in holding his pupil's attention. In May of 1732 his father purchased a captaincy for his son, and with it came greater military responsibilities. Camp life, drill, and duty now began to dominate Louis-Joseph's life, and before long he and his regiment found themselves shifted to the Rhine frontier, where war was brewing over the succession to the Polish crown.

In 1733 after a year of constant alerts and countermanded orders, the French army crossed the Rhine. Not long afterward Montcalm found himself involved in his first major action, the siege and capture of Phillipsbourg, where he distinguished himself and caught the eye of the corps commander, Marshal Charles Fouquet, Duke de Belle-Isle. The conflict itself was short-lived, and by 1735 the Hainaut Regiment found itself stationed in southern France, not far from Candiac. A few months later his father died at Candiac, leaving Louis-Joseph the title of marquis, a considerable estate, and a sizable debt to match. Although its beginnings were auspicious, these were to become some of Montcalm's fondest years. The next year an old friend introduced Louis-Joseph to Angelique-Louise Talon de Boulay, and by October the two were married. Angelique was the descendent of two old and powerful families, which not only alleviated some of the marquis' financial burdens but secured him a number of influential political allies as well. The following years saw Montcalm rise rapidly through the ranks, no doubt as a result of his new family connections. The days, however, were spent mostly at Candiac, where he and his wife tended to their estates and their growing family.

Louis-Joseph, Marquis de Montcalm-Gozon de Saint-Veran. An experienced soldier and product of French military nobility Montcalm spent almost as much time fighting with the governor as he did the English. Against the latter he rolled off an impressive string of victories while his skirmishes with the former eventually divided the defenders of New France and would ultimately play a part in the colony's downfall. (*National Archives of Canada*)

In the early 1740s the political scene of Europe was once again changing. War clouds gathered over Austria, and by 1742 another War of Succession broke out, this time revolving around Austrian claims and Prussian ambitions. Montcalm found himself posted in Frankfurt as aide-de-camp to the General Marquis de la Fare, one of the officers that he had so impressed at Phillipsbourg, and the man who had arranged the introduction to his wife. The French army, under command of Montcalm's old patron Marshal Belle-Isle attempted to hold its position in Germany and Bohemia but, after being defeated by an Anglo-Austrian army at Dettingen, was forced to conduct a disastrous withdrawal to the French border. Even with this turn of events, Belle-Isle, had not forgotten his protégé and his efforts while serving with the rearguard during the retreat. Backed by Belle-Isle's influence, Montcalm was able to purchase the colonelcy of the Auxerrois Regiment, which was destined for the Italian theater. It was here, in Italy, that Montcalm made a name for himself, participating in some of the most grueling campaigns of the war. On May 15, 1746, at the Battle of Piacenza, Montcalm's regiment was shattered by an Austrian cavalry attack. The marquis, thrice wounded, rallied his regiment, only to see it broken by a second charge. As the Austrians reformed, he again rallied his troops, but a third charge swept away what was left of his position leaving the now five-time wounded colonel an Austrian prisoner. Montcalm spent a year in Milan with little hope of repatriation. His wife's and friends' pleas for his exchange fell on deaf ears, that is, until Belle-Isle was appointed commander of the armies of France. One of Belle-Isle's first actions was to secure Montcalm's parole, and after a general prisoner exchange, he promoted the marquis to the rank of brigadier general on Christmas day 1746. Again, Montcalm found himself in Italy, and again disaster awaited, this time at Assiette in July 1747. Belle-Isle's brother, in command of the French army, attempted to storm what he believed was the poorly defended Austrian-Piedmontese position along the heights of Assiette. What he found instead was a hornet's nest of fortifications, man-traps, and prepared positions. The results were predictable. The Chevalier Belle-Isle was cut down while planting the French flag at the summit, and by the end of the day over a quarter of his men lay scattered over the rugged mountainside, including Montcalm, who, after lying severely wounded in a ditch for hours, was carried off the field in a litter.

The wound ended the marquis' campaigns in Italy. He returned home to Candiac and in October of 1748 received the news that the war was over. With the conclusion of hostilities his regiment was incorporated into the Flanders regiment. The move meant that the marquis had lost his position and the sizable investment that came with it. A month later, however, his service to the crown was rewarded with the commission of *mestre-de-camp* and authorization to raise a cavalry regiment, which would bear his name. For the next eight years Montcalm returned to the idyllic earlier days of life on his estate. His time was spent tending to his lands, his regiment, and his family.

This would change with Montcalm's appointment to Canada in March 1756. The marquis' orders were identical to those issued to Dieskau. His authority extended to the discipline and command of the regular army units, while overall authority rested with Governor Vaudreuil. In addition, as it was clear that an official declaration of war between Britain and France was imminent, the king was sending two battalions of the La Sarre and Royal Roussillon regiments and four hundred recruits for the Free Companies of the Marine along with the marquis.[15]

To face the daunting task placed before him, Montcalm was fortunate to have several talented officers on his staff. Accompanying him was his aide and chief of staff, Captain Louis-Antoine Bougainville. Montcalm was instantly pleased with Bougainville. "A very pleasant, bright young fel-

Louis-Antoine Bougainville, later Admiral and Count de Bougainville. Bougainville would participate in several major actions in North America, rising to the rank of Colonel and being placed in command of Île aux Noix the last French stronghold in the Champlain Valley. This portrait shows Bougainville has he appeared during the American Revolution while in command of the French man-o-war *Auguste* at the siege of Yorktown. (*Library of Congress*)

low," he wrote his wife a few days later.[16] The last comment was something of an understatement. The twenty-six-year-old had already published a two-volume treatise on integral calculus, which earned him a membership in the Academie des Sciences and the patronage of Count D'Argenson. In addition to this, he had served as secretary to Marechal Mirepoix, who had been named special ambassador to the English court after the turmoil in the Ohio Valley in 1754. During this brief stay in London, Bougainville had so impressed the Royal Society of London that they ignored the current political climate and made him a member in January 1756. Somehow, he also found time to become an accomplished sailor, a regarded navigator, and an officer in three different French regiments. A man who combined "elegance with depth," as one biographer has characterized him, he was destined to become much more, but at the moment his career was just beginning.[17]

His second in command was François-Gaston Levis, the Duc de Levis. Levis was from an ancient and noble family, impoverished but with excellent political connections. He entered the army in 1735, served on the Rhine during the War of Polish Succession, and by the age of seventeen had obtained a captaincy in the Regiment de la Marine. Along with Montcalm, Levis had been a member of the disastrous retreat from Bohemia and had fought gallantly at Dettingen in 1743. He spent several more years in Germany distinguishing himself in a number of battles and sieges. In 1746 his regiment was shifted to Italy where he obtained a post as assistant chief of staff in the forces commanded by his cousin Duc de Levis-Mirepoix, eventually earning himself a temporary appointment to colonel in the process. Brave, competent, and as calm as a mountain lake, the cash-poor Levis accepted the post as Montcalm's second in command primarily for its salary, which he viewed as a step toward obtaining his own regiment.[18]

As with Bougainville, Montcalm was pleased with Levis. The same could not be said of his third officer François-Charles de Bourlamaque. The difference, however, seems to have been nothing more than a poor first impression. Bourlamaque was a captain in the Regiment du Dauphin, a fairly high-standing French regiment, when he was assigned to Montcalm's staff with the new rank of colonel. He had served under Count Saxe during the War of Austrian Succession, seems to have had some engineering experience, was a veteran of the battles of Fontenoy (1745) and Rocoux (1746), and had recently been rewarded for the work he had done on a new infantry drill manual.

There were two other individuals assigned to the marquis' staff, both military engineers. The first and senior of the two was Captain Jean-Claude Lombard de Combles. Combles had been a royal engineer since 1743 and was a veteran of the War of Austrian Succession, where he had acquired extensive experience in the construction of fortifications. His assistant was Jean-Nicholas Desandrouins, a twenty-seven-year-old captain who had only recently graduated from the military engineering school in Mezieres. Both men were to act as replacements for the three engineers captured on *Alcide* and *Lys* the year before.[19]

Shortly after Montcalm's arrival at Quebec he met with Vaudreuil, and it was agreed that the general should quickly march his army to the newly constructed Fort Carillon on the Ticonderoga Peninsula, not only to forward work on the fortifications but also in anticipation of a renewed colonial campaign against the French strongholds on Lake Champlain. This assumption proved correct. The British plans for 1756 called for Shirley, who was now in command, to lead two regiments of British regulars against Fort Frontenac on Lake Ontario, while a New England army of five thousand men under General John Winslow of Massachusetts would assemble at Fort William Henry to launch an attack against Fort Carillon and Fort St. Frederic. Facing severe manpower issues Shirley suspended all western

General Francois-Gaston Levis. Montcalm's second in command would demonstrate his abilities on numerous occasions, and just as importantly, he remained neutral in the ongoing feud between Montcalm and Vaudreuil. He would assume command with Montcalm's death after the Battle of the Plains of Abraham on September 13, 1759, and in April 1760 he defeated the British forces occupying Quebec at the Battle of St. Foy, but with insufficient artillery and munitions he was unable to retake the French colonial capital. He would surrender with the French regulars at Montreal later that year. (*New York Public Library*)

operations and halted the British regulars at Albany. Here they would stay as news arrived that spring that Shirley was being recalled and that General John Campbell, the Earl of Loudoun, was being dispatched to replace him.[20]

From this point command issues, illness, and Montcalm's actions undermined the British campaign of 1756. On June 7 Major General Daniel Webb, Loudoun's third in command, landed at New York City. Webb forwarded letters from the ministry on to Shirley in Albany, but he did not personally go to assume command. Instead, he waited for two weeks for the arrival of Loudoun's second in command, Major General James Abercromby who, along with two regiments of reinforcements, dropped anchor at New York City on the sixteenth. Four days later the two British officers, along with contingents of the newly arrived regiments, set off for Albany, and on June 25, Abercromby officially assumed command from Shirley.

Upon taking command, Abercromby quickly found himself in a quandary. Scattered about the posts north of Albany were nearly five thousand colonial troops preparing to assault the French forts on Lake Champlain. Shirley had planned on uniting this force with the 44th and 48th

regiments, but with the arrival of Webb he had not carried through with
the plan. The question then became would the colonials, who had raised
their forces under terms that exempted them from service with British regulars, agree to this junction of forces. When Abercromby inquired into the
problem, he was informed that the colonials would regard such an act as a
breach of their enlistment contract, which would automatically release them
from service. Perplexed, Abercromby decided to leave the problem for
Loudoun and busied himself with the four regular regiments now encamped in and about Albany.[21]

Loudoun finally arrived on July 22 carrying a formal declaration of war
between France and England, which signified the official start to a conflict
that was already entering into its third year in North America. By the end
of the month Loudoun was in Albany demanding that Winslow's army be
placed under his authority, but he found the colonials unwilling to yield
their contractual rights in such matters. Loudoun pointed to his authority
and threatened the New Englanders, but it was clear that the matter had
reached an impasse. Winslow had given little if any ground, and Loudoun
was not in a position to push any farther. As much as he would have liked
to have disbanded the colonials and thrown their officers into chains for
insubordination, he could not. First, although he had little regard for their
military abilities, he still needed them to help guard the New York frontier.
Secondly, such an action would have guaranteed a political firestorm, pitting his authority against the assemblies of New England. Although his
authority extended over these bodies, alienating them at this point would
make his tenure in North America miserable, as many would view this use
of royal authority as a threat to their existence and would never cooperate
again.[22]

It almost didn't matter. Winslow's army, unfamiliar with camp discipline
and hygiene, had fallen prey to sickness and disease. By August over a quarter of the provincials were listed as unfit for service, with up to a score being
buried each day at Fort William Henry and Fort Edward. Efforts by
Loudoun and his officers helped rectify these issues, and in late August it
appeared that Winslow would make an attempt on Fort Carillon, but
Loudoun suddenly suspended all operations when news arrived that Montcalm had captured the British posts at Oswego after a three-day siege.[23]

Loudoun would shift to the defensive for the rest of the campaign, but
one element of note that has bearing on our subject was a detachment the
general had sent to reinforce Oswego a few weeks earlier. Under the command of Webb this detachment, consisting of the 44th Regiment and the

John Campbell, the 4th Earl of Loudoun. Loudon's authoritarian style created problems with the colonial legislatures, but it was the aborted siege of Louisbourg and the fall of Fort William Henry that were the primary motives behind his recall. (*National Galleries of Scotland*)

New York Independent Companies, had only reached German Flats when news of the capture of Oswego reached them. Upon hearing the reports, Webb advanced to the Oneida Carrying Place, but after doing so, he elected to retreat back down the Mohawk River, blocking Wood Creek and laying waste to all the English posts being erected at the Carrying Place, even though he had no orders to do so. Many were left to question the decision, viewing it as rash and unnecessary measure.[24]

By the fall of 1756 Loudoun had come to the conclusion that the objective of next year's campaign should be Quebec. Striking at Quebec served several purposes. First, it would draw Montcalm and the bulk of Canada's military resources to the siege, which in turn would lessen the burden of defending the frontier. Second, it held prospects of bringing the war in North America to a quick conclusion. Third, it avoided a land campaign along the Albany-Montreal corridor with all its expenses, organizational problems, and delays. The general requested that a large British expedition be sent to rendezvous with his 5,500 regulars to carry through with such a venture. Many raised an eyebrow at the idea of attacking the French colonial capital while leaving the French naval fortress of Louisbourg in the expedition's rear free to challenge its supply lines, and one in particular, the new first minister, William Pitt, was not interested in taking this risk.

2

THE FALL OF
FORT WILLIAM HENRY

THE ASCENSION OF WILLIAM PITT TO THE HEAD OF THE BRITISH government brought a drastic change to the prosecution of the last French and Indian War in North America. Dubbed "The Great Commoner," which derived from his popular appeal and stirring orations, Pitt was to become the architect of the modern British Empire. A tall, sinewy figure who had suffered from gout in his youth, he had cut short a military career to assume his eccentric grandfather's seat in Parliament, a seat that had been essentially purchased by the latter's diamond fortune. From the onset of his tenure in government, Pitt had shown himself to be a prodigious nationalist, and though he had assumed his position by perhaps less than genuine means, in domestic affairs he became an ardent advocate of wringing the vice and corruption from the government, even if this required portraying fact as fiction and fiction as fact in doing so. Whatever his failings, Pitt's popular support and fiery dialogues placed him in a position where he could not be ignored. Looking to broaden their political support, the newly formed Newcastle administration appointed him paymaster general of the army in 1746, a politically lucrative post he held until a falling out with the administration in late 1755.

In the fall of 1756, the Newcastle ministry began to crumble under a string of military setbacks. Crowds jeered the duke at every opportunity, and Parliament began to question his foreign policies. It was at this time that all eyes turned toward Pitt. His popular support, backing by the merchant class, members of the army, the navy, and even the clergy, made him an ideal candidate for inclusion into a new government. Even the king, who viewed "The Great Commoner" with a skeptical eye, realized that Pitt, regardless of whatever agenda he might bring to the table, would at the very least restore public faith in the government. In October of 1756 Pitt was approached by the lord chancellor to ascertain the conditions of his inclusion in the government. Pitt's terms were straightforward; he wanted a free hand to conduct the war as he saw fit, not only free from Newcastle's interference but from the king's as well. After several rounds of negotiation and a number of concessions on both sides, Newcastle agreed, and in June 1757, the Newcastle-Pitt government was formed.[1]

Pitt believed that England's wealth and fortune was directly tied to her colonies. Most would not argue this point, but Pitt took the relationship to the extreme. For the war in Europe (the Seven Years' War) he would set aside ample sums of money and for political reasons a handful of troops, but in general he would leave the bulk of the fighting to Britain's Prussian allies. His reasoning looked beyond the conclusion of the conflict and dictated its prosecution. A successful war in Europe, he argued, would offer little in regard to Britain's future, but in the colonies it was different. New avenues of trade would be derived from territorial concessions and the elimination of French competitors. And at the center of this newfound wealth would be Britain, a position that would eventually place her first among European powers. Although no one at the time would call it such, it was the seed of empire. It was in the colonies, particularly the American colonies, where the future lay, and as such, he wrote Newcastle, it was where "England and Europe are to be fought for." Whatever it took, in terms of men, money, and material, was of no consequence. His intentions were to expel the French from North America, India, Africa, or wherever else he found them. To some, he justified the effort by speculating on the advantages these captured colonies would offer at the peace table, while to the king he spoke of his real intentions, the merits of an enlarged dominion.

After studying the military situation in America, Pitt concluded that it was too confused for those formerly linked to its prosecution to rectify. As such, he inserted his own authority and would direct the war effort from London. He would determine the targets, the timing, the troop allocations, and would make all the necessary arrangements with the colonial governors. In essence he was to be the conductor and his generals the musicians in orchestrating the reduction of Canada.[2]

Pitt's first attempt at managing the American war would not go well. Loudoun had been waiting in New York City since late March 1757 for his promised reinforcements and the approval of his plan to attack Quebec. When Prime Minister William Pitt's directives finally reached him at the beginning of May he found that Louisbourg was to be the focus of this year's campaign, and if time permitted, to be followed by an attack on Quebec. The general was directed to assemble his forces and transport them to Halifax, where he would rendezvous with Admiral Francis Holburne and some eight thousand reinforcements sent from England. Although the orders differed from Loudoun's suggested plan, it was an approach that "in a great measure," he wrote Pitt, "coincides with the preparations I have made."[3]

The orders, however, created a problem. The change undermined one of the basic tenets of Loudoun's original plan, that being the inherent safety of the colonial frontier. Loudoun rightly believed that, if he besieged Quebec, the entire French army would be tied to its defense leaving it with insufficient resources to mount a major effort elsewhere. Now with the late shift of targets to Louisbourg, the defense of the frontier took on an even greater importance, especially along the Hudson-Champlain corridor where the French were likely to mount some type of attack while the bulk of the British army was away at Louisbourg.

To counter French movements in this area, Loudoun assigned his third in command, Brigadier General Daniel Webb. Webb had at his disposal the 35th Regiment, the third battalion of the newly raised 60th, and 5,500 provincials levied from New England, New York, and New Jersey. It was a force of nearly 7,500 men supported by a reserve of militia, several established forts, and despite French raiding efforts that spring, a sizable fleet of small vessels still operating on Lake George, which would prevent the French from moving their artillery up the lake. It was a considerable force that Loudoun, Governor Charles Hardy of New York, General James Abercromby, and Webb all agreed was sufficient. With his orders in hand, and the defense of the New York frontier established, Loudoun loaded his six regular regiments and Rogers' ranging companies onto transports in New York Harbor and departed for Halifax on June 5.[4]

For Governor Vaudreuil, the opening of the campaign season was proving problematic. Although he had successfully guided Canada through the

The Great Commoner, William Pitt. Pitt's rise to power changed the tone of the conflict in North America. The war was to be personally directed from his desk in Whitehall with the mentality that no effort was to be spared to expel the French from the continent. This approach initially faced a number of setbacks, but with the high-level focus of so many resources it ultimately sealed the fate of New France. (*Library of Congress*)

first two years of the conflict, the advantages he had gained over the English were slowly being undermined by the state of the colony. The fall harvest had been a miserable one, and only a concerted effort on the part of the government and the citizenry had prevented widespread famine. The governor informed Versailles of his plight and attached an urgent plea for provisions, troops, and munitions, but as of yet none had come, and it was not certain when they would. To complicate matters, there was the question of where the next English attack would fall. Here Vaudreuil acted in a preemptive fashion and launched a winter attack on Fort William Henry in late February 1757. The 1,500-man detachment, led by the governor's brother, Rigaud, marched across the frozen skin of Lake Champlain and Lake George, arriving in the vicinity of Fort William Henry on March 17.

Rigaud's orders were twofold. First, if the fort could be taken by surprise, he was authorized to make an attempt to seize the structure, otherwise the primary objective of the expedition was to destroy the enemy vessels pulled ashore near the fort. If this latter element could be accomplished Vaudreuil was certain that it would delay any expedition originating from the fort by several weeks or even months. The first part of the mission proved impossible, as the garrison, commanded by recently promoted Major William Eyre, was alert and soon discovered Rigaud's presence. While this was sufficient to prevent an attack on the fort, it did not prove enough of a deterrent to stop the French from accomplishing their primary goal. Amidst the slanting snowfall, the occasional discharge of the fort's cannons, and the sporadic flashes of musketry, Rigaud's men burned a number of storehouses near the fort, two hundred bateaux, three small barks, and the sloop *Loudoun* still on the stocks a few dozen yards from the fort. With his provisions running low and nothing else to be accomplished, Rigaud returned to Fort Carillon on the morning of the twenty-third.[5]

Vaudreuil was pleased with the results of the expedition, but as the weather improved rumors of British attacks abounded. Fort Carillon seemed the most likely target. A number of informants and prisoners stated that New England was once again raising troops to seize this strategic point. There were other signs as well, indications that Loudoun was organizing a larger effort to be directed either at Louisbourg or Quebec. If it was the latter, supply shortages or not, the governor would have no choice but to muster every man available to the defense of the colonial capital. If, however, British intentions were focused on Louisbourg, which was too far removed for him to provide any significant assistance, it offered an opportunity to shift to the offensive and strike at Fort William Henry and Fort Edward.

By early July the governor had a much clearer picture of British intentions. A prisoner taken in Acadia informed Vaudreuil that Loudoun was to rendezvous with a British fleet at Halifax for some maritime expedition. The information was in keeping with that from captives taken along the frontier and scouting parties operating near Fort William Henry, who reported little effort on the part of the English to repair the damage done by Rigaud's expedition. Over the course of the month, additional prisoners and reports from arriving vessels made it clear that Loudoun was concentrating on besieging Louisbourg, and along the New York frontier, he had left a handful of regulars and five thousand provincials with orders to remain on the defensive. In addition to these reports Vaudreuil was informed that a strong French squadron had entered Louisbourg. This all but ruled out any attack on Quebec, as Loudoun would not dare enter the St. Lawrence River with a French naval threat behind him.[6]

The information coincided with the arrival of the first ships from France carrying a handful of reinforcements, a thousand barrels of flour, and a large quantity of salt pork. It was not nearly enough, but for the moment it effectively lifted the shortages at Quebec and Montreal. They also brought good news. The king had granted all of the governor's requests. Provisions,

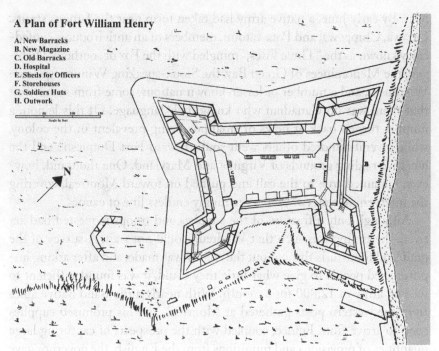

A Plan of Fort William Henry

A. New Barracks
B. New Magazine
C. Old Barracks
D. Hospital
E. Sheds for Officers
F. Storehouses
G. Soldiers Huts
H. Outwork

Fort William Henry. Designed by Captain William Eyre and built by Johnson's New England troops, the famous fort would have a very short life. (Hulbert, *The Crown Collection of Photographs of American Maps*, Series I I/1. [1910])

munitions, artillery, and almost three thousand men had left French ports in March. There was even more. Two battalions of the Berry Regiment originally destined for India were being diverted to Quebec to bolster the colony's defenses.

In addition to these reinforcements, others were arriving from the west. Using the successful capture of Oswego as a backdrop, Vaudreuil had sent envoys out to the nations of the Great Lakes region, urging them to take up the hatchet against the English and join the French in the next year's campaign. The effort had gone far beyond the governor's hopes. News of the plunder from the capture of Oswego had spread quickly throughout the region, making the French envoy's task much easier than expected. Lured by the prospects of prisoners and booty, and urged on by Canadian partisans such as Charles Langdale, Louis Villiers, and Charles Noyelles de Fleurimont, nations from as far away as Lake Superior pushed their canoes onto the cool lake waters and began congregating near Detroit in late

May. By early June, a native army had taken form near the famous straits. Ottawa, Chippewa, and Potawatomi, members of an anti-Iroquois confederacy known as the "Three Fires," mingled with the Fox of southern Michigan, the Menominees of Green Bay, the Sioux-speaking Winnebago from Wisconsin, and a number of lesser-known nations, some from so far west that there was no Canadian who knew their language. Of this legion, a number turned back at news of smallpox being prevalent in the colony, while several hundred others went south toward Fort Duquesne and the lucrative raiding grounds of Virginia and Maryland. One thousand, however, remained true to the call and pushed on toward Montreal, covering the intervening waterways in a seemingly endless line of canoes.[7]

Although only a fraction of the supplies and troops requested had arrived, the timing was such that Vaudreuil could not wait. A survey of the grain and foodstuffs throughout the colony was made, and after asking impoverished people to give what little they could, it was found sufficient to feed an army of 12,800 for a month. With nearly a thousand native allies from the western posts gathered at Montreal, and his promised supplies soon to arrive from France, coupled with the prospects of capturing large quantities of provisions and munitions from the English, the governor gave the order in early July for Montcalm to proceed against Fort William Henry and Fort Edward as soon as sufficient forces could be mustered at Fort Carillon.

While Vaudreuil correctly assessed British intentions and was able to concentrate his forces in the Champlain Valley, the siege of Fort William Henry and the massacre that followed was only made possible by a series of British mistakes. Montcalm, although directed to move against Fort William Henry and Fort Edward, was much more realistic about the operation. The latter post he all but ruled out given the distances involved and his current supply situation. As for the former post, reports from Rigaud's expedition pointed to a well-made sandbox fort that would require heavy cannons and large mortars to reduce. These guns, which given the current supply situation were irreplaceable, would have to be transported up Lake George on pontoon barges. This meant that Montcalm had no intentions of moving on Fort William Henry until he had established naval superiority on the lake.[8]

It is at this point that the first of the British mistakes were made. The untimely death of Richard Rogers and many of the Rangers at Fort William Henry to smallpox, coupled with the activity of French and Indian war parties that were consistently intercepting Ranger patrols a few miles from the

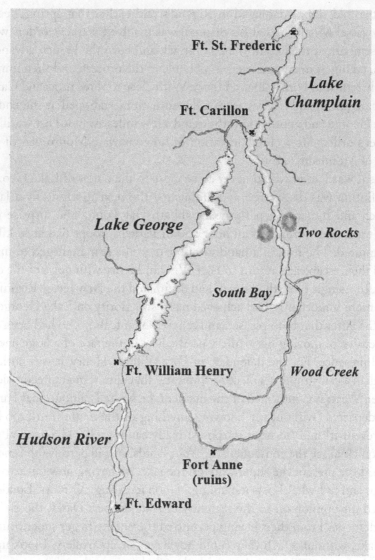

A map of the French and British posts from Fort Edward to Fort St. Frederic at Crown Point, c. 1757. (*Author*)

fort, led the commander of Fort William Henry, Lt. Colonel George Monro, to order a reconnaissance in force down Lake George. On the evening of July 23 Lt. Colonel John Parker's 350 New Jersey and New York troops arrayed in twenty whaleboats and two bay boats pushed away from the wharfs at Fort William Henry. With the exception of a few whaleboats, and two old sloops damaged in Rigaud's raid earlier that spring, nearly every vessel Monro had at his disposal was involved. Parker's orders were to disembark at the end of the lake, attack and burn the French advanced posts, taking as many prisoners as possible in the process, and then immediately return to Fort William Henry. With close to three thousand Canadians, regulars, and natives from a dozen nations stationed at the end of Lake George and another four thousand a few miles away at Fort Carillon, Parker's orders are a clear indication of how unaware Monro was of the state of Montcalm's army.[9]

As it was Parker would never come close to the outlet of Lake George. His flotilla was discovered and ambushed the next morning by a large French and Indian war party near Sabbath Day Point. The surprise was near total, and within half an hour 250 of Parker's troops had been killed or captured. The rest, in a handful of boats to the rear, managed to make good their escape and return to Fort William Henry with news of the disaster. In a single blow the French had decimated the New Jersey Regiment and, more importantly, had achieved naval superiority on Lake George. It was the latter that both pleased and relieved Montcalm, who had been apprehensive of moving his artillery up the lake in the face of a large enemy naval presence. For the defenders of Fort William Henry, it was nothing less than a catastrophe, "a piece of stupidity" that almost guaranteed a siege. When Webb was informed of the incident, he wrote Loudoun that Parker had departed "without my knowing anything of the matter until too late to prevent it" and "to what purpose I really cannot tell." The general was also quick to see the consequences. "Your Lordship will perceive the enemy have at the present the superiority on the lake, we having now but two old sloops and five whaleboats remaining." Upon receiving this news, Loudoun passed his opinion on to the secretary of state, Robert Darcy, the Earl of Holderness. "From their having permitted the enemy to get superiority of the lake, without which they could not have got up artillery, I look upon that place and garrison, as lost, with the whole troops there."[10]

Loudoun's assessment would prove to be correct. With the path before him now clear Montcalm sailed up Lake George with an army of close to seven thousand men and landed near Fort William Henry in the early morning hours of August 3. By mid-afternoon French troops had invested the fort and the nearby entrenched camp and had seized control of the Fort Edward Road. With sporadic skirmishing dominating the remainder of the day, Monro finished his third letter to General Webb at Fort Edward, speaking to the French siege and Montcalm's initial surrender demand, which he had refused. It was still unclear to the colonel how many men the French had and how many cannon they had brought, but in either case he was determined to hold out, for "I make no doubt that you will soon send us a reinforcement."[11]

The next morning Montcalm made a number of adjustments to his lines which pinned the British against the waters of the lake. When this was complete, he ordered the army's supplies to be landed and passed the task of reducing the fort over to Captain Jean-Nicholas Desandrouins of the Royal Engineers. Desandrouins' first action was to trade his blue coat of the French Royal Engineers, a color frequently worn by the English militia, for a white one of the French regulars. He then spent the morning of August 4 conducting a detailed reconnaissance of the British stronghold. The positioning of Montcalm's forces and the terrain before him left little doubt how the siege would proceed. First, the artillery would be landed in a protected ravine at what became known as Artillery Cove some seven hundred yards from the fort. From here the main trench would be started in a southwestern direction. When the work had progressed far enough, a pair of firing parallels would be dug. The first would be constructed along a branch to the left, and the second along a path cut a little farther forward to the right. At five hundred to six hundred yards from the fort neither battery was close enough to seriously damage the fort's walls. Instead, they would cover the continuation of the main sap, which after negotiating a small marsh, would push forward into the garrison's gardens along the fort's western wall. Here a final set of parallels would be constructed at point-blank range, about a hundred yards from the structure, close enough to guarantee a breach in the fort's wall.[12]

With the approach decided upon, it was agreed to wait for nightfall to land the artillery and begin work on the trenches. In the meantime, the engineer set his men to work preparing fascines and gabions which would be used to buttress the freshly dug trenches. While this was being done Desandrouins walked the terrain again and again looking for roadblocks and problems with his plan, and when he was satisfied, he and several of his staff marked out the opening stages of the main sap, the first two parallels, the communication trench, and the road to move the artillery forward.

For the defenders the day was spent skirmishing with French and Indian war parties. Although sizable reinforcements had arrived the day before the French landing, swelling Monro's garrison to 2,300 men, and making any French attempt to storm the works unlikely, there were signs of trouble when a mortar and one of the fort's two eighteen-pound guns split after just a few shots. There was also little in the way of information from Fort Edward. Monro had received a letter from Webb's aide, Captain George Bartman, that morning urging the Scot to hold on and pledging that the general "is determined to assist you as soon as possible with the whole army if required," but since then he had heard nothing.[13]

While Webb would have liked to march to Monro's aid, the problem was that he did not have the forces available to carry out this task. With the recent transfer of over 1,000 men to reinforce Fort William Henry, Webb was left with only 1,600 men at Fort Edward. The general's obsession with the safety of Fort Edward, which he rightly viewed as the lynchpin of the New York frontier, had led him to assign half his command to securing the fort's supply lines and garrisoning the smaller posts along the Hudson below Fort Edward. It would now take several days to gather together these forces. Webb had also written Sir William Johnson and the colonial governors a few days before, urging them to call out their militia and send it to Albany with all haste, but as of yet none had arrived.

The poor allocation and positioning of his forces aside, Webb was about to make another mistake. A few broken and incomplete reports had reached the general but proved of little help when a trio of Rangers led a Canadian officer into Webb's office on the morning of August 4. When questioned as to the strength of the French army, Lt. Jacques Vaudry de la Chesnaye, who only a few hours ago had been captured on the Fort Edward Road, informed Webb "that he was assured" it "consisted of between eleven and twelve thousand men," four thousand of which were Canadians, three thousand regulars, and the rest Indians. And cannon? Webb asked next. He had personally helped move thirty of various calibers over the portage road to Lake George. The other militia units, he had been told, moved another six as well as four large mortars. Webb flinched at the news. But there was more. La Chesnaye informed him thirty ships stocked with provisions, munitions, and two regular regiments of Old France had recently arrived at Quebec and that the French had no fear of the latter place being attacked, having received news a few weeks before that a French fleet had defeated an English squadron at the mouth of the St. Lawrence.[14]

La Chesnaye's inaccurate report on the size of the French army could not have been better directed than at the jittery Webb. The entire episode made the general's head spin. Strangely, the general accepted the prisoner's report without question, which only magnified his terror. The question no longer became one of reinforcing Monro, and the safety of Fort Edward and the New York frontier. If Fort William Henry fell before the promised reinforcements reached him, Montcalm could sweep south and destroy Webb's strung-out army in piecemeal fashion. Unclear of French numbers, and just as unclear as to when the militia and his other forces could rendezvous with him at Fort Edward, the next morning Webb dispatched a cautionary letter to Monro explaining his situation.

> Fort Edward August 4th, 12 o'clock at Noon
> Sir
> I am directed by General Webb to acknowledge the receipt of three of your letters, two bearing the date about nine yesterday morning, and one about six in the evening by two Rangers, which are the only men that have got in here, except two yesterday morning with your first acquainting him of the enemy being in sight. He has ordered me to acquaint you he does not think it prudent (as you know the strength at this place) to attempt a junction or to assist you till reinforced by the militias of the colonies, for the immediate march of which repeated expresses have been sent. One of our scouts brought in a Canadian prisoner last night from the investing party which is very large, and have possessed all the grounds five miles on this side of Fort William Henry. The number of the enemy is very considerable, the prisoner says eleven thousand and have a large train of artillery with mortars and were to open their batteries this day. The general thought proper to give you this intelligence, that in case he should be so unfortunate from the delays of the Militia not to have it in his power to give you timely assistance, you might be able to make the best terms [that] were left in your power. The bearer is a Sergeant of the Connecticut forces and if [he] is happy enough to get in will bring advices from you. We keep continual scouts going to endeavor to get in, or bring intelligence from you.
> I am & c.
> G. Bartman, Aide-de-camp[15]

A few hours after sunset two hundred men began hauling the three-dozen French cannons ashore. Desandrouins oversaw the opening stages of the operation as one at a time the artillery barges and boats pulled astride a makeshift dock or were beached to unload their iron contents. It was delicate work best left to the direction of a handful of experienced operators if one wished to avoid extracting one of the two-thousand-pound guns out of the lake. Satisfied with the progress, Desandrouins proceeded to the main trench. There was no mistaking what was occurring as the tempo of pick, axe, and saw drifted over the mountain waters. Three hundred and fifty men, mostly Canadian militia, toiled under the protection of nearly a thousand regulars who stood guard nearby, while another one hundred and fifty pioneers cut a road for the guns from the landing site. The fort's cannon only fired occasionally throughout the night, more in an attempt to remind the attackers of the stronghold's presence than to cause any real damage. At 4 a.m. the work party and their guards were relieved. In the span of eight hours Desandrouins men had accomplished wonders. With the exception of some tangled trees and brush the ground proved easy to move. The main sap had been advanced some eighty yards, the left parallel was started, the ground for the right parallel was broken, and a communications trench between the two had been started as well.[16]

At dawn the fort's defenders could clearly make out the work parties perfecting the lakeside parallel and forwarding the communications trench to the southwest, but there was little they could do to dissuade the effort beyond showering the area with artillery fire. The French and their Indian allies responded by "peppering away" at the gun crews and anything else that appeared to be within musket range, occasionally checking their fire when clouds of grapeshot rippled through their positions. The day's activities had only resulted in a handful of casualties on both sides, but for the defenders there was another cost. By the end of the day both of the fort's thirty-two-pound guns had split and the last eighteen-pounder exploded on the ramparts, injuring several of its crew. Montcalm had yet to open his batteries, and already the heaviest pieces of the fort's arsenal and one of its mortars were out of action.

Late that afternoon as Desandrouins' troops began to assemble for another evening's work, Bartman's August 4 letter to Monro was handed to Montcalm. It had been found in the jacket of a British Ranger who had been slain near the Fort Edward Road. Montcalm nodded as he went through the letter, finally passing the bloodstained document on for Bougainville and some of his staff officers to read. All quickly understood the confident look on the general's face. Webb had greatly overestimated the size of the French army, which coupled with the delays in calling out the colonial militia, gave Montcalm free reign for at least several days, if not longer. Nor was the marquis as anxious about the prospect of a British relief column as he had first been. Most of it would consist of raw militia who would have to march up a narrow, wooded road occupied by several thousand Canadians and Indians. Indeed, the marquis and his officers even began hoping that the English would attempt such a foolish move. Visions of Braddock and the Bloody Morning scout would pale in comparison to

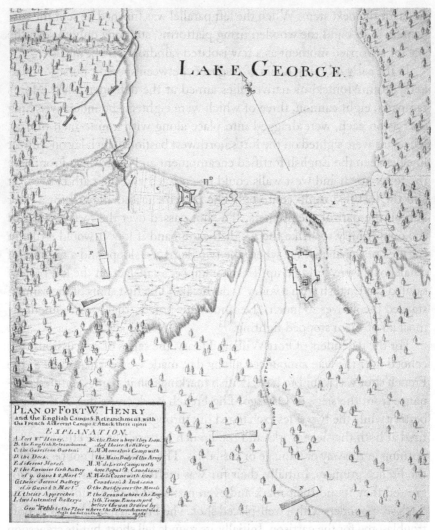

LAKE GEORGE.

PLAN OF FORT Wm. HENRY
and the English Camps & Retranchment with
the French different Camps & Attack there upon
EXPLANATION.

The siege of Fort William Henry, August 3–9, 1757. (*Norman B. Leventhal Map & Education Center, Boston Public Library*)

the ambush that would transpire. Just as importantly, a victory here would cement Fort William Henry's fate and probably seal that of Fort Edward's as well.[17]

That night Captain Desandrouins and seven hundred men worked feverishly to complete the left parallel and the communications trench to the right parallel. The engineer moved between the different digs, encouraging his men, questioning what they needed, and seeing to the preparations for the next steps. When the left parallel was finished he sent the carpenters in to build the wooden firing platforms, stopping only to scan the sky for a worried moment as a few isolated raindrops struck his face.

In the early morning hours of August 6, between sporadic bursts of musketry from Montcalm's native allies aimed at the defenders on the fort's ramparts, eight cannon, three of which were eighteen-pounders weighing over a ton each, were dragged into place along with a nine-inch mortar. The guns were sighted on the fort's northwest bastion, which lay on a direct line between the English fortified encampment and the battery. From here the fort's north and west walls could be engaged and the path between it and the fortified camp contested. The placement also allowed for a poor aim on the part of the gunners. If a shot passed over the fort, it still had the opportunity to strike the English camp, and if low, it would strike in the area of the anchorage where the two damaged sloops and a number of whaleboats were still tied up. To the engineer's satisfaction the left battery saluted the English with a volley at daybreak. "The first shots of the cannon startled the natives so much," Desandrouins noted, "that for a moment almost all of them stopped fighting."[18]

For the defenders of Fort William Henry, the series of concussions that echoed over the lake announced a long day, made worse when some of the French shot was found to have British markings on it, being captured ordnance from the siege of Oswego. The French work crews dug at the right battery while the two sides exchanged fire throughout the day. The English fired at both the siege works and the French battery, but the effort yielded nothing in the way of damage or casualties. The same could not be said for the French gunners. Initially, their fire was ineffective, but as the day progressed they found their mark and even managed to dismount one of the fort's six-pounders with a well-placed shot. The French mortar proved more troublesome for the garrison. Initially, its rounds fell short, but its crew soon found the range and began lobbing shells onto the fort's parade ground, causing a number of casualties and forcing those not on the ramparts into the bomb-proof shelters. Late in the day, the engagement was punctuated by a lucky shot which carried away the pulley on the fort's flagstaff. A resounding ovation could be heard from the French lines as the Union Jack fluttered to the ground. To the cheers of the garrison, a pair of volunteers quickly grabbed the flag and climbed the pole to refasten it. The vocal encouragement, however, soon subsided when a subsequent shot struck the pair, decapitating one of them and sending his wounded companion tumbling to the ground with the flag still in his hand.[19]

Matters were only slightly better within the English entrenched camp. Several men within the compound were killed or injured by stray shots. Colonel Frye's tent was leveled by an errant cannonball and the sentry standing guard outside of it killed. Amazingly, a pair of Rangers managed to run the French and Indian gauntlet and arrived before Monro a little before two o'clock that afternoon. The understandably excited pair mentioned that Webb expected to be joined shortly by William Johnson and a number of Mohawks, but when Monro pressed them for the rest of the message it was relayed to him in such a garbled manner that he "could not rightly understand it." Puzzled as to what was transpiring at Fort Edward, Monro wrote his third letter of the day to Webb. He informed the general that yet another twelve-pounder had split, forcing him to replace it with a pair from the fortified camp, a move he could ill afford to take, and that the French were clearly erecting another battery to the northwest of their current one. As for his garrison's status, they were holding, although "if the reinforcements we had reason to expect from your letter . . . had arrived on time," he added, "our situation probably would have been better."[20]

At Fort Edward the situation had moved from nervous to apprehensive to near panic in the span of a few days. Every day Bartman pressed Captain Christie in Albany for news on the militia, and every day Christie forwarded another urgent appeal on to the colonial governors. The state of affairs prompted Webb to convene a council of war on the morning of August 5. Colonial Colonels Phineas Lyman, Samuel Angel, and Beamsley Glazier, Captain Thomas Ord of the Royal Artillery, Major Henry Fletcher of the Regulars, and engineers James Montressor and Harry Gordon listened as Webb outlined their "disagreeable situation." Because of poor planning on the part of the general, there were only 1,600 men at Fort Edward. The rest of his command had been ordered to the fort but had yet to arrive. Nor had any of the militia, whose current status was unclear. As Webb anxiously paced about the room, two questions were posed. First, whether or not it was practical, given the current circumstances, to march to the aid of Fort William Henry. The consensus was no. The next question, as to whether or not Fort Edward could be defended, was more pressing, and at length it was agreed that it was proper to retreat toward the gathering militia, and once joined with them, make a stand at some suitable location. This then led to a third question. If the army did retreat, was Fort Edward to be razed? Would not a small garrison at least delay the French and give the militia and the army more time to cover the upper part of the province? Colonel Montressor, tasked with preparing the fort for either a siege or demolition, pressed the general for an answer, but the best he could get from Webb was that everyone should be "ready to march at a minute's warning."[21]

The next day Webb had a change of heart, and at the core of this were two men. At nine o'clock that morning William Johnson arrived with 150 Mohawks and 1,500 militia from Albany and the surrounding area. Webb's outlying detachments also began to arrive, bolstering his numbers to the point that he directed Bartman to inform Monro that three armies totaling five thousand men had been collected in the woods about Fort Edward and would soon march to his relief. The second element behind Webb's about-face was Lord George Augustus Howe, who arrived at Fort Edward on the evening of the sixth. The new colonel of the 3rd Battalion of the Royal Americans was a popular and thoroughly professional soldier whom James Wolfe, the future victor of Quebec, referred to as nothing less than the best soldier in the British army. Howe's arrival must have startled Webb, for even Loudoun did not know that he was destined for America. The dynamic and politically well-connected Howe created conflicting emotions within Webb, which focused to the same point. First, it lifted some of the pressure off of the indecisive commander, bolstering his confidence and giving him for the first time a professional opinion on which he could rely. Second, it made Webb far more conscious of the repercussions of his actions. Whatever transpired from this point on was certain to reach the highest levels of the government and the army through Howe's correspondence.[22]

For Monro and his garrison, the morning of August 7 started in an ominous fashion. At 6 a.m. Desandrouins and his men announced the completion of the right battery with a volley from eight heavy cannons, a six-inch mortar, and a pair of seven-inch howitzers. A few moments later, the left-hand battery joined in, punctuating the clear advantage that Montcalm possessed in artillery. For nearly three hours, the French guns pounded the fort and the entrenched camp. At nine o'clock, after a double salvo from both batteries, the guns fell quiet. A few minutes later, a French drummer tapped out the "parley."

Under the protection of a flag of truce, Bougainville, the drummer, and an escort of fifteen grenadiers walked out of the trenches. At the foot of the fort's glacis, they were met by a like number of Englishmen who asked them what they wanted. Bougainville responded that he had a letter for the fort's commandant. After a blindfolded tour of the fort and the fortified encampment, during which the garrison did everything possible to deceive the Frenchman, he found himself before Colonel Monro and his officers.

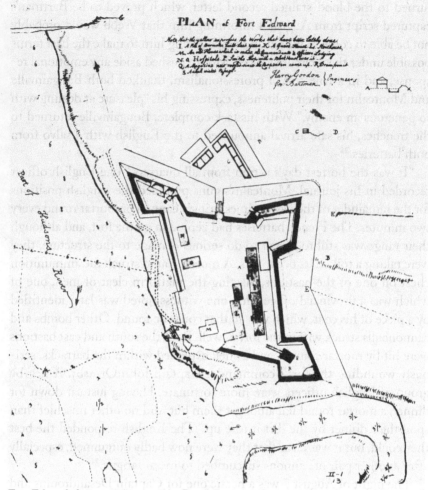

Fort Edward, from a 1757 survey by Royal Engineer Captain Harry Gordon. The fortification had undergone a major transformation from when Dieskau first considered storming its walls. While there was still work to do, by August 1757 Colonel Montressor was able to report that the structure now mounted thirty-nine cannons, the heaviest of which were eight eighteen-pounders, six nine-pounders, and four large mortars. (Hulbert, *The Crown Collection of Photographs of American Maps*, Series I I/1. [1910])

Actually, Bougainville had two letters. The first, from Montcalm, announced the second. "One of my reconnaissance parties returned last night with prisoners and obtained the letter," the first note began, "which I am sending you, because of the generosity I profess towards those against whom I am obliged to wage war." With the introduction complete, Monro turned to the blood-stained second letter, which proved to be Bartman's captured script from August 4 informing him that Webb would probably not be able to come to his aid and empowering him to make the best terms possible under these circumstances. Monro pushed aside any emotional response, and in a true test of professionalism, thanked both Bougainville and Montcalm for their politeness, expressing his "pleasure at dealing with so generous an enemy." With his task complete, Bougainville returned to the trenches, his safe arrival announced to the English with a salvo from both batteries.[23]

"It was the hottest day's action from all quarters," one English officer recorded in his journal. Montcalm's guns pounded the English positions for the remainder of the day, at times firing a cannon or mortar round every two minutes. The French batteries had zeroed in on the fort, and although their range was still too great to do serious damage to the structure, they were taking a toll on its occupants. A mortar round struck the ammunition chest on one of the bastions, blasting the platform clear of men, one of which was a provincial officer that one witness noted was later identified by a piece of his coat, which was all that could be found. Other bombs and cannonballs struck within the fort as well. Both the south and east bastions were hit by mortar rounds, and a shell exploded within the barracks, seriously wounding the fort's commander Captain John Ormsby. A nearby group of English officers were more fortunate. Having just sat down for dinner, a mortar round fell amongst them but "did no other mischief than spoil their dinner by the dirt it tore up." The English responded the best they could, but it was clear that they were now badly outgunned, especially after another pair of cannons succumbed to metal fatigue.[24]

The night of August 7 was a hectic one for Captain Desandrouins and his staff. With the first two batteries completed, work was directed back toward advancing the main trench. The problem was a small marsh, perhaps a hundred yards in width, in the path of the sap. Siege craft of the day, however, had an answer for this problem in the form of a dry trench. The wet expanse would be crossed by building a causeway of fascines, felled trees, and stones. To shield movement across this earthen bridge, gabions and sandbags would be placed along the sides to form walls, and the entire length would be covered to further protect the troops and workers. At the head of three hundred militiamen Desandrouins spent the night seeing to this task and the digging of a third parallel at the northern edge of the swamp. Around eleven that evening they were interrupted by a handful of musket shots in the gardens to the west of the fort. The shots were quickly followed by war whoops, which moved like a wave along the heights surrounding the fort. One by one the native war chiefs called out their names, each answering the calls of the previous leader. The event made it clear to the French engineer and his pioneers that there was no fear of a sally by the garrison.

At daylight the English could make out the efforts of their industrious enemy and turned their remaining cannon against it. Although it would have been safer to suspend the works until nightfall, the decision was made to press on with the night's work. "The workers went ahead with such ardor that it was finished that very forenoon," one French officer noted, "in spite of the brisk cannon fire and musketry of the enemy."[25]

The French batteries responded to the English, and both sides fired throughout the day, the hollow thump of the French mortars adding timing marks to the cacophony. In the background flurries of musketry ebbed and flowed as the French Indians jockeyed for position and exchanged fire with the garrison from their former garden. In all, it was a bad day for the defenders as the French gunners, having found the range, began to regularly drop mortar rounds into the fort. For Monro the siege was reaching its climax. His garrison was exhausted, his casualties mounting, and his supply of artillery dwindling as yet more pieces failed under the strain of prolonged firing. In what was to be his last message to Webb, he complained of Bartman's letter falling into Montcalm's hands and of the exaggerated reports that the French were eleven thousand strong. "If they really had those numbers," he informed the general, "they might have demolished us at once." With little more to say, he concluded his note in simple terms, "Relief is greatly wanted."[26]

On August 8, with his detachments back at Fort Edward and another thousand militia a day's march from the fort, Webb had Bartman pen a letter to Monro, informing him of the general's intention to march to his relief when the militia arrived. "You may depend, upon their arrival, that he will not fail to march to your assistance," Bartman informed the beleaguered commandant. Until then, "We wish most heartily that you may be able to hold out a little longer and hope soon to have it in our power to relieve you from your present disagreeable situation." It was the news that the besieged commander had been waiting for, and had either the letter of August 6 or that of August 8 actually reached Monro it seems likely that the veteran Scot would have carried on with his defense. But the first, after a three-day odyssey, arrived in his hands too late while the second never reached him, being intercepted by the French on the evening of the ninth.[27]

With the end approaching on the night of August 8 Desandrouins and five hundred men pushed the main trench into the garrison's gardens along the fort's western wall. The defenders blazed away with musket and clouds of grapeshot at the shadowy figures digging a few hundred yards away, but it did little to deter them. When the trench came to within a hundred yards of the fort, Desandrouins ordered two long parallels dug, and when complete, the heavy cannons were dragged into place. The young captain took his turn along with the pioneers coaxing stuck gun carriages forward through the earthen maze. It was back-breaking, dangerous work, but by daybreak a dirt-covered Desandrouins was able to stand before Montcalm and inform him that "the trench was in a very good state and the batteries ready to fire."[28]

It proved unnecessary. The British understood as well as their enemy that the fort was doomed and surrendered the next day. Montcalm, not in a position to feed the captured garrison, had granted Monro full honors of war, meaning that the British were free to leave with their personal armament and effects under oath that they would not serve in North America for eighteen months. At least that was the agreement. Instead, a number of native allies who had been promised the spoils of the victory, but now believing that they had been deceived, beset the British column as it formed up to march to Fort Edward the next morning.

At first it was simply a matter of looting by a few hundred individuals, but news quickly spread and soon a thousand or more swirled about the perimeter looking for their opportunity. When the situation began to turn to outright plunder, Monro complained to Captain Dominique Nicolas de Laas, who with two hundred men from the La Reine regiment, had been assigned to escort the column. De Lass advised "giving up our effects," pointing out that the besiegers "would not be satisfied until they had got all the baggage." For the sake of his men Monro complied, but this only escalated the demands, which now encompassed almost anything which attracted their fancy: hats, watches, swords, horses, and even the soldiers' clothing.

Somehow through the confusion, the British column began moving forward "with great difficulty." The regulars at the head of the column had secured some means of protection as de Laas had his men draw closer, flanking either side of their formation, but "woe to all those who brought up the rear, or to stragglers whom indisposition or any other cause separated however little from the troops." As it slogged forward, the column continued to be waylaid, but as of yet, it had been more an act of theft and pillaging than anything else. This was shattered when a war cry echoed from the back of the column. Ten, fifty, then hundreds of war whoops rang out as the crowd fell upon the soldiers. Several French sources blamed the Abenaki for starting the massacre, claiming they were avenging some grievance against the English, while at least one British source claimed that the war cry came from a Canadian partisan. Both are an attempt at a simple explanation, but given the confusion that existed, it is unlikely that either were true.[29]

Regardless of who started the assault, its effects were immediate. Over a thousand men descended on the unarmed column. Initially, the tomahawk and war club reigned, and perhaps as many as forty or fifty Englishmen fell before their wielders, but the massacre was short-lived. As with Parker's men a few weeks before, once the attackers saw that the English were offering no resistance, they turned to taking prisoners. The latter were far more valuable than scalps, for they could be sold, traded, or incorporated back into the tribe to make good war losses, and at the moment the choices seemed endless. Later English accounts would claim hundreds slain in the murderous frenzy, but this is not in keeping with the guiding philosophy of a "mourning war," which dominated North American native warfare. Nor is it in keeping with the reality of the situation. Had over a thousand warriors besieged the unarmed column with the intent of slaying all involved, it is unlikely that anyone would have survived.

Of course, for those involved, none of this mattered. The column acted like an accordion under the attack and then flew apart as panic overcame discipline. A number of troops in the front, some with harrowing tales of capture and escape, managed to make their way to Fort Edward with the news. Order was established with the arrival of Montcalm and more French troops, but by then the event had already subsided. Montcalm was able to ransom several hundred prisoners who, along with Colonel Monro and those who had found refuge among the French escorts, returned to Fort Edward a few days later.

For those who escaped it was a scene that burned in their minds, conjuring up the familiar New England stories of Indian atrocities, which never far from the surface now blazed across the countryside. "To what a pitch of perfidy and cruelty is the French nation arrived!" the newspapers spat forth. "Would not an ancient heathen shudder with horror on hearing so hideous a tale?" The stories of what transpired rippled through colonial taverns and forums with the number of slain and captured growing with each rendition. Sgt. Jabez Fitch, who had spent the siege at Fort Edward, perhaps put it best. "This and yesterday are ye two most sorrowful day(s) that were ever known to New England."[30]

The actual cost in lives is difficult to assess. On August 9 2,308 British soldiers were given their parole. By mid-August some 1,000 of these men had reached Fort Edward in one fashion or another, and by the end of the month the number had climbed to almost 1,800. Vaudreuil made good on his promise and secured the release of two hundred or so prisoners from the native nations stopping at Montreal. They embarked on three different vessels in late September along with ninety men from Parker's ill-fated expedition and by mid-October were back in British hands. Some fifty others were deemed too sick to move and remained behind. By the end of the year two thousand of the garrison could be accounted for. As for the remaining 308, a number were returned or escaped over the next few years. Others died in captivity, not necessarily from violent means but from the same diseases and epidemics that plagued the local population. In all, 267 soldiers and a score of camp followers never returned home from the campaign. It is clear, however, from the accounts of the witnesses that priority was given to prisoners over scalps, implying that not all of the missing were killed in the attack. For the families involved, however, the details of their loved ones' fate made little difference, all that mattered was that they left Fort William Henry, never to return.[31]

3

RANGERS AND PARTISANS

BY EARLY SEPTEMBER THE CAMPAIGN OF 1757 WAS COMING TO AN end. While the memories of the "massacre" still burned brightly in British and colonial hearts, it did not translate into military action. Webb, now reinforced by the militia, had decided not to risk the New York frontier and march to Monro's aid, although by the time he had arrived at this decision the fort had already surrendered. Instead, he worked on improving Fort Edward and garrisoned it with several thousand men awaiting Montcalm's next move and Loudoun's return with his brigade of regulars. Webb would soon be able to breathe easier. Montcalm was never interested in risking his army by advancing on Fort Edward. He ordered Fort William Henry destroyed and within a week had returned to Fort Carillon with his captured supplies.

It now became a war of small raids, defensive preparations, and waiting as the two armies eyed each other from their respective strongholds. On August 29 Montcalm turned command of the Lake Champlain frontier over to Levis and departed for Montreal. The latter personally conducted a reconnaissance of the area about Fort William Henry in early September, and finding no signs that the English had returned, he departed, leaving

Bourlamaque with two regiments of regulars and a number of Marines to continue work on the fort. The regiments of La Sarre, La Reine, Languedoc, and Guyenne moved back to Fort St. Jean and Fort Chambly where they would be in position to support Fort Carillon should the English attempt a late move against it. Later that month Vaudreuil and Montcalm both celebrated reports that Loudoun had called off his plans to besiege Louisbourg. With the enemy showing nothing beyond making defensive arrangements, Vaudreuil gave the official order to end the campaign in early October. The garrisons of Fort Carillon and Fort St. Frederic were filled out, and on October 20 Bourlamaque departed with the regiments of Royal Roussillon, Bearn, and the remaining colonial troops. The regiment of Guyenne would winter at Fort Chambly, while the rest of the French army marched into winter quarters in the interior.[1]

Although several scouts had indicated that Montcalm had withdrawn to Fort Carillon, Webb's apprehensions did not disappear until Loudoun's returning regulars entered Fort Edward on September 18. Although thoughts turned toward an official end to the campaign, it would not be until early November that Loudoun saw fit to withdraw to winter quarters. Until then work continued on Fort Edward and the southern posts along the Hudson. While his army focused on their defenses Loudoun turned to administrative matters. One of these concerned Robert Rogers who, along with his ranging companies, had settled back into their old encampment on Rogers Island across the river from Fort Edward.

Formed in late March 1756 by the acting commander in chief in North America, Governor William Shirley, the Rangers were a strange unit from their inception. Although they were not a provincial unit, they had the flavor of being one, reflected in part by their rank and file which was drawn almost exclusively from New Hampshire, Western Massachusetts, and upper New York. Nor were they a regular unit like the Independent Companies of New York. Unlike the latter, which possessed permanent funding, the Rangers were paid from the commander in chief's contingency fund. The nature of this subsidy meant that they held no permanent status. They were a temporary unit existing only as long as the commander in chief deemed them necessary. The arrangement also extended to their rank. The officers were technically commissioned under a warrant granted by the commander in chief, placing them above provincial officers, yet their commissions were not considered regular commissions issued by the king like those of the regulars. Their pay also reflected their unique status. The officers were paid almost the same as regular officers, but the enlisted men made substantially more than the average British soldier and nearly twice that of a provincial soldier.

These issues aside, the most important element of the independent status was that it afforded Rogers the leeway to discipline his troops as he saw fit. Rogers understood that standard measures of discipline did not fit his men. By their very nature, the men best suited to the task were rough, independent-minded individuals, spirited men who did not take well to the whip or confinement and were likely to simply vanish one evening if they thought that they or one of their friends had been mistreated. The problem Rogers encountered was not unlike that faced by many French leaders, and like them, he arrived at the same conclusion; the only way to lead such a group was by earning their respect. As such, Rogers set the example and asked nothing more from his men than he was willing to do himself.[2]

While the value and necessity of the Rangers was clear to every British commander in North America, how to deal with the Rangers in terms of their incorporation into British military control proved a major problem. As might be expected, Rogers' men did not adapt well to British military discipline. The regular officers were aghast at the lack of control exercised over the Rangers, and even many provincial officers, notorious for their lax enforcement of military regulations, raised a questioning brow at what they saw. Numerous incidents between the Rangers and a string of British officers ensued, and it was only through the intervention of Rogers and the British commander in chief in North America, as well as moving the Rangers camp to Rogers Island, that matters were defused.

In keeping with his earlier orders from Pitt to raise additional Ranger companies, Loudoun attached fifty-five British volunteers to Rogers' command. The idea was that these British soldiers, after learning Rogers' methods and tactics, would form the nucleus of regular-army ranging companies, two of which would be attached to every British regiment in North America. Although it was not called such at the time, it was the germ of light infantry companies—elite, fast-moving, self-sufficient units that were to become prevalent in the military affairs of the late eighteenth and early nineteenth centuries. At the moment, however, it was just an experiment on the part of Loudoun, and much of this experiment depended upon Rogers' ability as an instructor and the cadets' ability to absorb the lesson plan. In the former there was little doubt. From the onset Rogers had proven himself an excellent teacher. It was true that many of his men were backwoodsmen, as able as himself to navigate the perils of partisan warfare, but surprisingly, a large number were not cut from this cloth. Sailors, shoe-

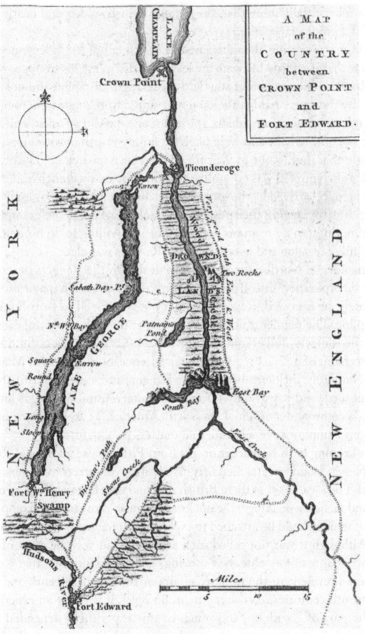

A contemporary map from *Gentleman's Magazine* showing the contested area from Fort Edward to Crown Point. (*New York Public Library*)

makers, fugitives, and a wild assortment of adventurers were scattered through the ranks. Yet regardless of their background, Rogers managed to mold most into Rangers, instilling in each the rules of wilderness warfare. As for the second component of the experiment, that being the cadets' responsibility to quickly learn Rogers' lessons, that remained to be seen.[3]

With a cessation of formal army operations, Rogers' four companies, including his new cadet company and what was left of his brother's company from the debacle at Fort William Henry, returned to their old activities, as did their counterparts to the north. As the leaves passed through gold and crimson, browned, and gathered in wind-strewn piles, the two sides sought each other out. The French and their allies fell upon isolated homesteads and circled the woods about Fort Edward, while the Rangers probed north, reporting on the state of the French defenses on Lake Champlain and occasionally seizing a prisoner or two in the process.

For the most part the scouts were uneventful, at least from the perspective of enemy action. Instead, the real skirmishing was with the British regulars who were slowly becoming a more prominent part of Ranger life. It was almost inevitable. Rogers had done his best to isolate the Rangers from British military authority, but with the inclusion of so many regulars within his scouting expeditions and a garrison of redcoats at Fort Edward, some sort of disturbance was bound to occur.

The first of these situations took place in mid-November when Captain James Abercrombie of the 42nd Regiment, Lt. Matthew Clerk of the Royal Engineers, and Lt. Jan Hollandt, a Dutch engineer in the Royal Americans, accompanied a large scouting party led by Captain John Stark. It would be reasonable to believe that one of Washington's future generals simply did not like redcoats, but this was not the case. Perhaps Stark expected Abercrombie to behave as Brigadier General Howe had done on earlier scouts with the Rangers, asking questions, listening to advice, and making a genuine effort to learn the art of woodland warfare. Instead, Captain Abercrombie, although clearly out of his element, defaulted to his superior rank and began issuing orders, which only made Stark bristle. Not a man to let his feelings or grudges go unanswered, Stark did just about everything in his power to annoy Abercrombie. On the march to Ticonderoga, he let his men fire at game and snubbed any objections made by Abercrombie as to their conduct or how to best proceed. It was the beginning of a long feud between the two men, one that was to show itself again near Ticonderoga the following year and one that was destined to reach a conclusion on a humid summer day at a place called Bunker Hill.

Almost a week later the scouting party arrived at Ticonderoga. Abercrombie and the two engineers, under the cover of a dozen Rangers, moved forward that afternoon and, from the vantage point of Mount Defiance, studied the fort splayed below them. A few hours later they returned and a council of war was convened. Abercrombie wanted to attack and burn the thirty or so bateaux he had seen along the water's edge, but Stark and his officers were not interested. It was dangerous work for little reward. The loss of a few boats would not amount to anything and certainly was not worth the risks involved. Instead, another plan was put forth. The Rangers would lie in ambush along the Fort Carillon–Fort St. Frederic trail in hopes of surprising a wood-cutting party whose tracks they had noticed on their arrival. With a plan arrived at, Abercrombie took command and positioned half the three-hundred-man force along either side of the road, while the other half at the makeshift camp was ordered to relieve them at midnight. The Rangers, aware that no one would appear on the trail at night, promptly ignored Abercrombie and returned to their camp for a good night's rest. This not being enough, Abercrombie then complained that, contrary to his orders, sentries had not been posted, and when he sent Clerk to speak to Stark about it, the latter claimed to have found every man "asleep under his blanket."[4]

The next morning the ambush was set, and about mid-morning a few Frenchmen came out of the fort to cut wood. After watching them for two hours and realizing that the trap would not net anything else, Abercrombie ordered a small detachment to cut the work party off from the fort. These Rangers, however, were soon seen by the enemy, prompting Stark to "set up the Indian hollow, upon that the whole party jumped up and yelled as if Hell had broke loose, and all fell a firing at a few men running away." The Rangers chased the French toward the fort until within range of the cannons, which were now firing to cover the work party's retreat. Stark and his men taunted the garrison for a few minutes, firing off their muskets and shouting "God Save King George" in hopes they would induce a sally from the fort, but when it became clear that this was not going to happen, they began their march back toward Fort Edward without, Abercrombie claimed, a rear guard, which he and his comrades were forced to form for the safety of the detachment. The expedition and conduct of the Rangers had not impressed Abercrombie, and in his official report to Loudoun he informed the general that if the Rangers were to remain part of his forces that "it will be necessary to put some regular officers among them to introduce a great deal of subordination."[5]

Major Robert Rogers. The dynamic leader of one of the most famous military units ever raised may have proven a constant source of irritation to his British supervisors, but each realized that they could not do without his services. Although perhaps never equaling the abilities of his French counterparts, such as Langy and Marin, Rogers became a master of the "*Petite Guerre.*" More importantly, unlike these men Rogers had a knack for passing on what he had learned and for molding men into Rangers. (*Anne S. K. Brown Military Collection, Brown University Library*)

Over the next week tensions were further heightened between the Rangers and the regulars when Abercrombie presented the commandant of Fort Edward, Lt. Colonel William Haviland, with a list of twelve Rangers "unfit for service" based on his observations during the recent scout. Haviland, of the same mind as Abercrombie and a disciplinarian whom the Rangers incessantly irritated, had the men dismissed from the service without even consulting Rogers or soliciting the opinion of their commanding officers. In early December the matter came to a boil when a near riot broke out on Rogers Island after a pair of Rangers caught stealing rum were given a number of lashes at the whipping post. The matter was further aggravated when a rumor began to circulate that the offenders had been unjustly subjected to the punishment. As the pair sat in the guardhouse serving out the remainder of their sentence, a crowd inflamed by the story of their innocence chopped down the whipping post and then marched on the guardhouse demanding the pair's release. The matter, already mutinous by regular military standards, became more so when one of the disgruntled Rangers leveled his musket at Captain John Shepherd, who was attempting to restore order.

Shepherd knocked the weapon aside and, with the help of a few supporters, secured the Ranger and dispersed the crowd.

The incident might have died right there, but Haviland, having caught wind of what had transpired, demanded that Rogers send him the mutiny's ringleaders for questioning. When Rogers complied, Haviland had the men clapped in irons and thrown into the fort's guardhouse. He then directed Rogers to hold a formal hearing into the episode, but when Rogers requested that his men be returned so he could question them, Haviland refused for fear that they would be the target of another rescue attempt. Rogers held his inquest during the second week of December, but it accomplished little. It seemed that every Ranger questioned was somewhere else when the alleged mutiny took place. Even Shepherd, who was at the center of the incident, refused to testify against the mutineers. The response was easy to understand. The Rangers resented Haviland's meddling with their affairs more than the actions of the mutineers and closed ranks. The message sent was simple: the Rangers would deal with their own.[6]

Haviland, incensed over the results of the inquiry, summoned Rogers to the fort. The commandant wanted to hang the mutineers in his hands, but Rogers warned him that if he did that it would not be in his power to prevent most of the Rangers from deserting. Haviland fired back "that it would be better if they were all gone than to have such a riotous sort of people." The colonel then compromised. If Rogers handed over the ringleader of the mutiny, only he would be hanged and the rest released. Rogers, not trusting Haviland and realizing the effect such an action would have on his men, refused. With nothing accomplished beyond the creation of a personal feud, the two men parted ways after Haviland informed Rogers that he would make his recommendations to General Loudoun and that the matter now had become one for him to decide.[7]

As he shuffled back to his camp, Rogers realized that Haviland's report was certain to paint his command in a poor light to Loudoun, especially when placed beside Abercrombie's earlier criticisms. Given the expense of the Rangers, their unorthodox conduct, and their recent lack of success, the report might well prove the end of the ranging companies. What he desperately needed at the moment was a report of his own—yes, a stunning scout, one that would overshadow Haviland's comments or at the very least temper their sting. As he finished crossing the frozen Hudson and weaved his way through the Rangers' scattered huts, he made up his mind. Better to act than do nothing.

A few days later Rogers and 150 of his men left their camp to conduct a reconnaissance of the French position at Ticonderoga. Setting out on the afternoon of December 17 the detachment spent the evening encamped near the burnt remains of Fort William Henry, where they uncovered a cache of artillery shells and cannonballs buried by the French earlier that summer. Amidst the increasing snowfall, the group made its way north along the western side of the lake, skirting the French advanced post near the head of Lake George, and by the twenty-fourth found themselves within a few hundred yards of Fort Carillon, having encountered nothing beyond a set of day-old tracks.

After briefing his troops on rendezvous points in case they were forced to retreat, an ambush was laid out. Twenty men were advanced along the path connecting the fort and the sawmill on the La Chute River, while Rogers and the main force dispersed themselves in the snow-covered timber a few hundred yards to the rear. By 11:00 a.m. the trap had snagged its first victim, a sergeant of the Marines who, having involved himself in some financial misdealing at the fort, was attempting to desert. Rogers listened closely as the prisoner supplied him with information on the garrisons of Fort Carillon and Fort St. Frederic, as well as news of French endeavors underway at Montreal. Although outnumbered more than three to one, the information proved useful enough that Rogers began contemplating taking the fort. He had several factors working for him in this respect. First, it was Christmas Eve, which meant that the garrison might be lax in its guard duties, especially if the usual festivities were being observed. Second, the French were still unaware of his presence and more importantly his numbers. If a portion of the garrison could be enticed to sally out, there was a chance, albeit remote, that his Rangers might be able to slip behind them and seize the fort via a *coup de main*. And even if seizing the fort proved impossible, at the very least it would afford him an opportunity to lure the unsuspecting French into an ambush.

To accomplish either of these Rogers had to first find a way to draw the French out of their fortifications. Around noon just such an opportunity presented itself. A lone French hunter returning from an earlier foray approached the Rangers' advanced guard. Rogers ordered several of his men to give away their positions with a few shots and pursue the Frenchman into the cleared area about the fort before seizing him. After a brief chase the surprised Frenchman gave up in full view of the garrison. Along the fort's walls the sentries sounded the alarm, but the fort's commander, Captain Louis-Philippe le Dossu d'Hebecourt of the La Riene Regiment, was not interested in taking Rogers' bait. Suspecting that the English might try something, Hebecourt had previously canceled the scheduled midnight mass, closed the canteen, and doubled the guard.

Rogers spent the next few hours showing small detachments of his men feigning retreat and occasionally sniping at the fort, but it was pointless. Under orders, the garrison simply watched from behind the safety of the fort's walls. His plan frustrated, Rogers turned his attention to a herd of oxen that had mistakenly been allowed to roam just outside of the range of the fort's cannons. The Rangers slaughtered all seventeen of the animals before turning to the piles of neatly stacked firewood situated close to the fort. Several piles were set ablaze with small incendiary charges, which elicited a response from the fort in the form of a few cannonballs. With the French proving uncooperative and with little else to be done, Rogers moved off under the cover of darkness and began his trek back to Fort Edward.[8]

The next morning Captain Hebecourt sent out a patrol under one of Rogers' counterparts, a lieutenant by the name of Wolf, to survey the damage. Wolf returned a few hours later with news that the English had departed. He found a few cords of firewood burnt and all the escaped oxen slaughtered. In addition, he presented the fort's commandant with a small English firebomb that had failed to ignite and a letter that had been pinned to the horns of one of the oxen. "I am obliged to you sir," the letter began. "For the rest you have allowed me to take and the fresh meat you have sent me. I shall take good care of my prisoners. My compliments to the Marquis of Montcalm. (Signed) Rogers, Commander of the Independent Companies." Wolf may have smiled at his adversary's audacity, but Hebecourt was not amused and forwarded Rogers' "thank you" note along to Quebec. Both Governor Vaudreuil and Commissary Doriel viewed the contents of the note as an "ill-timed and very low piece of braggadocio," but Montcalm, after reading the letter, was more pragmatic, writing, "The billet of Captain Rogers is some of this partisan's customary gasconnade. Perhaps we can dampen his spirit."[9]

Rogers' actions during this patrol accomplished what he had hoped. When he returned to Fort Edward, he found orders to report to General Abercromby at Albany. Contrary to any fears Rogers might have had, the meeting with Abercromby went well. Rogers impressed Abercromby by recounting the actions of his latest scout, and when the question of his men's conduct arose, the Ranger captain deflected the issue by implying that Haviland had made more of the matter than it deserved. The remainder of the meeting dealt with Rogers' rank, which he proposed be raised to at least captain-commandant in lieu of an offer of a provincial colonelcy and his willingness to recruit additional ranging companies. It was, in all, a cordial encounter designed by Loudoun to gauge Rogers and his command. When it was over, Abercromby informed Rogers that Loudoun wished to speak with him personally, and armed with a sealed letter from Abercromby to Loudoun, Rogers set out for New York City the next day.

Any confidence Rogers may have taken from this preliminary meeting with Abercromby was ill-founded. While he was conducting his latest scout, Haviland's letter and Captain Abercrombie's earlier report had reached Loudoun, creating serious questions as to the future of the Rangers. On December 18 Loudoun asked General Abercromby for his opinion as to expanding the Rangers. Given the evidence before him, Abercromby was not for increasing Rogers' corps. Their conduct, which would prove difficult to deal with if their numbers were multiplied, and their high pay were certainly instrumental in reaching this conclusion, as was news that Lt. Colonel Thomas Gage was to raise a regiment of lightly armed troops, which Abercromby was convinced "would discharge all the functions of the Rangers in a short time."

Although Abercromby was not for augmenting Rogers' corps, neither was he for disbanding it. With a sprinkling of regular officers added to their ranks and a regular officer placed over their head, the Rangers would prove an invaluable asset, and even if Gage's light infantry regiment was established, Abercromby was of the opinion that they should be continued "for this ensuing campaign under such regulations as your Lordship thinks proper." Rogers' meeting with Abercromby, regardless of what Rogers might have thought, did little to change the general's feelings on the matter. In the letter Rogers carried, Abercromby informed Loudoun that much of his conversation with the Ranger leader, particularly those elements regarding his rank, was a "good deal of nonsense." He was still unsatisfied with Rogers' explanation as to the conduct of his men, and as a product of the British military establishment, he chafed at Rogers' forecast that most of his men would desert if the mutineers in custody were punished. Still, in regard to Rogers himself he was forced to admit that, "I think him so necessary and useful a man that I should be extremely sorry to part with him . . . Without him these four Independent Companies would be good for nothing."[10]

Rogers met with Loudoun on January 9. When Loudoun launched into a sermon on mutinies and their effect on unit discipline, the Ranger must have questioned his recent confidence, but when it came time for him to speak, he saw a glint in Loudoun's eyes when he pointed to Haviland's bias against his command. He had been fortunate. Loudoun, like Rogers, had issues with the commander of Fort Edward, and as such, was inclined to side with Rogers. The moment settled all other matters in Loudoun's mind.

In the best interest of the service, the mutineers would be returned to Rogers who would then promptly dismiss them from the service. His corps would be increased, not by the eight companies Rogers proposed but by five, one of which was to be a native Mohegan company commanded by one of Rogers' current lieutenants. Recruiting, uniform, and pay issues were resolved in turn, leaving only one question, that of Rogers' rank. Loudoun was aware that New Hampshire had offered Rogers a colonelcy, but he was not in the position to counter the offer with a regular commission. The best he could do was convince Rogers that the issue would be revisited in a more favorable light once the new companies were raised. It worked. Armed with Loudoun's directives and a promise of future rank, Rogers returned to Rogers Island with the news and was soon issuing orders to several of his officers to begin recruiting the new companies.[11]

In the meantime, the Partisan War continued. The Rangers, after having been flooded by a January thaw that sent the waters of the Hudson spilling through their camp, conducted several scouts over the next few weeks. Most were aimed at gauging the ice on Lake George and Lake Champlain. This was an important question, as two plans for a winter strike against the French were being advanced. The first was a scheme purposed by Rogers. His Christmas scout against Fort Carillon had sparked his interest in seizing one of the French forts via a *coup de main*. The plan, however, called for a strike against Fort St. Frederic, not Fort Carillon. The reasons were simple. Fort Carillon was too heavily garrisoned and too closely guarded for such a plan to succeed, but Fort St. Frederic, located farther down the lake, was another matter. With Fort Carillon covering its southern approaches, the French were not expecting an attack on this stronghold, as indicated by its smaller garrison of 150 or so. The operation would be based on deception. Rogers would take his four hundred Rangers and circle west around the prying eyes of Fort Carillon to arrive at a point on the lake somewhere north of Fort St. Frederic. Once there, he would wait until they could ambush or capture a French supply convoy coming from Fort St. Jean. When this was accomplished, a portion of his men would assume the roles of the French sleigh drivers, while others hid in the back of the sleighs. The remaining troops would follow close behind this ruse, and when the commanding officer of Fort St. Frederic opened the gates to receive the convoy, the entire lot would rush in and take the fort by storm. Once Fort St. Frederic was taken, Fort Carillon would be cut off and vulnerable to attack. In Rogers' mind, this audacious effort would unhinge the entire French position on Lake Champlain.[12]

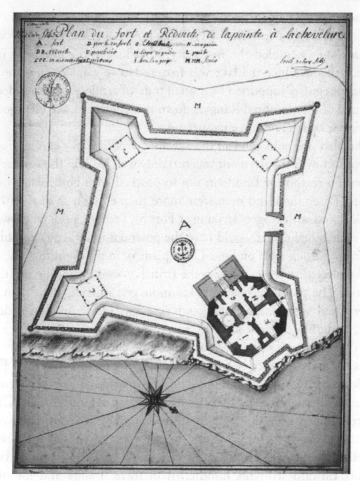

Plan of Fort St. Frederic at Crown Point circa 1737. (*National Archives of Canada*)

When presented with the idea, Loudoun directed Rogers to consult with Abercromby over the details and execution of the plan, but in fact, he dismissed it outright. The general had his own venture underway to seize Fort Carillon, one that called for the use of the Rangers and one which he had no intentions of calling off to satisfy Rogers' daring scheme. Since late autumn Loudoun had pushed forward a plan for a winter expedition against the fort. The idea was not new. Shirley had unsuccessfully attempted to convince the New England colonies of the merits of such an attack years before during King George's War (1744–1748). Loudoun, however, employing British regulars and Rangers, did not have to convince anyone to execute such a plan. The details of the expedition had been handed over to the capable Brigadier General Howe, who throughout the early winter months had assembled the necessary provisions and equipment in and around Albany. Once the lake was frozen, Howe would lead some three thousand regulars supported by a small train of artillery and preceded by a vanguard of four hundred Rangers down the length of Lake George to invest Fort Carillon and force its surrender.

The plan was bold, held all the advantages of Shirley's earlier proposal, and with Howe's involvement was certainly well led. On the surface there seemed no reason for Loudoun not to proceed with both plans, his and Rogers. Three thousand men were more than enough to deal with Fort Carillon, and with Rogers striking at Fort St. Frederic prior to Howe's attack, such a dual thrust would have the potential to inflict a deathblow to the French strongholds on Lake Champlain, or in the event that one of the attacks faltered, at least still leave the British in a commanding position on the lake. The problem, however, was more one of equipment than manpower. There were simply not enough snowshoes to equip Howe's detachment, and thus Rogers and his men would be required to use their snowshoes to break a path for the British regulars.[13]

As preparations moved forward with Howe's expedition, the French struck at Fort Edward. Eager to squash the bravado of Rogers' recent raid, Vaudreuil dispatched a war party under Ensign Jean Langy to Fort Carillon in late January. Langy, a Marine officer of whom the normally critical Montcalm remarked, "understands the petty war best of any man," wasted little time, and by the afternoon of February 7 had arrived in the vicinity of Fort Edward with his hundred-man force. Langy and his officers watched from the woods as an English woodcutting party, finished with its day's work, slowly made its way back to Fort Edward. The natives in his party wanted to attack immediately, but Langy nixed the idea. The English were too close to the outlying defenses of the fort. Not to worry, though, he informed them. They would have their chance tomorrow.

Langy and his men were up early the next day, peering quietly from the tree line while white puffs from their breath dissipated in the morning air. Around nine o'clock the fort's gates swung open and two parties emerged. The first was a covering party of twenty-five men from the 27th Regiment, followed shortly thereafter by a larger party of unarmed provincials dragging sleds behind them. Langy watched their movements closely. As he had noticed the day before, both parties followed a snow-packed trail that led toward the woods; they had no choice, the snow was several feet deep, and none were wearing snowshoes. Langy passed the word that once the attack started, his men were to drive the English off the trail. Once in the deep snow, they would be easy targets for his snowshoed forces. All waited for the signal as the English shuffled closer, then with a thunderous war whoop, the trap was sprung. The brunt of the attack fell on the covering party, who, as Langy had hoped, were forced into the deep snow. Floundering, they were driven "back into ye woods like so many sheep or cattle where they were tomahawked, killed, and scalped." The provincials, being closer to the fort, were luckier, losing only three of their number, but the covering party was decimated. Thirteen of the twenty-five members, including the sergeant in charge, were killed, five were carried away prisoner, and of the seven who made good their escape four were wounded. Rogers and his men organized a pursuit, but it was for naught; Langy had too much of a head start. Two days later the bodies of the fallen were recovered and one was found to have a note pinned to it addressed to Captain Rogers. The French, too, were capable of low pieces of braggadocio.[14]

Within a few days the attack had passed out of mind, as amidst the constant flurries sleigh loads of provisions began arriving at Fort Edward. Captain Stark and Lt. Mathew Leslie of the regulars moved forward with a small party to break a trail to the lake and test the ice one more time as the contents of the sleighs changed from provisions to ammunition, artillery, and scaling ladders. The fort was abuzz with anticipation, which only heightened when Stark and Leslie returned with news that the lake was frozen solid.

Not far behind Stark was Lt. Wolf and a small party of French bearing letters addressed to Loudoun. Wolf entered Fort Edward under a flag of truce on February 17 under the guise of delivering letters from Vaudreuil regarding a prisoner exchange. The real reason, however, had more to do with Langy's prisoners speaking of an upcoming English offensive and reports that a large number of sleighs were moving between Albany and Saratoga. Haviland quickly saw through the deception and did not allow Wolf to spend long at the fort. Fortunately, there was little for him to see. None of Howe's troops had moved up from Albany, and the incoming supplies, to protect them from the elements, had already been stored out of sight. While Wolf waited for Haviland to pen a response to his letters, a smirking Rogers prodded him about the effects of his recent raid and the fresh meat he had left them at Carillon. Wolf gave a half-hearted nod as an acknowledgement of the Rangers' success and then warned him "to be careful of himself when he came again." Rogers scoffed at the remark, which proved to be an ominous forecast.[15]

Although Wolf had not gleaned any details concerning the upcoming English offensive, at Fort Carillon Captain Hebecourt was convinced that one was coming and braced for the worst. As it turned out, he had little to fear. Howe met with Leslie and several of the officers involved in the expedition to determine whether or not it should proceed. There were no issues in regard to provisions or troops; both had been seen to, and the lake was certainly capable of handling the movement of the troops and their supplies. What was of concern was the weather. A bitter cold front had taken hold of the area. Several of the members of Stark and Leslie's party, mostly hardened woodsmen, had returned from the short scout with cases of frostbite. For three thousand regulars unaccustomed to such severe weather the implications were clear. There was also another problem, a shortage of snowshoes. Rogers had been ordered to make seven hundred pairs in November, but the January flood of Rogers Island consumed a large number under construction, leaving only four hundred pairs available for the operation. The three hundred missing snowshoes, although a convenient excuse later used to explain why the expedition was called off, was not the issue. Leslie had found the snow four to five feet deep on and about the lake. Whether four hundred, seven hundred, or a thousand snowshoes existed did not matter. It would not be enough to pack a trail hard enough to support the troops much less the provision sleighs and heavy artillery. The conclusion was clear, and on February 27 the expedition was abandoned.[16]

Rogers took some delight in the cancellation of Howe's expedition, for it seemed to imply that his plan to seize Fort St. Frederic would go forward. Instead, Haviland dispatched Captain Putnam and 115 men to make a scout of Fort Carillon, and then, in a clear breach of discipline on his part, publicly announced that Rogers and four hundred of his men would be sent out immediately upon Putnam's return. Rogers was rightly furious over the announcement and implied that Haviland, still smarting over the results of the Ranger mutiny, had purposely attempted to sabotage his operation. Rogers' fears became more pronounced when Putnam returned with news that there were up to six hundred French Indians encamped in the vicinity of Fort Carillon, and minus one man, who had apparently become separated from the detachment. The loss of one of Putnam's men and the report of a large French force about Ticonderoga unsettled the Ranger captain, but not as much as the orders Haviland passed to him the next day. Rogers was to take 180 men and scout the area about Ticonderoga. Rogers was stunned by the orders. If his plan was off, so be it, but to reduce his detachment to 180 men in the face of news that six hundred French Indians were at Fort Carillon, and after one of Putnam's party, who was armed with information that Rogers was to conduct a scout within a few days, was missing and potentially in enemy hands, smacked of something else. It appeared that Haviland was sending him and his men into a trap. "What could I think!" Rogers wrote in his journal. "To see my party, instead of being strengthened and augmented, reduced to less than one half of the number first purposed. I must confess it appeared to me (ignorant and unskilled as I then was in politics and the arts of war) incomprehensible; *but my commander doubtless had his reasons, and is able to vindicate his own conduct.*"[17]

On the afternoon of March 10, a gloomy Rogers shuffled out of Fort Edward at the head of 172 Rangers and eight Volunteers. The detachment only proceeded as far as Half Way Brook where it made camp. The following evening was spent at the First Narrows, and by the twelfth the detachment was slowly working its way up the eastern side of Lake George. A few hours after sunrise, the Rangers spotted a dog running across the lake. As the animal was likely part of a French war party, Rogers moved the column into the woods along the shoreline and sent out small patrols in search of the creature's masters. Nothing was found, but Rogers, acting more cautious than normal, crossed the lake and encamped at Sabbath Day Point. From here he and his men spent the rest of the day monitoring the lake with the "prospective glasses" they had brought. At nightfall the detachment moved forward until the advanced guard under veteran Ranger Lt. Bill Philips reported seeing a campfire on the east shore a few miles from the abandoned French posts at the head of the lake. Rogers halted the column, ordered his men to drop their packs, and moved across the lake to attack the enemy encampment, but it proved a false alarm. Philips had mistaken the glint from a "bleak patch of snow" for a fire, which Rogers added in his journal "in the night, at a distance, resembles it." With the attack called off, the detachment retraced their steps back to the west side of the lake and made camp for the evening.[18]

The Rangers fixed themselves a meal on the morning of the thirteenth and shook off the cold while Rogers met with his officers. All were of the opinion that the detachment should don their snowshoes and proceed by land at this point. The lake route before them, although easier to traverse, was too risky, being visible to the enemy from a dozen vantage points. Rogers agreed, and at seven o'clock the column moved forward, taking a route nearly parallel to the Trout Brook Valley, while consciously keeping to the backside of the ridge along the western shore of the lake to conceal their movements from any enemy scouts. At noon Rogers ordered a halt. For three hours the detachment waited at the base of Bald Mountain, or as it is known today, Rogers Slide. Part of the reason was the snow, which at over four feet deep was proving difficult even on snowshoes, but the real motive behind the stop was that Rogers wanted to give time for the daily French patrols that traversed the region to return to Fort Carillon. He would then move up the Trout Brook Valley and set up an ambuscade to catch them when they returned the following morning.

Around 3 p.m., when he felt reasonably sure that the French patrols had left the area, Rogers gave the order to move out. The main column had marched a mile and a half along the backside of Cook and Bear Mountains when one of the advanced scouts reported a party of a hundred French and Indians moving toward them down the frozen skin of Trout Brook. It was not exactly how he had planned it, but since the ambush had come to him Rogers wasted no time in taking advantage of the opportunity. He ordered his men to drop their packs, wheel left, and form a skirmish line along the eastern bank of brook.[19]

Rogers' belief that his patrol had been compromised by Haviland's reduction in its size and the earlier disappearance of one of Putnam's Rangers, along with another man captured during a raid against one of Fort Edward's supply convoys a few days later, proved partially true. As it turned out, neither of the missing men betrayed his party's presence in the area; the French discovered this by other means. But Haviland's reduction of his force from 400 to 180 men was to have dire consequences. Under normal circumstances 180 men would be more than enough to deal with any patrols launched by the winter-weary garrison of Fort Carillon, but unfortunately for the Rangers, the fort had recently received some unexpected visitors.

On March 12, while Rogers and his men were resting at Sabbath Day Point, Marine Ensign Raimbault Laperriere De La Durantaye, along with a number of Canadians and colonial cadets, arrived at Fort Carillon with two hundred Mission Iroquois and Nipissing. Vaudreuil had dispatched this force to follow up on a pair of recent raids by Langy against Fort Edward. The latter was still at Fort Carillon to greet the newcomers, although most of his original force had departed for points north. For the fort's commandant, Captain Hebecourt, the arrival of Durantaye was a mixed blessing. The next morning Durantaye's men requested brandy and provisions from the commandant, informing him that they planned to rest at the fort

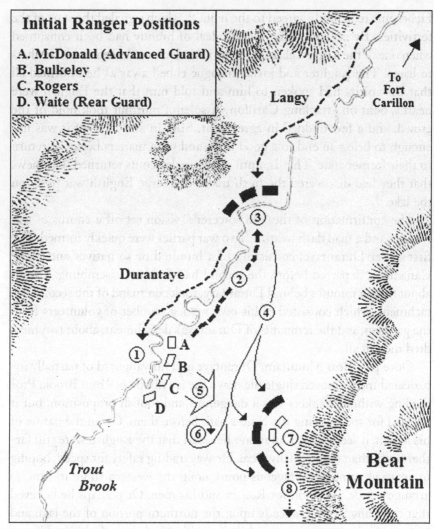

Initial Ranger Positions

A. McDonald (Advanced Guard)
B. Bulkeley
C. Rogers
D. Waite (Rear Guard)

Langy

To Fort Carillon

Durantaye

Trout Brook

Bear Mountain

A sketch of the Battle of Rogers Rock. Letters A through D show Rogers' deployment at the start of the engagement. 1. The Rangers ambush and rout Durantaye's detachment. 2. Half the Rangers set off in pursuit of Durantaye's retreating forces. 3. The Rangers are ambushed and routed by Langy's detachment. 4. Langy advances. 5. Rogers orders a fighting retreat to the foot of Bear Mt. 6. Waite's rear guard is surrounded and annihilated. 7. The Rangers position near dusk. 8. Ranger retreat after nightfall. (*Author*)

a few days before pushing south. Hebecourt was familiar enough with custom to realize this meant a few days of drinking and revelry on the part of the raiders, consuming what little supplies he had left after a hard winter.

Hebecourt reluctantly agreed to the request, which signaled the start of the festivities. By mid-morning a good deal of brandy had been consumed when one of the natives, claiming to be a witch doctor, called to his brothers to listen. The laughter and jovial dialogue ebbed away as he informed all that the spirits had spoken to him and told him that the English were nearby, bent on attacking Carillon. A solemn murmur took hold of the crowd, and a few nodded in agreement. Still, in and of itself it was not enough to bring an end to a good time, and soon matters began to return to their former state. That is, until six Abenaki scouts returned with news that they had discovered the fresh tracks of a large English war party on the lake.[20]

The confirmation of the "old sorcerer's" vision set off a chorus of war whoops and a mad dash to arms. Two war parties were quickly formed. The first under Durantaye, consisting of a hundred or so natives and a few Canadians, departed before the second had finished assembling. Langy, about fifteen minutes behind Durantaye, took command of the second detachment, which consisted of his own men, a number of volunteers from the garrison, and the remnants of Durantaye's detachment, about two hundred men in all.

Once past Bear Mountain, Durantaye and his vanguard of partially intoxicated troops moved single file down the icy ribbon of Trout Brook. Proceeding without flankers was a dangerous and foolish proposition, but it allowed for speed, being the easiest path before them. Given the nature of his march, it seems that Durantaye believed that the English were still farther south than they actually were. He was trading safety for speed, hoping to arrive at some advantageous point along the western shore in time to arrange a rude reception for Rogers and his men. Or perhaps he believed that the Rangers were already upon the northern portion of the lake and was attempting to circle around their position in hopes of placing his war party between them and Fort Carillon, effectively cutting their retreat to Fort Edward. In either case he guessed wrong and was now about to pay for his lack of precaution.[21]

Rogers had stumbled across a textbook ambush. He occupied the higher ground along the east bank of the waterway, which gradually fell away before him until it reached the streambed and began an ascent from the foot of the opposite mountain. It was a natural parabola in which his unsuspecting enemy would soon find themselves at the vertex. The Ranger leader deployed his men along this ground in four loose divisions drawn out to envelope the entire French column with one volley. Ensign Gregory Mc-

Donald, in charge of the advanced guard, formed the northernmost point or head of the line, followed by Captain Charles Bulkeley's contingent, Rogers' contingent, and ending with a dozen men of the rear guard under Ensign James Waite. Here the Rangers waited behind rocks, bare trees, and whatever other cover the ridge afforded, their breath thundering in their ears as anxious little puffs drifted from their stilled forms.

Their patience was soon rewarded as the head of Durantaye's column shuffled into sight. McDonald let it pass by, as did Bulkeley and Rogers. Finally, when it had reached Waite's position, Rogers fired at the column, a signal that was followed by the successive detonation of over 150 muskets. The French column disintegrated and broke into a disorganized flight back up the stream just as the Rangers came screaming down the embankment, brandishing tomahawks and scalping knifes. Rogers claimed that above forty French Indians collapsed under the Rangers' guns or fell before their hatchets in the frantic retreat. It was a well-executed ambush and a complete rout, but like the unfortunate Dieskau a few years before, it was not to be victory. For a quarter of an hour the Rangers pressed their advantage, and in doing so they had become scattered, half occupied in chasing their adversary up the valley and half occupied in scalping and picking over the dead.

Suddenly, the jubilance of victory was shattered by the sound of a hundred muskets rolling down the valley. Those Rangers in pursuit of the fleeing French had raced headlong into an ambush set by Langy's detachment. Two hundred guns decimated the Rangers' ranks. Captain Bulkeley and three of his officers were instantly cut down, while Ensign McDonald and Lt. Increase Moore received mortal wounds. In all, a score of Rangers fell victim to the attack. Langy's men surged forward under an umbrella of shouts and war whoops, and within minutes the hunters had become the hunted. Rogers and those still at the original ambush sight were jolted into action. Realizing that he could not make a stand at his current location, Rogers ordered his men to higher ground at the base of Bear Mountain. With Langy's force hot on their heels it was a costly retreat. By the time the Rangers redeployed themselves on higher ground, over fifty of their number lay scattered across the winter landscape, including almost every member of Waite's rearguard, who found themselves cut off in the hasty retreat.[22]

Langy's contingent, fueled by the effects of brandy and maddened at finding the scalp of one of their war chiefs in a Rangers jacket, recklessly threw themselves at the horseshoe-shaped formation Rogers had established across the face of the mountainside, but the Rangers' concentrated firepower blunted their initial surge. The battle now settled down into a more static affair. Rogers juggled his men to support his position as the more numerous French pushed on his wings and front. Again, the French pulled back in response to the Rangers' fire, only to rally and press forward anew, compressing the Rangers' position and, when it did not break, sliding back down the mountainside once more.

So far, Rogers was holding his ground, but doing so was costing him too many men. Numbers were now becoming the real issue. The engagement was turning into a battle of attrition, one that he could not hope to win. As the sun began its descent toward the peaks of the Adirondacks, Langy and Durantaye attempted to envelope Rogers' position. They placed a screen of skirmishers along Rogers' front and launched a large party of Indians at his right flank and a similar body of Canadians against his left flank. Lt. Philips informed Rogers of the movement of the first group, which appeared to be aimed at seizing a piece of rising ground on the Rangers' right as a prelude to circling behind their defenses. Rogers gave Philips eighteen men and ordered him to take possession of the hill before the enemy reached it, and then fearing that Langy might attempt a similar move on his other flank, he dispatched Lt. Edward Crofton with fifteen men to bolster the position there, reinforcing him not long after with another ten men under volunteer Captain-Lieutenant Henry Pringle of the 27th Regiment. The moves salvaged the Rangers' position for the moment, but now Rogers' center was so weakened that the "enemy pushed on so close in the front that the parties were not more than twenty yards apart and often times intermixed with each other."[23]

Rogers looked at the falling sun and urged on its trek. He had lost over a hundred men, beaten off four attacks, and still clung to a tenuous position on the snow-strewn mountainside. Night was his ally. If he could hang on until it arrived, he stood a chance of breaking off the engagement and withdrawing under its cover. Langy also looked to the west as the muskets flashed in the lengthening shadows. Over an hour had passed since his initial attack, and he now had less than that to finish off the English before darkness offered them a chance at escape. Now was the time for a final push. Langy ordered a general assault on the Rangers' position, and at his urgings the French and their allies pitched forward like the onslaught of an angry bull.

Rogers' center, progressively weakened by detachments and enemy action, finally gave way. The Ranger leader ordered the thirty or so men about

A painting of the Rangers' position in the later stages of the Battle of Rogers Rock. Although the battle decimated the Rangers' the tenacity shown by the corps won them not only the respect of their opponents, but a flood of new recruits as well. (*New York Public Library*)

him to retreat back up the mountainside, effectively collapsing his horseshoe defense. The Rangers now formed a line with Philips on the right, Rogers in the center, and Crofton on the left. Even this, however, only bought a few minutes. The French were pressing too hard, making the next decision unavoidable. Philips was nearly surrounded and informed Rogers that he would seek terms if the French would give them, otherwise he would make a stand down to the last man. With Philips unable to extract himself, Rogers abandoned his position and scrambled over to the hill being held by Crofton and Pringle. Here the unequal battle continued, until with twilight upon them and his forces cleaved in two, Rogers gave one last command, Ranging Rule number ten: "If the enemy is so superior that you are in danger of being surrounded by them, let the whole body disperse, and every one take a different road to the place of rendezvous."[24]

The flight of Rogers' Rangers was perhaps the lowest moment of the unit's existence. Ironically, it also led to one of the lasting legends of the area and one that would eventually rename Bald Mountain to Rogers Slide. Many of the fleeing Rangers were tracked down in the rising moonlight, but Rogers managed to stay one step ahead of his pursuers as he scaled the western face of Bald Mountain. When he reached the summit, he glanced down at the near vertical drop of almost a thousand feet to the lake below.

As he listened to the shouts and sporadic gunfire closing in on his position, the Ranger captain considered tempting his luck by riding down the incline sitting on his snowshoes. It was but a thought quickly replaced by a better idea. He loosened the thongs on his snowshoes and then, without moving them, turned to step into them so that they were now worn backward. He then retied the thongs and retraced his steps until he encountered a defile along the southern face of the mountain, which he used to descend to the lake below. His pursuers, a number of French Indians, reached the summit just in time to see Rogers scampering down the lake. When they examined the tracks before them, they became convinced that the Englishman they witnessed had slid down the face of the thousand-foot cliff. Such a man, they concluded, was being "watched over," which effectively ended any thought of pursuit.[25]

At least, so goes the legend of Rogers Slide, which although colorful, quickly fails to hold under closer scrutiny. Among other issues the most important inconsistency concerns the pursuers. Was he pressed by pursuing French Indians who bore witness to his final movements down the lake? Doubtful. If the legend is to be believed, Rogers would have reached Bald Mountain around eight o'clock that evening. It is difficult to believe that victorious French Indians, after winning a pitched battle, would have passed up the opportunity to pick over the spoils of their victory to chase this lone figure for nearly two hours in the dark. Some of the Rangers were certainly caught at the start of their flight, but it seems more likely that any pursuit that actually did occur did not last very long.

Whatever his actual path, Rogers met up with a number of his men at the rendezvous point at Cook's Bay on Lake George. Here, with a few volunteers, he passed the evening waiting for any stragglers. The rest of his men, including a number of wounded, were sent off toward Fort Edward. Three Rangers sent ahead of the survivors arrived at Fort Edward around noon on the fourteenth with news of the battle and an urgent plea for help. Haviland responded immediately, dispatching Captain Stark up the lake with all the Rangers he could lay his hands on. That evening Stark met Rogers near Sloop Island, and by the next afternoon what was left of Rogers' detachment began filtering into Fort Edward, Rogers himself being the last to enter the fort around five o'clock.[26]

For the young Ranging Corps, the Battle of Rogers Rock was a crushing defeat. Of the 180 Rangers and volunteers that departed with Rogers, only fifty returned, eight of whom were badly wounded. For those left behind in the retreat, death or capture awaited them. Bill Philips' detachment, which Rogers was forced to abandon, did seek terms and surrendered to the French, only to be set upon by their allies when a number of fresh scalps were found in their possession. They tied the captive Rangers to trees and subjected each to an agonizing death, all except Bill Philips. While they were engrossed in this grisly work, the old Indian fighter managed to free one hand, and then cutting himself loose with a pocketknife that he opened with his teeth, escaped into the night. Captain-Lieutenant Pringle and his comrade Lt. Boyle Roche, both volunteers on the ill-fated expedition, miraculously avoided capture when the Rangers dispersed. Familiar with neither the terrain nor snowshoes, they spent the next several days on a hopeless winter odyssey led about by a deranged Ranger who saw Indians and familiar landmarks wherever he looked. When the Ranger died on the nineteenth the two officers, nearly dead themselves from exhaustion and exposure, surrendered to the garrison of Fort Carillon the next day. Three other Rangers also fell captive and were led back to the Nipissing villages as "live letters to their friends," never to be heard from again. The rest, 125 in all, lay scattered across the Trout Brook Valley and the side of Bear Mountain, covered in a thin dusting of spring snow.[27]

For the French it was sweet revenge. Rogers' green jacket was found on the battlefield, his commission from Shirley tucked away in one pocket. The discovery convinced the French that Rogers was one of the dead. An Indian chieftain even claimed to have scalped the English partisan, which only added credence to the belief. The French commanders Langy and Durantaye both had accolades heaped upon them. The latter was promoted as a reward for his part in the action, and the former solidified his place as Canada's greatest partisan fighter. Officially, the French losses were tallied as eight Indians killed and seventeen wounded, along with two cadets and a Canadian wounded. The numbers are questionable, especially given Rogers' initial ambush of Durantaye's detachment, which several French reports confirmed. The real French casualty figures may never be known, but Captain Hebecourt may have come closest to the truth when he informed Bourlamaque shortly after the battle that the results were wonderful, though "it cost us dearly through the loss which we suffered."[28]

For the colonies, Rogers' defeat, albeit a heroic one, was yet another in a long series of setbacks. The war in North America was preparing to enter its fourth year and had not gone well for the British colonies. Oswego was gone, Fort William Henry was gone, Braddock was dead, Webb recalled in disgrace, French war parties raided the colonial frontier from Maine to Georgia, and Louisbourg, Fort Carillon, Fort St. Frederic, and Fort

Duquesne were still in French hands. For all the expense, all the manpower, and all the effort put forth, there was nothing to show beyond a few initial successes in Nova Scotia, and even these were in constant jeopardy of falling back into the enemy's hands.

The colonists were not alone in these thoughts. In London Pitt set down the reports of Loudoun's failed campaign against Louisbourg and the fall of Fort William Henry next to a growing pile of letters from the various colonial governors pleading for assistance. He studied a map of the British American colonies with a frown and found he agreed with the governors. A more concerted effort was required on the part of Britain to turn the tide.

4

"AN IRRUPTION INTO CANADA
BY THE WAY OF CROWN POINT"

ON MARCH 7, 1758, CAPTAIN JOSHUA LORING (R.N.) ARRIVED AT
Abercromby's headquarters at Albany. Unlike Abercromby, Loring was not new to the American colonies, or even Lake George.
A native of Massachusetts, Loring had been instrumental in the planning
of Governor William Shirley's successful Louisbourg expedition in 1745.
His actions would earn him a lieutenancy in the Royal Navy. Loring would
serve through the rest of King George's War (1744–1748) before being
placed on half-pay (reserve) status with the military reductions after the
conflict. At the start of the Seven Years' War he had returned to service
and spent the summer of 1756 building a number of vessels on Lake
George. In mid-December 1757 he was promoted to captain of the twenty-
gun HMS *Squirrel*, but it does not appear that he ever served on the vessel,
given that shortly thereafter he was dispatched to North America to deliver
Pitt's correspondence to Abercromby.

Abercromby opened the first letter. While the snow accumulated on the
rooftops of Albany, Abercromby quietly reread the portion of the first letter
which appointed him the new commander in chief of His Majesty's forces

in North America. Pitt's words brought forth a sense of satisfaction that his talents and long service to the king had been officially recognized. These thoughts, however, quickly passed. He had not opposed Loudoun's conduct of the war as others had and had certainly not actively sought out the position that was now thrust upon him, given that more than anyone on the continent he understood the obstacles his predecessor had faced.

Pitt's second letter contained explicit instructions for the upcoming campaign, a copy of a circular letter addressed to the various colonial governors, and a copy of a letter addressed to Governor DeLancy of New York. Pitt laid out the ambitious details for the campaign of 1758. The French were to be attacked simultaneously on three sides. To the east, fourteen thousand men and a sizable fleet would be assembled at Halifax by late April with the aim of besieging Louisbourg at the first possible opportunity. To the west, a smaller contingent of seven thousand provincials and regulars under the command of Brigadier General John Forbes would launch a similar effort against Fort Duquesne in the Ohio Valley. Abercromby was to personally lead the third element of the campaign, deemed "an irruption into Canada by the way of Crown Point," with the forces not tasked for either of the other two enterprises. In keeping with his plan to direct the war effort from London, Pitt neatly laid out the forces at the general's disposal. They amounted to eight regular battalions, a number of recruits to be forwarded to fill out these units, the four New York Independent companies, and a detachment of the Royal Artillery, some 9,447 men by the minister's count. Fearing that such a force would not be sufficient after detachments were left to guard the frontier and in keeping with his philosophy of utilizing the military capabilities of the colonies, Pitt took the unprecedented step of calling upon the governments of Massachusetts, Connecticut, New Hampshire, Rhode Island, New York, and New Jersey to provide "at least twenty thousand men to join a body of the King's forces for invading Canada by the way of Crown Point."[1]

Based on his previous dealings with the colonial assemblies, Abercromby must have shaken his head at the news, but matters in regard to such details had changed, taking much of the responsibility, and in a like fashion much of the control, out of the general's hands. Pitt would deal personally with the colonies to oversee and direct such efforts. Abercromby needed only to assist and encourage the various colonial governors, to monitor their progress, and to direct the point and time of their rendezvous with the regulars. Pitt had seen to other matters as well. The provincials would be provided for and provisioned by the regular commissaries, which would free the colonies of the burden of creating their own supply lines—establishments which had proved nothing but an entangled mess in the past. There were other incentives as well, aimed at both reducing the time needed to raise such a force and facilitating a speedy rendezvous with the regulars. First, the colonies would only be asked to provide for the cost of levying their troops, their basic clothing, and their pay, all of which would later be submitted to Parliament for proper compensation. Arms, tents, and munitions would be provided out of the king's stores. It was understood that the first of these might pose a problem, as the number of men to be raised was likely to exceed the number of arms currently available. To rectify this shortfall, an additional ten thousand stands of arms and four thousand tents would be dispatched from England. In the meantime, the governors were ordered to inventory and assemble what serviceable weapons they had to cover their immediate needs. As if this was not enough, Pitt removed one of the past obstacles to colonial participation by seeing to issues created by provincial ranks, such as those that plagued the union of Winslow's forces with Loudoun in 1756. From now on, provincial officers would rank equally with regular officers up to the rank of colonel.[2]

In addition to his efforts to raise a sizable colonial force, Pitt covered another contingency by informing Abercromby that Governor DeLancy of New York would be tasked with the construction of the necessary bateaux and larger vessels required to protect the movement of the troops and assure naval supremacy on Lake George. Commodore Joshua Loring, who had delivered the letters to Abercromby, would be placed in command of this little navy and would oversee the immediate building of these vessels under both the guidance of DeLancy and the general.[3]

After reading all the letters in the packet before him, Abercromby sat back and reflected on his situation. Beyond seeing to the initial details of the troop deployments for the three campaigns, it was clear that his position as commander in chief in North America was really nothing more than that of an independent command. Forbes, and as it would turn out Major General Jeffery Amherst, would each direct their own campaign without any real input from Abercromby, as in reality, each was being controlled from London. In some sense this arrangement relieved him of a number of responsibilities, which might otherwise deflect his attention away from his own campaign. He sighed and stared out the window at the snowfall. Perhaps this was for the best, he concluded, given the daunting task that now lay before him in raising, supplying, and marshalling together an army of nearly twenty-seven thousand men.

The general's first act was to scrap the existing plans formulated by Loudoun for the upcoming campaign. Just as it had last year, the first minister's insistence on directing the war effort from London bore fruit for the hard-pressed French. Loudoun's plans for 1758 had earmarked troops and supplies for campaigns against Fort Duquesne, Louisbourg, Fort Carillon, and Fort Frontenac. He had carefully arranged his troops and selected their winter quarters to allow for an earlier effort against each of these targets. To the southwest, Fort Duquesne would be attacked by two thousand regulars and as many provincials, all currently stationed within the southern colonies. In addition to these troops, Loudoun had secured invaluable allies in the powerful Cherokee nation, who agreed to support the venture with five hundred men.

To assault Louisbourg, Loudoun planned to use the 5,400 regular troops under General Peregrine Hopson, who had remained in Nova Scotia after the previous year's effort had been called off. These troops would be augmented by a number of New England provincials. The New Englanders could be quickly deployed from the various coastal towns and cities, and as the operation called for a formal siege, the provincials' skills in constructing the required field works made each worth two regulars. By these arrangements the entire force could be in place to strike at Louisbourg in April, long before the yearly French supply and naval reinforcements had reached the fortress. To the northwest, one of Loudoun's colonial specialists, Captain John Bradstreet, would lead an attack on Fort Frontenac with eight hundred irregulars. Bradstreet would construct the necessary boats in early spring, move up the Mohawk River, and cross over to Lake Ontario to strike at the unsuspecting fort before the garrison received its spring supply convoys from Montreal.

The last element of Loudoun's plan was Fort Carillon. As we have seen, the general originally planned to capture the French fort in a winter campaign. Although this was called off, the supplies, munitions, and artillery Howe had carefully assembled at Fort Edward were left in place to facilitate an attack at the earliest opportunity. Loudoun had concentrated eight regular regiments at Albany during the winter, and four more were within easy reach down the Hudson River. His plan was to take advantage of the climate, which typically opened the waters of Lake George a fortnight before those of Lake Champlain. He would use this window of opportunity to march on Fort Carillon with his regular regiments, Rogers' companies, and a handful of colonial auxiliaries, striking at the stronghold before it could be reinforced from Montreal. Against such a force the fort's winter garrison

Major General James Abercromby. An efficient administrator and staff officer, the aging Scot struggled to cope with the frustrating colonial legislatures and found himself out of his element as a field commander. Portrait by Allan Ramsay. (*The Papers of Sir William Johnson, Vol. X*)

of four hundred or so would be doomed. The older and weaker Fort St. Frederic would follow in short order, and by late May the entire French position on Lake Champlain would be in British hands, leaving Loudoun free to press on to Montreal.[4]

On the surface, Loudoun's plans differed little from those laid down by Pitt. Three of the targets, Louisbourg, Fort Duquesne, and Fort Carillon, were included in the latter's December letter. What was different was the methodology put into place to accomplish these goals. Loudoun's arrangements were the product of two years' experience in North America. He understood the seasonal weakness of his enemy and carefully selected the resources assigned to each target; regulars against Fort Carillon because they could be marshaled together quickly, provincials for Louisbourg because of their proximity to transport and their superior construction skills, irregulars for Fort Frontenac because of their ability to travel light and navigate the numerous portages to be crossed, and a combined Anglo-Native expeditionary force to traverse the forests of the Ohio. In each instance he put these resources into place to allow for an early campaign to take advantage of his enemy's inherent vulnerability.

For Pitt, tucked away in his office in London, strategy and planning were nothing more than an arrow on a map and a few lines in a letter. Powerful allocations of troops and supplies were assigned to his targets without regard to their current location, the delays of mobilization, and the nightmare of logistics involved in their transportation. He failed to grasp what Loudoun had learned and reorganized British forces in North America into his own vision of victory, regardless of the consequences.[5]

At least in Abercromby, Pitt had found what he was looking for, an officer who would unwaveringly follow the minister's directives, but the selection was also a good one in terms of Abercromby's strengths as an organizer. Through his family's excellent political connections, Abercromby entered the king's service in 1717, purchasing the rank of ensign in the 25th Foot at the age of eleven. It would be several years before he actually joined his regiment, but by 1736 he had attained the prominent rank of captain in the 1st Regiment of Foot, the Royal Scots. With promotions proving slow, Abercromby began focusing on politics. In 1734 he was elected to Parliament and a few years later became the lieutenant governor of Stirling Castle, a prestigious but primarily honorary position. With the outbreak of the War of Austrian Succession, the advancement opportunities he had sought became available. In June of 1742 he was promoted to major, and after his participation in the Battle of Culloden Moor in April 1746, he was made lieutenant colonel of the first battalion of the Royal Scots. In September and October of the same year, he served as quartermaster general during St. Clair's unsuccessful expedition against Port L'Orient, France, and later proved himself a competent staff officer while campaigning in the Netherlands until a severe wound at the siege of Hulst in 1747 forced him to return to Scotland. Here he entered into semi-retirement, focusing his efforts on politics until at the outbreak of the Seven Years' War he was made a major general and assigned as Loudoun's second in command in North America. While serving under Loudoun, he had demonstrated an ability to tackle the difficult paperwork and logistical details that had frustrated so many British officers in North America. Loudoun even wrote the commander in chief of the British Army, the Duke of Cumberland, that "Abercromby is a good officer, and a very good Second Man any where, whatever he is employed in."[6]

Although the fifty-two-year-old veteran's health was in question, his disposition was better suited to Pitt's needs. Reserved to the point of being quiet, he was a tactful man, not prone to the angry outbursts and hardline tactics of his predecessor, which had thoroughly alienated many within the colonies. If it could be said that Abercromby had alienated no one under his command, it could just as easily be said that neither had he inspired anyone. The general was viewed as somewhat methodical, even slow by some accounts, attached to an old school of military protocol and thought, poor qualities for a leader who might find himself forced to quickly size up a situation and act during the throes of battle.[7]

Fortunately, Abercromby was assigned a number of officers, which more than covered his shortfalls. First among these was Abercromby's executive officer, Lord George Augustus Howe. Pitt, who referred to Howe as "a character of ancient times; a complete model of military virtue," had envisioned that Howe would be the real leader of the campaign, and in this he was not mistaken. Howe, the third Viscount of the name, and the elder of three brothers, each of whom would figure prominently in American history, was a distant relation to King George I. These connections served him well when, in 1745 at the age of twenty-one, he entered the army as an ensign in the 1st Foot Guards. By May of the next year he had obtained a captaincy in this prestigious unit, and throughout 1746 and 1747 he served as aide-de-camp to the Duke of Cumberland, participating in both the Battles of Culloden Moor and Laufeldt during this period. By May of 1749, after just four years in the service, he had reached the rank of lieutenant colonel.

Howe's rapid rise through the ranks of the British army was certainly influenced by his family's connections, but just as important, if not more so, was his inherent aptitude for his chosen profession and his winning personality. Both of these elements came into play when Howe arrived in North America in 1757 as colonel of the 3rd Battalion of the Royal Americans. His presence at Fort Edward during the siege of Fort William Henry bolstered the jittery Webb and restored some form of order to his command. After the siege, Loudoun was quick to recognize Howe's talents. In September he was made colonel of the 55th Regiment, and in November he was given command of a detachment sent to the relief of German Flats in upper New York. A few months later, after being promoted to the rank of brigadier general, Loudoun entrusted him with the command and planning of what turned out to be an aborted winter expedition against Ticonderoga.

Unlike other British officers, Howe's charm, open mindedness, and serious devotion to his studies won him the immediate admiration and friendship of the Rangers, particularly of John Stark, whom he accompanied on several scouts to study not only the layout of Fort Carillon but the methods and tactics of the Rangers as well. Soon he was applying what he had learned to his own regiment. The soldiers' coats were cut down, Indian leggings were issued, and hats were trimmed to better facilitate movement through the brush. Unnecessary items were discarded from their persons, gun barrels were blackened, and every man from the general on down was expected to carry on his back what was required to subsist in the woods for a week. "You would laugh to see the droll figure we all make," wrote one officer of his regiment. "Regulars as well as provincials have cut their coats so as scarcely to reach their waists. No officer or private is allowed to carry more than one blanket and a bearskin . . . No women follow the camp to wash our linen. Lord Howe has already shown by example by going to the brook and washing his own."[8]

While in Albany, Howe refused to occupy the quarters set aside for him, choosing instead to encamp like the rest of his troops in a tent outside the town, devoid of furniture, which he viewed as absurd for an army in the field. He ate what his troops ate from a private's mess kit and suffered through the same discomforts of wind, rain, and cold. These actions alone would have won the general the respect and admiration of his troops, but the nature of his personality, his quest for studying a problem from perspectives other than his own, cemented his position among his charges. Ann Grant, a young denizen of Albany at the time, noted Howe's conduct in this regard.

Above the pedantry of holding up standards of military rules, where it was impossible to practice them, and the narrow spirit of preferring the modes of his own country, to those proved by experience, to suit that in which he was to act, Lord Howe laid aside all pride and prejudice and gratefully accepted counsel from those whom he knew to be best qualified to direct him.[9]

Here was a rare leader indeed, and all knew it, from Pitt down to the newest Massachusetts private. Howe was a binding force, unafraid to employ new ideas and support them by personal example, which was a command philosophy closer to the methods of the French partisans than his fellow British officers. He was the leader Shirley had aspired to be, and what the former governor and general felt was necessary to unite the British forces in North America into a single cohesive unit: an admired commander among the regulars with authority over them, while at the same time being able to motivate the provincial troops by holding their respect and confidence.

Behind Howe and third in command was Brigadier General Thomas Gage. Gage, the son of a prestigious Irish peer, entered the service in 1741 and, like Howe, rose quickly through the ranks primarily through purchase and his family connections. By 1743 he was a captain in the 62nd Foot and

General George Augustus Howe. (*New York Public Library*)

a few years later participated in both the Battles of Fontenoy and Culloden Moor. He served throughout the remainder of the War of Austrian Succession, becoming a major in 1748 and lieutenant colonel of the 44th Regiment in 1751. In 1755 he came to North America with Braddock, and after being slightly wounded at the Battle of the Monongahela, he developed a better appreciation of warfare in the wilds of America. Gage displayed great personal courage during the battle but was later criticized for failing to secure a crucial hill with the advanced guard under his command. The charges leveled by Braddock's aide-de-camp Robert Orme, although true, never took hold and were vehemently denied by Gage.

With the death of the 44th's commander in the engagement, Colonel Peter Halket, Gage assumed command of the regiment and for the next few years served as one of the senior British officers in North America, establishing a reputation for himself as a capable soldier and an effective administrator. Most recently, he had used the opportunity presented by Loudoun's annoyance with Rogers to raise a light infantry regiment, designated the 80th, at his own expense. Employing officers recruited in the colonies and a number previously tutored by Rogers, it was hoped this unit would eventually replace the Rangers, who had proven an expensive and somewhat unpredictable necessity. The move, along with his political connections, brought with it the rank of full colonel and shortly thereafter an appointment to brigadier general. It also brought Gage a number of admirers who fostered the mistaken belief that he was something of an expert in the area of wilderness warfare, an impression that he did little to dissuade.[10]

The last member of Abercromby's immediate staff was Lt. Colonel John Bradstreet, recently promoted to acting deputy quartermaster general in North America. Under Pitt's orders, Bradstreet was to be assigned to Forbes' Fort Duquesne campaign, but Abercromby, in one of his few changes to the minister's directives, reassigned Bradstreet to his own campaign, not under his official title as deputy quartermaster general but as commander of the colonial bateaux service. The reasons were as obvious as they were necessary. Bradstreet was familiar with the terrain to be traversed by Abercromby's army and was a well-known expert in the construction and management of small boats, huge numbers of which would be required to move the army and its supplies down Lake George. He was of far more use in this role than that of quartermaster general, the functions of which could be continued by Captain Gabriel Christie, who Abercromby insisted had done a superb job.

One of the colonial specialists that the British army had come to rely on, John Bradstreet had begun his career in 1735 as an ensign in the 40th Foot stationed in Nova Scotia. A native of the island, he soon left the service and with his brother established a lucrative business trading with the French garrisons in the area. With the onset of King George's War, Bradstreet used his extensive knowledge of Louisbourg to influence Governor Shirley to launch an attack on the fortress. He was made lieutenant colonel of the 1st Massachusetts Regiment for his efforts and participated in the siege and eventual capture of the French stronghold in 1745. The next year he was made a captain in the 51st Regiment and later that year was rewarded for his services by being appointed lieutenant governor of St. Johns, Newfoundland. In 1751 Bradstreet went to England and a few years later returned to America with Braddock. In the campaign of 1755 he was assigned to Shirley's command, which fell short of its goal of capturing Fort Niagara. The following year Shirley included Bradstreet's recommendation to attack Fort Frontenac into the army's operations and placed Bradstreet in command of the task. Shirley's recall and the state of the British garrison at Oswego resulted in the attack being postponed, although Bradstreet distinguished himself in keeping the supply lines to the garrison open, skirmishing with French raiding parties on several occasions in the process. When Loudoun assumed command, Bradstreet's long association with Shirley did not affect his standing with the new general. This was due to

General Thomas Gage, left. (*Yale Center for British Art*) General John Bradstreet, right. (*National Park Service*)

some political maneuvering by Bradstreet, but for the most part it reflected the real talent he had shown in managing the transport of troops and supplies across the wilds of North America. In late 1757 he was made a captain in the Royal Americans, and throughout Loudoun's tenure as commander in chief, he acted as *de facto* quartermaster general and aide-de-camp to the general, eventually convincing Loudoun to allow him to lead an attack on Fort Frontenac in the spring of 1758.[11]

Driven by ambition, a desire for promotion, and motivated by an urge to counter any questions of loyalty raised by his Acadian ancestry, Bradstreet had proven himself as an "irregular regular." Indeed, he was one of a handful of the king's specialists, men like William Johnson and Robert Rogers, who filled a void presented by the application of traditional army methods in the nontraditional realm of North America. He was an exceptional officer, a keen problem solver, and a dynamic leader whom Abercromby would end up leaning on far more than he had expected.

One of the first governors to receive Pitt's circular letter of December 30 was Thomas Pownall of Massachusetts. Pownall was also one of the first to act upon the minister's directives. The governor immediately presented Pitt's plan to the Massachusetts Assembly. The monetary incentives, rank concessions, and demands placed on supplying and equipping the troops quickly won over the Assembly, which Pownall proudly reported, passed a unanimous resolution to raise seven thousand men as the colony's quota. The other northern colonies followed in short order. Governor Wentworth pressed New Hampshire for a thousand men, but the Assembly, which had already provided a good number of Rangers for the cause, would only agree to eight hundred men, limiting their service to nine months in the process. Although Connecticut had borne a heavy share of the war effort over the last several years, Governor Fitch had no such troubles and was able to inform Pitt with "great satisfaction" that his Assembly had agreed to levy five thousand troops. The citizens of his colony as a whole, he remarked, "seem to be considerably roused and disposed to promote this service." Rhode Island, claiming to have only six thousand men able to bear arms, of which many were currently employed at sea, agreed to raise a regiment of a thousand men. New York, basing their quota on a percentage of Massachusetts' allotment, proposed to muster 2,680 men, while New Jersey could only be convinced to levy 1,000 men, a number, Abercromby informed Pitt, that was "far short of their abilities."[12]

In all, the northern colonies agreed to raise 17,480 men, substantially short of the 20,000 Pitt had requested. Even so, it was a commitment never seen before in North America. By late April Abercromby was able to report that recruitment efforts were underway. The New York forces were nearly complete, although part had to be impressed, and Massachusetts had raised 4,796 of its 7,000 troops and would probably be forced to follow New York's lead to meet its quota. As for the other colonies, efforts were underway, but as of yet he had no clear picture of the numbers levied or projected dates of their contingent's completion. "Although by what proceeds," he informed Pitt, "I have met with several difficulties." The first of these dealt with the phrasing of Pitt's letter, which stated, "the whole, therefore, that his Majesty expects and requires from the several provinces, is levying, clothing, and pay of the men." Several of the colonies, in an attempt to reduce costs, were employing a strict interpretation of this condition, refusing to furnish their men with items such as cooking utensils, mess kits, and other camp necessities. The second problem concerned provisioning the recruits. The crown had agreed to provision all provincial troops, but this was clearly impossible until they reached the rendezvous point at Albany. To speed up the recruitment process, the general agreed to pay the enlistees per diem in lieu of their promised provisions.

The third problem was the most pressing, a shortage of arms. The promised ten thousand stands of arms from England had yet to arrive, and the royal magazines in Albany, New York City, and Boston, along with the various colonial stores, had been severely depleted by the previous year's campaign. The governors, in accordance with Pitt's orders, had collected what arms they could lay their hands on, but this had fallen far short of what was required. New Hampshire and New Jersey were the first to complain in this regard. Governor Wentworth pointed out that the scarcity of arms in his colony was delaying the recruitment of his contingent, while Governor John Reading of New Jersey asked for his men to be provided muskets out of the king's stores, claiming that "the colony is exceedingly bare in that article."[13]

In an attempt to alleviate this issue, Abercromby encouraged the colonial governors to have their men bring their own muskets, promising to monetarily compensate them for "those arms as should be spoiled or lost in actual service." The move was unorthodox, but as stated in a New York proclamation to the point, Abercromby felt that the recruits would prefer their own arms "to those furnished by the Crown, not only from their being much lighter, but as from their being accustom to them, they will be much surer of their mark with those, than arms they never handled before." It was a reasonable assumption, yet the approach did not yield the desired results, as many provincials, realizing the wear and tear their arms would be subjected to, asked to be compensated for the loan of their weapon to the king's service, an idea Abercromby rejected outright. The general continued to urge the governors to collect whatever arms they could lay their hands on, even after several raised questions as to whether or not they were required to do so. With a shortfall apparent, the general eventually gave orders to purchase what weapons could be found, procuring some 750 in this fashion and creating something of a black market for muskets in the process.[14]

By late May, long after the projected rendezvous date of May 10, the general was still struggling with the arms shortfall. Pownall had secured 2,399 muskets, over half of which were purchased at highly inflated prices. Indeed, some merchants had even gone so far as to collect old muskets and then resell them at new musket prices. Similar problems existed in the other colonies, but for Abercromby, New Jersey proved the most aggravating. Governor Reading informed him in late April that he had collected less than a hundred muskets and saw no prospects of finding more, as there were no public stores and few serviceable weapons to be found among the recruits. Still perturbed by the colony's failure to raise more than a thousand men, Abercromby responded in a manner that could have been directed at any of the colonies. "[I] cannot be satisfied with a bare assertion that no arms are to be found within your province," he lashed out at Reading, "when at the same time it is known, almost to everyone, that few, if any, of the people of the continent are without arms."[15]

Governor DeLancy, finding a scarcity of muskets within his province, turned to more drastic steps and looked to impress the necessary firearms. However, the New York council objected, and he could find no law on the books that allowed him to proceed in this manner. At Abercromby's request, he petitioned the town of New York to lend him its supply of a thousand muskets. The city council refused but was willing to sell them at a hefty profit. Abercromby was rightly furious at the response, but there was little he could do beyond venting and accusing the council of profiteering in matters of their own defense. Eventually, an agreement was reached in which the muskets were lent to the crown to be replaced by a like number taken from the shipment promised by Pitt, but it proved of little help. By the time the deal was struck, the arms from England were only a few days away. Even with these setbacks, DeLancy managed to secure 5,310 muskets by June 1, almost half of them purchased on the open market at exorbitant prices. Added to this were the efforts of Brigadier General Stanwix and James Furnis of the Ordnance Department, who had collected every gunsmith they could find in New York to repair and refurbish the arms collected from recruits, purchased, or scavenged for the cause. In a true display of organizational skill, Stanwix was able to report to Abercromby on May 29 that he had 2,500 functional firearms and would forward them on to Albany at the first opportunity.[16]

Even with the efforts of Stanwix and the colonial governors, by late May it was clear that there was going to be a drastic shortfall in arms. Approximately twelve thousand had been collected, far short of the troops' totals voted by the northern colonies. With his campaign already a month behind schedule, Abercromby saw no choice but to order the governors to forward their troops to Albany with or without arms. Many of the provincials, however, were understandably reluctant to march into territory traveled by French and Indian war parties without arms, leading to yet further delays. A frustrated Abercromby summarized his plight in a letter to Pitt.

I am under the greatest difficulties imaginable for want of arms; not only by reason of the real want, of them, but because the Provinces, knowing my distress make a handle of it, to retard their troops from joining me, alleging that men without arms can be of no service.[17]

It appeared that only the arrival of the promised arms from England would rectify the problem.

Just as pressing to the campaign was the matter of transportation. At least in this regard Loudoun's earlier plans gave Abercromby a head start. In February Bradstreet had begun recruiting bateaux men and constructing the boats needed for his raid on Fort Frontenac. When Abercromby's orders arrived in March, it appeared that this operation would be scrapped, and with his promotion to deputy quartermaster general that he would be transferred to Forbes' campaign, but neither proved to be the case. With a major transportation problem looming, Abercromby needed Bradstreet's expertise, and as such, he reassigned him to the Ticonderoga campaign and sent Lt. Colonel John St. Clair south in his place. Nor was Bradstreet's Frontenac venture cancelled, although the general and many of his officers were in favor of doing so regardless of Bradstreet's lobbying. It was only through the intervention of Howe that the operation was saved, but under the condition that it would only go forward once the army had secured Ticonderoga.

With life still remaining in his Frontenac enterprise, Bradstreet turned his efforts toward Abercromby's transportation problems. There were three issues to be faced. The first dealt with water transportation. To move an army of 20,000 men and their supplies, Bradstreet calculated that 1,500 bateaux would have to be constructed, a task, he estimated, that would take until mid-May so long as the materials and skilled labor were available. The latter proved hard to come by. The New Hampshire carpenter company under Colonel Nathaniel Meserve who had served in the area for the last two campaigns had been assigned by Pitt to participate in the assault on Louisbourg, creating a skilled labor shortage. Carpenters, however, were eventually found, many coming from the soldiers recruited in Massachusetts' coastal communities, and on June 7 the last bateau was completed in a ceremony that included a great bonfire and ample quantities of beer and rum provided by Bradstreet. Added to these vessels were hundreds of whaleboats sent by Massachusetts to act as scouting vessels and two warships built, outfitted, and commanded by Commodore Loring, although neither of these vessels was completed until the end of the summer.[18]

The second problem Bradstreet dealt with was bateaux men. When he took stock of his forces in March, he found that he only had 450 of the 800 men he had originally recruited for his attempt on Frontenac. The reason was simple. Frontenac was a fur-rich trading post, and Bradstreet had offered those joining him an incentive in terms of a cut of the booty if the mission proved successful. With the priorities changed to Ticonderoga, many of his men sought employment elsewhere. Efforts were made to find replacements by increasing the pay and bounty money for new recruits, and when this failed to yield the desired numbers, Governor DeLancy signed a warrant allowing Bradstreet to impress bateaux men working along the Mohawk River into service but with little success. Finally, with no options before him, Bradstreet was forced to draft men out of the New York provincial forces to fill out his ranks.[19]

The last issued faced by Bradstreet was that of land transportation. The numerous portages along the Hudson and the rude trail from Fort Edward to Lake George demanded a huge commitment in terms of wagons and teams. Johnson had fallen victim to this problem in 1755, and in the intervening years Loudoun had done much to improve the situation, but the size of Abercromby's army overwhelmed the measures put into place. When asked what was required and how long it would take to transport a month's provisions for twenty thousand provincials from Albany to Lake George, Bradstreet estimated that a thousand bateaux, eight hundred wagons, and a thousand oxcarts could accomplish the task in three weeks' time. Even more depressing was that the estimate did not include the provisions required for the six thousand regulars, the transportation needed to move the siege train to the lake, or the time required to repair the roadways and bridges along the route. Clearly, the army's requirements far surpassed anything to be found in the area. Bradstreet searched the three upper counties of New York with power to impress any transportation he came across, but at best he was only able to procure three hundred oxcarts and wagons. With such resources available, it was not until late May that the necessary supplies and equipment were in place at Fort Edward, and even this required a Herculean effort on the part of the troops, who were often forced to drag cannons and supplies by hand over the muddy portage roads for the lack of draft animals.[20]

Arms were not the only delays Abercromby faced. The colonial contingents were slow to rendezvous at Albany. By early June those regulars not occupied in forwarding supplies or guarding the posts along the Hudson were in place, but with the exception of the New York and New Jersey contingents, few of the colonial troops had arrived. This was blamed on a reluctance to march to the rendezvous without sufficient arms, but more could be attributed to the colonial logistical system, which, as Abercromby feared, was slow in mustering and organizing the allocated forces. By late May the first of the Massachusetts troops were on the move. The march

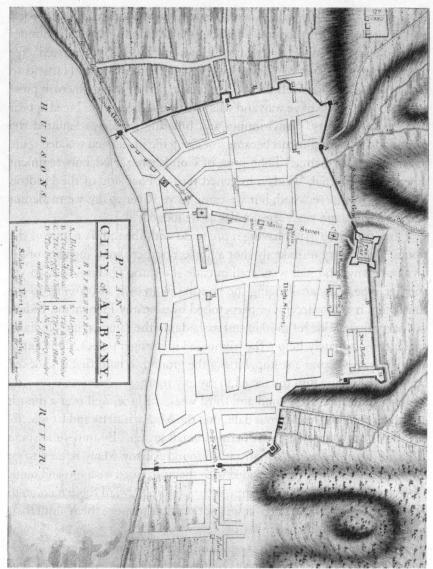

Albany, New York, 1758. (*Norman B. Leventhal Map & Education Center, Boston Public Library*)

across the western part of the colony proved more difficult than anticipated. Heavy rains swelled the creek and river crossings and turned the country throughways into ribbons of mud, all but halting any progress for days at a time. One Massachusetts soldier recalled a typical day. "We marched till about noon through mud and water, over hills and mountains, the worst way that ever was, and about 2 o'clock in the afternoon came up a thunder shower and wet us as wet as could be." Reverend Daniel Shute agreed, saying, "The greater part of ye way our Troops marched from Hatfield to Greenbush is inexpressively bad, and ye greater part of our regiment at present, with ye badness of ye way, and what with ye badness of ye bread appear to be unfit for duty." Provisioning and billeting problems haunted the march, and whole regiments became lost along the ill-defined wooded route to Albany, as Lt. Samuel Thompson of Col. Ebenezer Nichols' regiment noted in his journal. "Friday: marched on the East side of the Hudson River, and lost in ye wood; but we came to ye River again; we made but one good mile, and went seven miles as we judged."[21]

There were also issues having more to do with the militia nature of the troops. One sentry mistakenly shot a horse, another shot a member of his own company who had wandered outside the camp's parameter, and yet another, repeatedly challenging the hooting of an owl, and coming to the conclusion it was a deception perpetrated by a nearby French and Indian war party, flung aside his musket and dashed into the camp crying, "Indians, Indians!" Fortunately, before the frightened messenger panicked the entire camp, he tripped over a stump, hitting the ground so hard that it knocked out a tooth leaving him too dazed to say any more.

It was not until the second and third weeks of June, well over a month after the appointed rendezvous date, that the Massachusetts and Connecticut forces began arriving at Albany in small groups. By mid-June some 7,500 of these troops had congregated around Albany. Many refused to go any farther until they were provided with their promised weapons and tents. Abercromby's secretary, John Appy, attempted to forward these men on to Fort Edward but claimed that "it was not possible to move them" until their requests had been satisfied.[22]

Having long since seen to the preliminary details of Amherst's Louisbourg campaign and Forbes' Fort Duquesne expedition, Abercromby sent what armed detachments of colonials he could muster forward to reinforce the posts on the upper Hudson River. As for the rest of his provincial forces, many of which were reportedly still on the march, there was little he could do but wait for their arrival and the arrival of the promised shipment of arms from England.

Fortunately for the general, he would not have to wait long for the latter. On June 13 the convoy carrying the promised war materials entered New York Harbor, and by the nineteenth this cargo had reached Albany. With

Sir William Johnson. Although an unparalleled Indian diplomat and capable administrator, Johnson would only play a minor role in the Battle of Ticonderoga, although the following year he would oversee the British siege and capture of Niagara. (*New York Public Library*)

arms now issued to them the provincial forces around Albany began moving forward, one step behind the regulars, who under Howe's command had set up an encampment at the base of Lake George. Abercromby arrived at Howe's camp on the afternoon of June 26, and for the next several days spent time with his senior staff assessing the situation. Work had begun on two fortified posts, one near the remains of Fort William Henry and the other on the site of Munro's old encampment, both of which would be used as magazines for the expedition. Eight hundred bateaux and ninety whale-boats had been hauled up to the lake, but as of yet the artillery train had not arrived, nor had most of the provincials. When a roll was taken, it was found that only 5,960 provincials were present. The Rhode Island and New Hampshire Regiments were nowhere to be found, and only 475 of the promised Connecticut forces could be counted among those present. Even his regulars were short of the promised numbers, totaling some 6,370 in all. Of particular concern was the shortage of artillerymen. After sending off what was required for Amherst's expedition, Abercromby now found himself with only 124 of these crucial specialists, about half of what was promised to him.[23]

Also conspicuous in their absence was Sir William Johnson and his Mohawk contingent. Early in the planning of the campaign, Abercromby had written Johnson, urging him to use his influence to join him with as many

Iroquois as he could raise. At first things looked promising. The Iroquois, although neutral, seemed favorably disposed, but a French raid on German Flats in March quickly changed their attitude. The event spurred a council among the nations, and until the sachems finished their deliberations, the best Johnson could do was characterize the effort as "in a state of suspense." All was not lost, however. Regardless of how the council turned out, Johnson still held sway over the Mohawk, and after some deliberations, he was able to convince a number of men to join him; but the talks had taken time and it was not until June 18 that he was able to inform Abercromby that he would join him at Lake George "with all the Indians I can muster."[24]

A few days later Johnson followed this letter with another, asking for a few more days to gather together his detachment and a date from Abercromby as to when he would advance on Ticonderoga. Abercromby sympathized with Johnson's plight but emphasized his position. "I must again express my concern at being deprived of your aid and assistance . . . which we stand much in need of." He then informed Johnson that he intended to be at Lake George on June 26 and after a few days' preparation would move forward, "So that you have not a day to lose in joining us and if we should fall down the lake I shall leave boats for you to follow."[25]

Abercromby was clearly perturbed with the chain of events. He had pressed upon the colonial governors that speed was of the essence, and yet it was almost July and he was still waiting for these forces to arrive. Frustrated with the incessant delays, the shortage of arms, and the lack of colonial commitment, the general made up his mind to wait no longer.

5

MONTCALM AND VAUDREUIL

S BOTH ARMIES ENTERED WINTER QUARTERS IN THE CLOSING months of 1757 and the third campaign season in the Champlain Valley came to an end, the defenders of Canada realized that they had once again stood fast. In fact, so far, the severely outnumbered colony had done well against its enemies. Employing an aggressive defensive policy laid out by Governor Vaudreuil, its active populace and native allies had kept the English off balance, thwarting a number of their expeditions and even making some territorial gains with the seizure of Oswego and the expulsion of the British from the head of Lake George. In Nova Scotia, French policy, or lack thereof, had crumbled into a string of defeats which threatened the security of Louisbourg, but this had been dismissed as inevitable, and foolishly a large productive portion of the colony had been deemed lost. These misgivings aside, New France had weathered the storm. West of the Appalachians and along the Great Lakes French authority and influence still reigned, Louisbourg still guarded the entrance to the St. Lawrence, and in the Champlain Valley the colony's dominance remained firmly entrenched at Fort St. Frederic and Fort Carillon.

Although the English had not made any serious inroads into the defenses of New France, a more deadly enemy had. Famine, or at the very least near-famine, gripped Canada throughout the early months of 1758. As with the harvest of 1756, the harvest of 1757 had failed, pitting the colony against an enemy far more corrosive than the English and one that they could do little to defend against. "Misery commences to make itself felt," Bougainville recorded in his journal in early October 1757, upon hearing the gloomy forecasts arriving from Montreal. "The harvest is of the very worst in this Government, which is usually the granary of Canada." In response to the news, Vaudreuil took the unpopular step on November 1 of instituting a rationing program among the populace of Montreal, Quebec, and Three Rivers. There was little choice; the flour stores in Quebec and Montreal were nearly empty. The countryside had been stripped bare to put Montcalm's army into the field the previous summer, and the relief ships from France, which were being more routinely intercepted by the English, had scarcely covered this loss. A month later, to prevent the complete decimation of the cattle population, the governor announced that horse meat and salt cod would be issued to supplement the weekly allowance of beef.

The decree brought an angry mob of women to the governor's doorstep. They threw their horse meat at his door and demanded to see him. After a short standoff, Vaudreuil relented and admitted four of their number. The women berated him, bitterly complaining about the reduction in bread and their "abhorrence to eating horse meat," emphasizing that they would "sooner die than eat any." The pressed governor was probably tempted to test their resolve, but instead he calmed their fears, claiming that people had always eaten horse meat and that he had seen to it that the horses were killed carefully, in the same manner that cattle were. The words had some effect, but to make his point clear he informed the group as they were leaving that if there was any further civil disorder on their part, he would jail half the participants and hang the other half.[1]

There was trouble among the troops as well, whose rations were first cut in early October and then again in November. Taking a cue from the populace, a number of Marines at Montreal planned to refuse their allowance of horse meat. Upon hearing of the plan, Levis paraded the troops and informed them of the change in rations. He pointed out that towns in Europe had often eaten horse meat and that there was nothing wrong with its consumption. He planned on eating it, and they would eat it. Once the rations had been issued, he would listen to any complaints, but in the meantime his stance on the matter was to be clearly understood: anyone refusing to take his portion would be hung. He then cut himself the first piece and ordered his grenadiers to come forward and accept their portions. There was a little grumbling but no problems as the remaining troops came forward one at a time to take their share. In Quebec there were fewer problems with the garrison, and in keeping with Levis' example, Montcalm routinely served horse meat at his table in every fashion except soup, claiming to those he spoke with that it was much better than caribou, moose, or beaver.[2]

As the colds of January and February set in, the inhabitants of New France made do as best they could. For the moment, the excitement created by the rationing program had subsided, and all was calm. The troops settled throughout the countryside had an easier time than those located within the main towns, but as the winter progressed there was fear among the leadership that the lack of rations would leave them with an army too weak to fight when called upon. "The article of provisions makes me tremble," Montcalm informed the Minister of the Marine in late February 1758. "Notwithstanding the reductions in the rations the scarcity is greater than we should have believed." In early April matters got worse. Rations were reduced again, which coupled with the runaway inflation, caused mobs to gather about the doorsteps of Francois Daine, Quebec's chief of police. At this point the threat of hanging seemed preferable to a slow death, but the protestors scattered with a show of force. Earlier in the year, Montcalm had seriously considered transferring several regiments to Louisbourg because of the food shortage but decided against the move. Now he began to wonder if he had made the right choice. The garrison of Fort Chambly, which housed several companies of the Guyenne Regiment, reported that their stores were empty. At Fort Carillon Captain Hebecourt had quelled a mutiny over provisions, and in Quebec and Montreal even the horse meat and salt cod were running out.[3]

By mid-May matters had reached crisis levels. On June 1 the government would cease issuing bread, the supply of flour being exhausted. "I am at a loss for terms to describe our misfortune," Daine penned in a letter to the Minister of War.

The country has subsisted, up to the present time, only by the wise and prudent economy of our Intendant, but all resources are exhausted and we are on the eve of the most cruel famine, unless the succors which we are expecting from our monarch's bounty and liberality arrive within fifteen days at farthest . . . The supply of animals is beginning to fail; the butchers cannot furnish a quarter of the beef necessary for the subsistence of the inhabitants of this town, though they pay an exorbitant price for it; without fowls, vegetables, mutton or veal, we are on the eve of dying from hunger . . . The mechanics, artisans, and day-laborers exhausted by hunger, absolutely cannot work any longer; they are so feeble that 'tis with difficulty they can sustain themselves.[4]

The problem of subsistence which both haunted and weakened Canada lay not in any measures contrived by Vaudreuil or Montcalm but in the shortsighted policies of the past and the nature of the current conflict. There had always been an abundance of land to cultivate in Canada, but from its inception agriculture had taken a second seat to the fast profits of the fur trade. This alone was enough to retard agricultural growth, but other factors contributed to the problem as well. The first was the long wars with the Iroquois. To protect themselves from the native onslaught, farms clustered together in small communities for mutual protection. Such an arrangement meshed nicely with the seigniorial land system implemented within the colony, where a handful of individuals doled out portions of land to the inhabitants in return for services and a portion of the harvest. This medieval form of land management fostered small communities, which initially helped to defend the populace from the wave of Iroquois invasions, but after the Treaty of Montreal in 1702 this rigid approach proved an obstacle to agricultural expansion. The small amounts of land within the system were passed from one generation to the next, being continually farmed to a point of near exhaustion, while just beyond reach lay large tracts of land waiting to be developed. The unintentional efforts of the government also retarded any growth. Occasionally a bumper crop would lead to the export of foodstuffs to Louisbourg or the West Indies, but the leadership of New France, who carefully directed this trade, never saw this as an opportunity to expand the agricultural base and open markets for the colony. With little in the way of economic incentive, the focus of the typical Canadian farmer became self-sufficiency, to the detriment of himself and the colony as a whole.

In peacetime the margin associated with the agricultural system was small, but with the occasional supplement from France, it was, in general, able to cope with the needs of the colony. The war, however, upset this precarious balance. The system first strained to cope with the demands of the additional French regulars and the numerous native contingents raised, as well as with the militia demands placed upon the farming community. Together these elements threatened to overwhelm the agricultural base, but

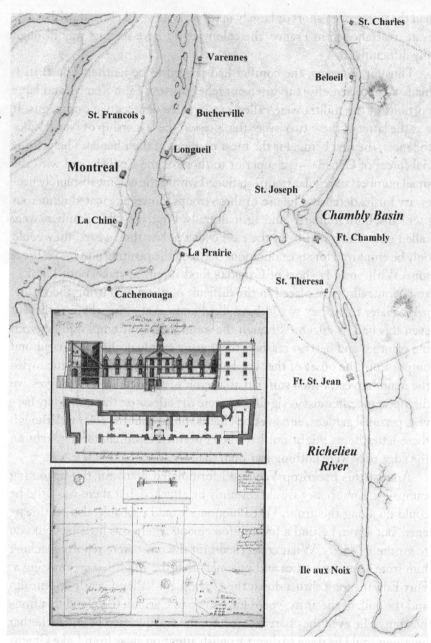

A map of the Richelieu Valley from Île aux Noix to Montreal, c.1758. A plan of Fort Chambly (top) and Fort St. Jean are also shown. A pair of rapids interrupt water communications between these two posts. This placed Fort St. Jean at the limit of northern navigation from Lake Champlain, and as such, transformed this post into a key anchorage for French warships and transports operating on the lake. (*Author*)

had the war proven short or largely inactive, it seems likely that, with moderate assistance from France, the colony could have seen its way through any difficulties.

Thus far, however, the conflict had proved to be neither. The British made a concerted effort to intercept relief convoys from France, and large portions of the militia were called out in three consecutive campaigns. It was the latter of these two issues that pressed the leadership of New France the most, the first being, for the most part, out of their hands. The provincial forces of Canada were superior to those of the English, and with the small numbers of regular troops stationed within the colony, absolutely necessary for its defense. The use of these troops, however, created numerous problems, both militarily and agriculturally. First, if sizable numbers were called out, which had been the case over the last three years, they could only be employed for short durations between the planting and harvest seasons. With nothing short of Canada's food supply at stake, both Dieskau and Montcalm were placed in the difficult position of starting their campaigns later than they would have liked and terminating them early. But even this had its effect. Although the militia was only employed between the planting and harvest seasons, there was a steady decline in agricultural output from the onset of the war. Part of this was directly concerned with the main harvest, which suffered as a result of their caretakers' progressive disappearance, but just as significant were the effects on the earlier hay harvest, personal gardens, and livestock herds throughout the colony. Although these latter items might not have been deemed essential, for a system on the edge they were nothing less than that.[5]

Amidst this backdrop Vaudreuil formulated plans for the upcoming campaign. Louisbourg would certainly be attacked, but there was little he could do along this front. Fort Duquesne would probably also be threatened, but again, beyond a few reinforcements, there was little he could do to ensure its safety. What concerned him the most were reports reaching him from scouting parties and prisoners that the English were massing at Fort Edward for a thrust down the Champlain Valley. Clearly Montcalm and the bulk of the army would have to go to Carillon to defend this frontier, but as he eyed the chart before him, the real question became whether anything could be done to divert English attention away from Lake Champlain. As he scanned the map, he realized that the opportunities and easy targets of the past were gone, that is, all except one. If he launched a powerful attack down the Mohawk River Valley toward German Flats and threatened Schenectady, he might panic the English into switching over to the defensive. It was a stretch, but in the past his enemy had shown an inclination to respond in just such a manner.

With his plan arrived at the governor penned a memoir to Montcalm outlining his goals and the general's instructions. Levis, at the head of 1,600 regulars, Canadians, and Marines, would assemble at Montreal and move down the Mohawk Valley from Oswego in early June. As for Montcalm, he would take the eight regular regiments on station, along with some five hundred to six hundred Marines, and a battalion of good Canadians, and proceed to Fort Carillon. From here he would assume a defensive position, feint an offensive, and concentrate on interdicting the English supply columns along the upper Hudson Valley. To help in this last task, the governor promised to support him with several hundred natives as soon as they could be raised.[6]

When he received the memoir, Montcalm could hardly contain his disbelief. The document began with a preamble describing how the governor had discussed the matter in length with the general and how they had come to an agreement on operations for the upcoming campaign. When? Montcalm pointed out. When had his advice been sought, for he could not recall the instance. The two had spoken over the winter on general matters concerning the colony's defense, but when had they formally met to discuss preparations for the upcoming campaign? Things got no better as he read on. He felt the overall plan was foolish. Fort Carillon and Fort St. Frederic were clearly the English objective, and they were massing to take both. How then would operations along the Mohawk River change this? Certainly, the English realized that if they took these twin strongholds any move by the French to the west would become meaningless. And given such, how would siphoning 1,600 troops from his command accomplish anything beyond making the enemy's task easier? Beyond this, his specific orders once he reached Carillon piqued his indignation. He accepted the small number of men assigned to him, some five thousand in all, realizing that the militia could not be deployed to his aid until the current provision problem had been alleviated, but the rest was a trail of contradictions and foolish ramblings. How would feinting an offensive accomplish anything? Reports were that twenty-five thousand English troops were to move against Fort Carillon. Did the governor really think that these forces would be dissuaded by the idle threats of a few thousand defenders?

The comment irritated him to the point that he wrote Vaudreuil "the proposition is so inconsistent that it must be a mistake on the part of your secretary." Nor was the idea of collapsing the enemy's offensive by interdicting their supply lines feasible. The task was a difficult proposition under the best circumstances, and with the forces at his disposal nearly impossible. These elements aside, it was the directives concerning the defense of Fort Carillon that angered the general the most. He was not to risk his army, but in the same breath he was to march against the English if the opportunity presented itself. He was to defend the portage, a position easily outflanked by an attacking army, and at the same time he was not to defend the portage but to withdraw to a suitable defensive position if a superior enemy appeared. It was a mass of contradictions and amateur tactics that made Montcalm's hand shake as he held the paper before him.[7]

For his part, Vaudreuil had been purposefully vague about the defense of the fort should the English attack. The reasons were not so much as to shift blame should things go awry but more because, not being privy to the circumstances that would unfold, he could not give the marquis a definitive course of action. Only Montcalm would be in a position to make this decision. Montcalm could have read between the lines and realized that the contradictions sprinkled throughout his orders were only suggestions, and the vagueness that he took for a shifting of responsibility was really a mandate to conduct operations at his discretion, but he did not. Had Vaudreuil simply stated the matter as such or had a better relationship existed between the two, this might have been understood, but at this stage the table had been set and neither man was willing to concede anything to the other. Montcalm penned a bitter response to the governor asking for clarification and justification in his obscure orders, turning what had been a rift into a true separation. In particular, he railed against the preamble that claimed he had been consulted on all military matters concerning the campaign, later writing in his journal of the incident that, "I declared to him positively that I would never suffer this fraudulent preamble to remain at the head of his instructions as a monument reflecting on my reputation."[8]

Not long after this affair another memoir reached the general. This time it was from Captain François Le Mercier, head of the colonial artillery, but Montcalm clearly saw Vaudreuil's hand in the letter. Le Mercier's memoir covered a possible move against Fort Edward to be conducted by Montcalm's army should the English repeat last year's maneuver and draw the bulk of their army off to besiege Louisbourg. Montcalm never took the document seriously, calling into question several of Le Mercier's assumptions concerning the strength of Fort Edward, the artillery necessary to conduct the siege, the mode of investment required to subdue the fort, as well as how the artillery and munitions would be moved the dozen or so miles from the head of Lake George to Fort Edward. Le Mercier countered, claiming that the marquis overstated the ability of the fort to defend itself, but without Montcalm's support the plan quickly became a dead issue.[9]

In late May a reprieve came to Canada in the form of several vessels from France carrying desperately needed provisions. It was nowhere near what was required to reverse the problem, but for the moment at least, the famine that threatened the colony was averted. The supplies also allowed Montcalm to begin deploying his troops along Lake Champlain. Given the late date the marquis viewed it as nothing short of providence that the English had not moved forward and overwhelmed Captain Hebecourt's weary little garrison at Fort Carillon. The regiment of La Reine already at Fort Chambly was immediately dispatched to Carillon, while the remaining regulars, augmented by a number of colonial and native auxiliaries, began converging on the forts of the upper Richelieu Valley. By mid-June Bourlamaque had arrived at Fort Carillon with the regiments of Languedoc and the two battalions of Berry, the latter of which were delighted to have ended their journey after a sudden summer tempest on Lake Champlain scattered their vessels and threatened to consume the occupants. Small parties of Nipissings, Hurons, Iroquois, and Canadians joined Bourlamaque over the next few days, and on June 30 Montcalm's flotilla arrived carrying the remainder of the French regulars.[10]

As both sides concentrated their forces, the "Petty War" along the lakes began to escalate. Behind this was a burst in English scouting activity led by the recently promoted Major Robert Rogers. Rogers did not wallow long in the misfortunes of his March defeat. Promotions were issued and replacements recruited. The odds and the gallant nature of the major's defeat did much to accelerate this last process. Rogers' reputation was spreading and with it came men more than willing to serve under the Ranger leader. By late April these measures made good most of the Rangers' losses, and after refitting his companies, Rogers decided that they were once again strong enough to move forward in force.

On the last days of the month, a five-pronged scout was launched toward the French forts in search of prisoners and intelligence. Captain Stark moved north along the west side of Lake George with his company, while Captain Jacob Naunauphtaunk with a detachment of Stockbridge (Mohegan) Indians shadowed him along the eastern side of the lake. Farther east, Captains Shepherd and Burbank moved toward South Bay and into the Drowned Lands, while the last element of the scout, personally led by Rogers, targeted the area about Fort St. Frederic. The Ranger advance proved a stunning success. Rogers nabbed three prisoners and took a scalp in an ambush near Crown Point, while Stark took six prisoners in two different incidents near Fort Carillon. Although Burbank and Shepherd returned empty handed, Captain Naunauphtaunk more than made up for their lack of success. On May 4 Naunauphtaunk and his party of nineteen Rangers lay in the woods across the lake from Fort Carillon when they observed three boats, apparently a large French wood-cutting party, approaching their position. Hardly believing his luck, Naunauphtaunk arranged his men in an ambuscade and when the first boat was pulled ashore opened fire. It was over almost as soon as it began. Seven of the boat's crew fell before the opening barrage and the rest, seeing themselves surrounded, quickly surrendered. The other two boats immediately reversed course, firing a few parting shots as they pulled for the safety of the west shore. Having scored a major success and fearing a French response, Naunauphtaunk set off for Fort Edward at once, arriving a few days later with his ten prisoners in tow.[11]

Not to be outdone, the French soon responded. In late May the Nipissing war chief Kisensik, looking to avenge the loss of his father the previous fall, joined forces with a small war party under the leadership of a Canadian partisan named Outetat. The combined force of forty French and Indians was moving south through the Drowned Lands when they came across the trail of twenty-six Rangers returning from a scout of Fort Carillon. Seizing the opportunity, Kisensik and Outetat raced forward and arranged an ambush along the western bank of Wood Creek. The Rangers, some twenty-five Stockbridge Indians under the command of Ensign Jonas Etowaukaum of Naunauphtaunk's company, walked into the trap the next morning. Threatened with encirclement, Etowaukaum and twelve of his companions managed to fight their way free and reach Fort Edward a few days later, but the rest were either killed or captured.[12]

In mid-June Rogers was back on Lake George. This time his orders came directly from Lord Howe. The major was to mark out a suitable landing place for the army at the north end of the lake and report on the French positions around Fort Carillon. On June 12 Rogers, accompanied by Captain Naunauphtaunk, Lt. Noah Porter, an ensign from the 55th Regiment, and fifty Rangers pushed out onto Lake George in five whaleboats. The party proceeded unmolested through the first narrows and a few days later arrived at the outlet of the lake. Here Rogers pulled the boats ashore along the eastern bank of the waterway, not far from the French advanced posts. The next day was spent fulfilling the first part of Lord Howe's orders, and

Major General John Stark. One of the original Rangers, Stark would command one of Rogers' companies. He retired from the Rangers at the end of 1759, but would be one of the first to take up arms against the British, commanding a New Hampshire regiment at the Battle of Bunker Hill and serving with Washington at Trenton and the Battle of Princeton. (*New York Public Library*)

several possible landing sites were located and marked. When this was complete, Rogers dispatched a few men under Lt. Porter toward Fort Carillon while he and three other Rangers ascended Rattlesnake Mountain (Mount Defiance) to sketch out the French positions about the fort. The remainder of his men, some thirty-five in all, he left to guard the boats under Naunauphtaunk's command.

Rogers had finished his task and was within a few hundred yards of the boats when a fierce fusillade erupted about the landing site. Rogers' old nemesis, Lt. Wolf, had discovered Naunauphtaunk's detachment, and with thirty-six French and Indians behind him, launched a three-pronged assault on their position. With Etowaukaum's defeat fresh in his mind and over-estimating the size of Wolf's detachment, Naunauphtaunk ordered a retreat back to the boats, but most of the Rangers had already deployed into a crescent to counter the French attack, and either never heard the command or simply ignored it. It was fortunate for Wolf that Rogers only had three men with him and that Porter, who heard the gunfire, did not march to the aid of his comrades, otherwise he would have found himself caught between two forces. As it was, Porter, thinking himself badly outnumbered, slipped past the battle and set out for Fort Edward, while the only course open to

Rogers was to circle around Wolf and rendezvous with his troops at the boats. This he was able to do without incident, and once at the boats he rallied his men and executed an orderly withdrawal back down the lake.[13]

Although Rogers had located a number of landing sites for the army, sketched out the French positions about Fort Carillon, and managed to extricate his force in the face of enemy fire, not all of his superiors were pleased with the results. The capture of three of Rogers' men, among them Ensign William Downing of the 55th Regiment, alarmed and angered Abercromby to the point that he accused Rogers of having exceeded his orders by proceeding too far down the lake and exposing his detachment to a superior enemy force. "This was an unlucky affair," the general wrote to London, "as they must learn a great deal from these prisoners."[14]

Much to Abercromby's worry, Rogers' men were not the only ones to fall into French hands. A patrol consisting of twenty-one Rangers under the command of Lt. Simon Stevens departed the advanced camp on Lake George on the evening of June 24 with orders to obtain intelligence on the French posts at the north end of the lake and to take a prisoner if possible. After landing a sergeant and three Rangers, who were to advance by foot toward Fort Carillon, Stevens' two whaleboats put ashore on a small island at the First Narrows. From here Stevens planned to break his detachment into several parties but had yet to do so when the island was suddenly beset by eighty French Indians led by Rogers' able counterpart Langy. With little in the way of options, Stevens prevented a massacre by surrendering his detachment on the promise of good terms. Stevens and his men were immediately taken to Fort Carillon, and although the Ranger lieutenant refused to cooperate with his interrogators, several of his men, continually threatened by their native captors, appear to have been more talkative.[15]

The reports coming from Stevens' men only confirmed what Montcalm had learned from Ensign Downing a few days before, that an English army of twenty to twenty-five thousand men was massing at the head of Lake George and would strike at Fort Carillon within the next few weeks. When the general reached Fort Carillon on the afternoon of June 30, he realized it was, in fact, worse than he had imagined. He found encamped about the fort eight battalions of regulars, weakened by the detachments assigned to Levis' expedition, a company of thirty-seven Marines, thirty-five Canadians, and sixteen Indians; a total of 3,058 troops with which he was to repel the attack of some 25,000 enemy troops.

When the returns from the fort's stores were laid before him, things became even more dismal. There were only nine days' worth of provisions and a few days emergency rations on hand. It seemed an impossible task. If the English attacked now, they would overwhelm his meager forces, and if they delayed a few weeks, his army would starve long before they reached Carillon. To complete the marquis' aggravation, his thoughts turned to Levis' detachment of several thousand well-provisioned men destined to strike a meaningless blow in a distant theater while the largest army ever assembled in North America was preparing to descend upon him. Although Bourlamaque had already forwarded the ominous reports from the prisoners on to the governor, Montcalm sent a courier on the evening of June 30 with a more urgent plea. The message was simple: send men, provisions, and more native scouts. The present circumstances demanded every resource New France possessed, and even then, the matter would still be in doubt. "What a country!" Montcalm penned in his journal later that evening. "What a war!"[16]

The next morning the marquis met with his staff and laid out his tactical arrangements. With so many enemy scouts lurking about and no screen of his own to hinder their actions, a semblance of strength was called for, otherwise it was feared that the enemy would seize the portage road in a sudden descent, calling the entire defensive position at the outlet of the lake into question. To this end, Montcalm ordered Bourlamaque to advance to the Lake George portage with the regiments of La Reine, Bearn, and Guyenne. Here he would erect a number of entrenchments to secure the possible English landing zones as well as construct a redan to cover the southern approach to the floating bridge over the outlet of the lake. Montcalm would personally lead the regiments of Royal Roussillon, 2nd Berry, La Sarre, and Languedoc forward to the bridge at the sawmill, posting the first two units on the southern bank and the last two on the northern bank of the river. The 3rd battalion of Berry would stay at the fort and continue work on the structure's defenses.

Covering the gaps in this arrangement was a problem. The marquis was short of Marines, which under normal circumstances he would have paired with detachments of Canadians and Indians to fill the voids. This left him with only one alternative, that of forming detachments of volunteers from the regulars. Two such units, each consisting of twenty-four men, were formed. The first was commanded by Captain Jean Duprat of the La Sarre Regiment and the second by Captain Antoine Bernard of the Bearn Regiment. Langy, a few Canadian partisans, and the handful of natives on hand were formed into small bands of scouts which moved out onto the lake at night and patrolled the banks of Lake George during the day. The decision to stretch French forces was risky, but as Bougainville put it, "Our situation is critical. Action and audacity are our sole resources."[17]

Over the next few days, work proceeded on the fort at a frantic pace. Crews hacked away at the rocky main ditch about the northern and western walls of the fort and put final touches on the parapets, demi-lunes, and glacis that covered these walls while others hauled water, food, and munitions into the fort in preparation for the expected siege. The army splayed across the La Chute Valley and the portage spent their time digging entrenchments and moving supplies and ammunition forward while Montcalm, his new chief engineer Captain Nicolas Pontleroy, Captain Desandrouins, artillery commander Lt. Louis Fiedmont, and Fort Carillon's commander, Captain Hebecourt, occupied themselves with surveying the terrain and formulating their defensive arrangements. There was some good news during this period. A convoy of thirty thousand rations arrived on the evening of July 1, enough for seven or eight days at the present rate of consumption. Men arrived as well but in pitiful numbers, given the circumstances. One hundred men arrived with the provisions convoy, Marine Captain M. de Raymond entered the camp on July 3 with 118, and another 150 Marines and Canadians appeared on the morning of the fifth. It was hardly what Montcalm had hoped for, but at least Raymond brought with him promising reports that the governor had called off Levis' expedition. The brigadier and his troops were pushing forward with all haste and were expected to be at Fort St. Jean by the fifth.[18]

July 5 proved to be a busy day for Montcalm. At 2 p.m. white flags were seen fluttering from the top of Cook's Mountain, a signal that boats had been seen on the lake. An hour later Langy's detachment returned from a scout on the lake with news that they had encountered, and for a short period of time, been pursued by fifty English whale boats after leaving Northwest Bay below the first narrows. Langy and a few volunteers had stayed behind to monitor the situation, but to all involved the implications were clear, the boats were the English advance guard. The drums beat out the call to arms, the troops reported to their respective posts, and all unnecessary equipment was ordered cleared away. Langy entered camp an hour later and reported what all had guessed; the British army was approaching. The fifty whale boats that had initially pursued his detachment had increased to a huge flotilla of boats and barges, all slowly making their way down Lake George.

The news spurred Montcalm to form several detachments for the express purpose of monitoring the progress of the enemy flotilla and observ-

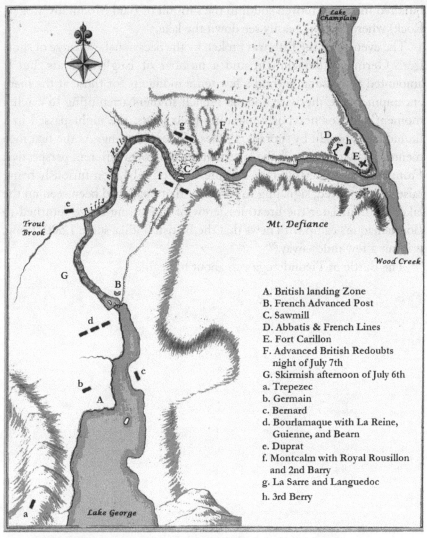

A. British landing Zone
B. French Advanced Post
C. Sawmill
D. Abbatis & French Lines
E. Fort Carillon
F. Advanced British Redoubts
night of July 7th
G. Skirmish afternoon of July 6th
a. Trepezec
b. Germain
c. Bernard
d. Bourlamaque with La Reine,
Guienne, and Bearn
e. Duprat
f. Montcalm with Royal Rousillon
and 2nd Barry
g. La Sarre and Languedoc
h. 3rd Berry

The disposition of Montcalm's forces on the evening of July 5, 1758. (*Author*)

ing their landing. Captain DuPrat's detachment was sent to the mouth of Trout Brook to guard the back route to Fort Carillon, Captain Germain of the La Reine Regiment was given 150 men and ordered to Contrecoeur's old camp below Bourlamaque's present position, Captain Bernard's Volunteers were sent forward with Germain and posted opposite his force on the east bank of the lake, while Captain Louis Trepezac of the Bearn Regiment, supported by Langy, took the largest detachment, a vanguard of nearly three hundred men, and moved south to the summit of Bald Mountain (Rogers Rock) where he could easily see down the lake.[19]

The evening of the fifth was broken by the occasional exchange of shots from Germain's detachment and a number of English scouts, but it amounted to nothing beyond a few tense moments for those at the main encampments. Otherwise, for the French soldiers attempting to catch a moment's rest or nervously manning their posts, the night passed in a humid haze, backlit by sporadic flashes of heat lightning. As the first moments of dawn traced out the lake, matters took on a different perspective. From atop Cook's Mountain, a white flag could be seen furiously being raised and lowered, signaling to all below that boats had been seen on the lake. An hour later the breathless crew of a scouting barge returned to Bourlamaque's camp with news that the British flotilla, some 1,500 strong, was but a few miles away.[20]

The Battle of Ticonderoga was about to begin.

6

LORD HOWE

THE HEAD OF LAKE GEORGE BUSTLED WITH ACTIVITY DURING THE opening days of July. Long lines of wagons from Fort Edward carrying provisions and munitions were staged into holding areas before their contents were loaded aboard awaiting craft. Bradstreet and his officers assigned vessels to the various regiments while work parties tended to the bateaux and whaleboats in need of repairs. More impressive was the loading of the expedition's artillery. Some eighteen cannon and twenty-six mortars and howitzers were manhandled onto newly constructed rafts, which were nothing more than a platform laid over two or three bateaux.[1]

Although the supply and transportation arrangements moved forward in an orderly fashion, the same could not be said for General Abercromby's army. The regulars were prepared. Their numbers were arranged into three brigades under senior colonels William Haviland, John Donaldson, and Francis Grant. The engineering brigade of 139 men was formed out of the ranks from volunteers with siege experience, and since Colonel Montressor was too ill to accompany the expedition, they were placed under the command of the new chief engineer, Lt. Mathew Clark. A similar draft was made to augment Major Ord's deficient detachment of Royal Artillery.

The provincials were another matter. Some three thousand of them marched into camp on the first days of July, and of these, many had only recently received their weapons and tents. As Abercromby's staff organized them into brigades, he and Howe met with their commanders. Here it was agreed that some form of rudimentary training was needed to make these units serviceable. Under normal circumstances weeks or months would be spent drilling raw troops in basic military maneuvers such as forming a front, deploying from a column to a line, or executing a wheeling movement, but there would be no time for this. A few days could be set aside for this work but nothing more.

Added to these problems was their officers' general lack of command experience and the troops' unfamiliarity with their newly issued firearms. This latter problem became readily apparent. Within the span of a week there were half a dozen accidental shootings and the wounding of a horse by a nervous sentry on the night of June 30. Even when the provincials exercised their weapons in a controlled fashion, the results were questionable, as Amos Richardson, a Massachusetts private, noted in his journal. "Had leave to shoot off all our guns, and we did, and there was a fine firing of them for a spell; and some of our men did shoot one of the regulars through the head which killed him dead." The event did little to bolster Abercromby's confidence in his colonial contingent.[2]

Whatever concerns the general might have had with his army, none of them were apparent to the French partisan Lt. Wolf, who now found himself in the midst of the largest collection of military might ever assembled in North America. Wolf and a small detachment had arrived at Fort Edward on June 19 under a flag of truce. The official purpose of his visit was to deliver Governor Vaudreuil's response to Abercromby's request to exchange Colonel Peter Schulyer and two other English officers for six Frenchmen currently being held in New York. No one, however, was confused as to the true nature of the French partisan's visit. It was clear that Wolf was sent to examine English preparations under the guise of a diplomatic exchange of letters.

Abercromby read Vaudreuil's letters, which asserted that under the surrender terms of Fort William Henry the year before, all French troops in English custody were to be returned. Hence, an exchange of prisoners was not the issue. The real issue, the governor insisted, was when the English government would honor this agreement and release all French prisoners. The matter had already crossed Abercromby's desk. Many of the New Hampshire and Massachusetts recruits captured the year before and released on their parole expressed concerns about enlisting in the current campaign. Abercromby answered these concerns by stating that the French had violated the terms of the capitulation with the "massacre" that followed the fort's surrender. Now he was prepared to make this stance official. He informed Wolf that in his view the agreement was "null and void," and within a few days he issued a proclamation among the colonial governments to the same effect. Wolf politely accepted the reply, and then with the attitude that one should at least try, he asked the general for an escort back to Ticonderoga. Abercromby smiled at the French officer and informed him that, in a few days' time, he would give him an escort of twenty thousand men.[3]

On July 4 the order was given for the army to embark the next morning. The timing puzzled some. William Johnson and his Mohawks were but a day away, and the New Hampshire Regiment, some eight hundred strong and reputed to be among the best of the provincial units because of the large numbers of woodsmen in its ranks, was but a day's march beyond that. Although the army already numbered some sixteen thousand, and the arriving numbers seemed small in comparison, it was the nature of these absent troops and not their numbers that mattered. Johnson's Mohawks and the New Hampshire troops were exactly what the general required from his provincial forces: scouts, flankers, and brush fighters who could act not only as an effective screen for the regulars but as a counterbalance to the French irregulars as well.

It seems that a number of points weighed heavily in Abercromby's decision to dispense with these units. First and foremost was his concern that he had already delayed too long and that each day lost at this point was another day the French had to reinforce Fort Carillon. Second, there was the timing of his attack in conjunction with Amherst's move on Louisburg and Forbes' march on Fort Duquesne to consider, both of which, to his knowledge, were already well underway. Third, and seemingly just as important, was the general's dim view of his provincials' fighting abilities. Given what he had seen, a few more, regardless of what was said about them, were not worth waiting for.

With the order transmitted the artillery stores and final provisions were loaded onto the boats, enough to supply the entire army for thirty days. In addition, each man was personally provisioned until the ninth and supplied with thirty-six rounds of ammunition. The regiments, provincial and regular alike, were formed up for review and the articles of war read to them. The provincials then cut their hats so they could be distinguished from any

French irregulars that might be encountered before all turned in for a restless night's sleep.[4]

At five o'clock the next morning, drummers began tapping out their martial tunes. Beneath threatening skies, the provincial and regular regiments formed ranks, and at the echoed commands of their officers, one after another marched down to the awaiting boats. At the patient urging and occasional insistence of Bradstreet's men, who commanded the boats, the vessels were loaded with little incident and pushed away from the shore at regular intervals. A few hours' time was required at nearby Sloop Island to arrange ranks before the signal was given to advance.

Never again would Lake George see such a display of military might upon its waters. At its head was a line of whaleboats holding Rogers' Rangers, Bradstreet's bateaux men, and the soldiers of the recently formed 80th Light Infantry Regiment. They spanned from shore to shore, a running skirmish line of nimble vessels forming the vanguard of the armada. Behind them were four slow-moving columns. The center two were occupied by the scarlet-clad veterans of the seven British line regiments, their grenadier companies forming a thin red line across the head of each column. To the left and right were the provincial regiments, forming the wings of the flotilla in a speckled array of blue jackets and buff shirts. Following a short distance behind were a pair of Connecticut regiments and the plodding barges of the Royal Artillery, their precious cargo lashed to makeshift decks under the constant supervision of Major Ord's men. The army's provisions and field hospital came next, several hundred vessels in all, slowly being ushered forward by Colonel Partridge's green-coated light infantry, who formed the fleet's rear guard. When merged with the pristine mountain waters it was a breathtaking sight. "I never beheld so delightful a prospect," one observer claimed after gazing upon the dozens of regimental flags fluttering in the cool breeze to the occasional skirl of bagpipes and the rattle of drums. Altogether nearly sixteen thousand men in over a thousand vessels were spread down the length of the lake in such a fashion that it was not until noon that the last boat disappeared from the watchful eye of those left to guard the encampment.[5]

Around dusk the head of the fleet pulled ashore at Sabbath Day Point to allow the slower elements to catch up. As the troops beached their vessels and clamored ashore, their spirits were dampened by a stark reminder of the price of overconfidence. Scattered across the beach was the remains of Parker's ill-fated expedition the year before. "We beheld there its melancholy remains," one British officer wrote. Bones, tattered clothing, and broken weapons dotted the beachhead. If the sight was an omen, it was quickly dismissed. Tents were pitched and campfires started to prepare a quick meal, and although it had not been a difficult journey thus far, most were happy to be back on land.

In Lord Howe's tent the brigadier met with a number of his officers, among them Captain Stark of the Rangers. Lying on bearskins, the men discussed the upcoming engagement and Howe's plans to invest the French stronghold, but sadly, the details of this conversation, which might have shed light on upcoming events, were not preserved for posterity. By 10 p.m. scouts sent forward to examine the landing place had returned, and the order was given to reembark. Many in the rear of the fleet had just reached Sabbath Day Point and never had an opportunity to go ashore. These troops, damp from their efforts, were left to frown at the sight of the hundreds of campfires purposely left burning in an attempt to deceive the French.[6]

By 4:00 a.m., the fleet was riding quietly in the waters of the Second Narrows about four miles from Ticonderoga. Just before dawn, a scout returned to inform Howe that he had discovered a French detachment encamped near the intended landing zone. At daybreak the fleet moved into position with Howe, Rogers, and Bradstreet at their head. When the flotilla had advanced to within a quarter of a mile of the landing zone, it became clear to the trio of officers that the French detachment was breaking camp in an attempt to retreat. With this, Howe ordered the Rangers, grenadier, and light infantry boats to advance to within a hundred yards of the shore. The troops then "lay upon their oars" for another fifteen minutes, an eternity for sixteen thousand anxious souls slowly bobbing before a thin stretch of sand and tall grass that disappeared into a panorama of dark forests and looming mountains. The hushed conversations and rattle of equipment subsided when a boat carrying a pair of engineers returned from a scout of the shoreline about a half-mile below the landing site. The report took but a minute. Satisfied, Howe rowed to the head of the grenadiers and gave the signal to land. A line of boats leapt forward under the power of their crews, covering the intervening distance in a matter of minutes. Rogers and his men were to the left and the light infantry to the right as Howe pulled ashore and formed his grenadiers into a line four deep. There were a few anxious moments as the Rangers and light infantry probed forward. The ground before them was clear of trees for several hundred yards, but the high grass and fallen logs made for an excellent defensive position. As it was, the French had chosen not to make a stand. The all-clear signal was given, and shortly thereafter the main elements of the army began landing.[7]

About a mile farther down the lake, Colonel Bradstreet's troops, along with a detachment of provincials, waded ashore to nothing more than a few scattered shots from retreating French sentries. Within minutes they had dashed over a log breastwork and were upon the abandoned remains of Bourlamaque's camp, having captured a few French stragglers in the process. The fact that the French had abandoned such a strong position surprised Bradstreet and his men, but if so, the nature of the retreat came as even more of a surprise. The French had left over a hundred tents still standing. Baggage was scattered about the camp, as were provisions in the form of sheep and poultry. Clothes, money, and personal papers were found, as well as a hogshead of wine. "Their terror was so very unaccountable," recorded one British officer, "that some of their officers even left their silver-hilted swords lying upon their camp tables, all of which became a prey to our irregulars."[8]

Thus far, Howe and Abercromby could not have been more pleased with how things had progressed. The landing had gone forward without the loss of a single man, and although the French had destroyed the pontoon bridge to the east side of the rapids in their retreat, this had been expected. As the army hauled its provisions ashore and went about the work of setting up camp, the two generals formulated their next move. Howe's plan was to invest Fort Carillon by marching the army in a flanking maneuver along the western side of the rapids until they reached the heights northwest of Fort Carillon. This maneuver would not only secure both ends of the portage road to the sawmill, a necessity if artillery was to be brought up against the fort, but if conducted quickly enough it would create a number of favorable scenarios for the attackers.

First, if they arrived at this position before Montcalm had retreated to the north bank of the La Chute River, they would cut his line of retreat back to the fort and his boats. Caught between Howe's force and the British landing force, Montcalm's army would be devastated. The second scenario was even more enticing. Scouts had indicated there were no fortifications built on these heights, which were still covered by belts of trees. If Montcalm chose to make a stand here, and the British army were to catch him on this ridge without field fortifications, the opportunity existed to destroy the standing army of Canada and capture Fort Carillon in an afternoon. The last and most likely scenario was that Montcalm had already retreated back to Fort Carillon. If so, then capturing the heights northwest of the fort would trap him on the Ticonderoga peninsula. Placed in an untenable position and facing a siege, the marquis would likely retreat back down the

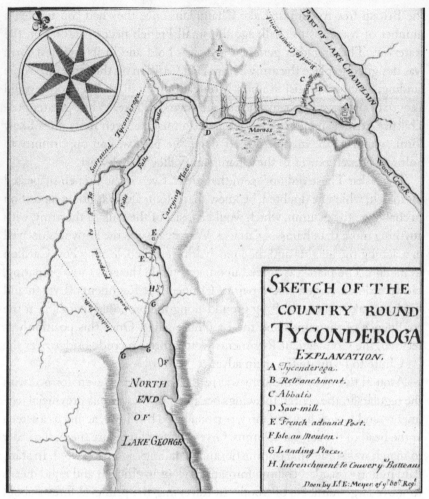

"Sketch of the country round Tyconderoga" by Lt. Elias Meyer, a Swiss Engineer in the Royal Americans, showing the British landings (G), the portage road to the saw mill, and the proposed march to invest Ticonderoga. (*Norman B. Leventhal Map & Education Center, Boston Public Library*)

lake with the bulk of the French army, either abandoning Fort Carillon outright or leaving a small garrison in the stronghold to simply delay the English advance.

In each case, Fort Carillon would fall into British hands, and since the deteriorating Fort St. Frederic to the north was incapable of withstanding a siege, even if Montcalm and his army did escape, they would have little choice but to fall back upon the Richelieu River. This in turn would leave the British free to contest Lake Champlain once they had constructed a number of warships to challenge the small French fleet operating on the waterway. The brigadier general's plan was bold and in its simplest form was designed to place the army before Fort Carillon on the same day as the landing, forcing a decision upon Montcalm, who in all likelihood would choose to preserve his army and retreat down the lake. While greater possibilities existed should the French make a mistake, even in its most likely form, which might include a brief siege, the plan was an opportunity to unhinge French power in the Champlain Valley at little cost.

The risks? These did not seem that great. Even if the French suspected his march, which he doubted, he knew that Montcalm was not in a position to challenge the column, which would consist of the bulk of the army, with anything more than harassing attacks. Worse case was the army was delayed in reaching the heights and the French army escaped, leaving Fort Carillon to its fate. The plan was agreed upon, and while the army was preparing, Howe ordered Rogers and a pair of Connecticut Regiments (Lyman and Fitch) to take a piece of rising ground along the proposed march, near the confluence of the rapids and the La Chute River. Once this position was secured, the Connecticut Regiments would throw a crude bridge over the La Chute to facilitate the main advance.

Around two o'clock the army was ready. Four columns were formed with the regulars in the center, the wings occupied by the various provincial regiments, and Gage's light infantry, personally led by Howe, acting as a screen at the head of the central columns. Given the terrain before them, the order to march was somewhat optimistic, and its failings soon appeared. In standard military practice, column formations were an efficient and rapid means to move large numbers of troops. In traversing the primeval forests about the outlet of Lake George, however, they proved less than satisfactory. With nothing in the way of a road before them and with visibility measured in terms of yards, the neatly formed columns soon became ragged clusters of men struggling to navigate over fallen trees and through hollows that inevitably broke their ranks and merged one column into the next.[9]

Somewhat impatient and less encumbered by their smaller numbers, Howe, elements of the light infantry, and a few New York provincials threaded their way through the woods ahead of the army. Around 3:30 p.m. the sound of movement ahead brought the vanguard to a halt. "*Que vi?*" a dim shape called out. "*Français!*" a quick-thinking light infantry officer returned. But no one was fooled. The response was answered with a shot and then another that ended any question of uncertainty. At the first sound of gunfire, Howe scurried into action. Major Alexander Monypenny, part of the brigadier's staff, witnessed what happened next.

When the firing began on part of the left column, Lord Howe thinking it would be of the greatest consequences, to beat the enemy with the light troops, so as not to stop the march of the main body, went up with them, and had just gained the top of the hill, where the firing was, when he was killed. Never ball had a more deadly direction. It entered his breast on the left side and (as the Surgeons say) pierced his lungs, and heart, and shattered his backbone. I was six yards from him, he fell on his back and never moved, only his hands quivered an instant.[10]

The head of Abercromby's army had run into Captain Trepezac's and Ensign Langy's detachment sent out to Bald Mountain the day before to monitor the English landing, or perhaps more correctly, Trepezac and Langy had run into the head of Abercromby's army. British participants in the upcoming skirmish were later convinced that they had encountered a prepared ambush, a retreating French detachment, or a forlorn hope sent out by Montcalm to harass the army's progress. In reality, none of these was the case.[11]

At daybreak Trepezac sent the two Indians in his party and a cadet from the La Sarre Regiment by the name of Granet to Bourlamaque's camp with news that the English boats were approaching in numbers too large to count. Bourlamaque, already aware of the situation and in the process of retreating, immediately ordered Granet and his native guides to return and inform Trepezac that his forces were withdrawing across the pontoon bridge to the eastern bank of the rapids. The trio set out on their return trip, but the natives, seeing that the English had begun landing operations, thought better of their task and abandoned Granet. The cadet pressed on, but disoriented in the woods, he soon fell prey to Bradstreet's men and was either killed or captured.

It is not clear if Trepezac waited for Granet's return or not, but given the time between the party's report of the English armada and the encounter with Abercromby's column, it seems likely he did. After a few hours, Trepezac and Langy concluded that something had happened to their courier. The question now was what to do. With the English army engaged in landing operations, Trepezac's mission was essentially complete. At this point, given the size of the enemy force, the only reasonable course of action was for him to lead his column down the backside of Bald Mountain and set out for Fort Carillon to report his findings. The logical route back would have been to follow the familiar Trout Brook Valley back to the La Chute River and then follow this body of water back to the sawmills, where Montcalm had posted the bulk of the French army. Trepezac, however, for some reason deviated from this plan. Bougainville later claimed that the captain's party, having lost their Indian guides (the two with Granet), became lost and blundered into the English columns, while Major Gabriel Malartic stated in his journal that Trepezac informed them that their guide, Langy, "had gone astray, and did not find out his mistake until three o'clock." Bougainville's explanation would be plausible if the detachment had been nothing but French regulars unfamiliar with the terrain before them, but this was not the case. Malartic's report is just as puzzling. The idea that Langy, the veteran of numerous scouts out of Fort Carillon, was lost in this stretch of woods is difficult to fathom, particularly when one considers the nature of the return route and that the engagement took place a good distance south of the La Chute River.[12]

It seems more likely that, once the party had cleared Cook Mountain, Trepezac made a conscious decision to turn south toward the English. Perhaps, as one account reasoned, he thought that Bourlamaque's detachment was still in place and that his troops might be of assistance, or perhaps he calculated that the English would attempt to force a crossing at the pontoon bridge, leaving him free to operate in their rear against their vulnerable supply or artillery trains.

Whatever the case, by mid-afternoon it seems that Trepezac had a change of heart. Whether it was the result of reports that Bourlamaque no longer occupied the advance camp or, as Marlartic claimed, because they were uncertain of their position, it was now decided that their best course of action was to reach the eastern bank of the Lake George rapids. In this they almost succeeded. The van headed by Trepezac and Langy reached the western bank of the white waters opposite a small island. Here Langy and a few others attempted to cross, but they found the current too strong and sent word back that they would have to look for another location farther downstream. The detachment had no sooner begun to retrace its steps when it ran headlong into the entire British invasion force.[13]

The opening exchange of musketry soon escalated from scattered shots to a steady crescendo as the French detachment and the British vanguard probed at each other in the dapple-lit woods. If at first the French thought that they had encountered a scouting party, it soon became apparent that this was not the case. As the provincial troops on the English right moved into the fray and elements of the 44th and 27th Regiments moved forward to support the light infantry, it became clear to Langy and Trepezac the scale of the numbers before them. The British line regiments, true to their training, formed a front and began firing in platoons. Soon, what had started as a few sporadic shots had erupted into an open engagement. One provincial soldier near the front of the action recalled, "Ye heat of the battle lasted but six or eight minutes in which time there was near as many thousand guns fired, which made a most terrible roaring in the woods." While another provincial, who with a comrade managed to take a number of prisoners, claimed, "The fire was so smart for some time that the earth trembled."[14]

Trepezac's men could not hope to hold against such overwhelming odds, but matters were about to get worse. Lyman's and Fitch's Connecticut Regiments had just reached Rogers who, true to his earlier orders, was stationed on a height of land near the confluence of Lake George rapids and the La Chute River. Rogers was now within a half a mile of Montcalm's forces posted at the sawmills and was speaking with General Lyman when the firing broke out to the rear of Lyman's regiment. Lyman immediately ordered his regiment to change front, and it was agreed that Rogers, with the bulk of his Rangers, would circle to the west to fall on the French flank. By this point, Trepezac's detachment was already in full retreat and found Rogers and Lyman almost as quickly as the latter found them. With their escape to the north and west barred by Lyman and Rogers, what was left of the French detachment scrambled east toward the rapids. The battle was now a running fight of sporadic shots, shouts, desperate men, and wholesale surrenders.[15]

For many of the provincials this was their first military action. Some, like Garret Albertson of the New Jersey Blues, unexpectedly found themselves in the midst of the fighting. Being farther back, the Jersey Blues did not come into action until later in the engagement. Nonetheless, Albertson saw more than he had bargained for. While moving through the woods, he spotted a fleeing French soldier at almost the same instant the man noticed him. The Frenchman snapped off a shot just as Albertson stepped behind the nearest available cover and fired his own piece. The shot missed and the Frenchman disappeared, leaving Albertson free to examine the musket ball embedded in the nine-inch sapling he had taken refuge behind. Albertson also witnessed the more vicious side of human nature later in the skirmish. One of his fellow soldiers, a man named John Hendrickson, came across a wounded French soldier. The Frenchman attempted to rise, most likely to surrender, but fell back to his knees in pain. When Hendrickson leveled his musket at the Frenchman, the latter pleaded for mercy, but Henderickson "granted none and shot him dead."[16]

For others, like David Perry of Prebble's regiment, the engagement was much different and reflected what most of the army experienced. When the firing first began, Colonel Prebble, true to military dictum, formed his regiment into a firing line among the trees. It proved a difficult proposition with raw troops. "At length our regiment formed among the trees behind which the men kept stepping from their ranks for shelter. Colonel Prebble, who, I remember, was a harsh man, swore he would knock the first man down who should step out of his ranks; which greatly surprised me, to think that I must stand still to be shot at." Although he never saw the enemy until the fighting was over, it proved an unnerving experience for the sixteen-year-old. "The whistling of balls and roar of musketry terrified me not a little," he later wrote of the experience.[17]

In fact, Perry's experience was reflected throughout most of the ranks not actively engaged. The regulars, in particular, perhaps still remembering the nightmare of Braddock's march, behaved poorly. An officer in the 60th Regiment described their conduct in a letter to a friend.

The moment that the fire was received in front, panic seized our soldiers; entire regiments flung themselves one atop the other, and even the general narrowly escaped being dragged off in the confusion by the fugitives. In vain did the officers cry out and offer opposition; nothing could stop 'em.[18]

Major William Eyre, in command of the 44th Regiment with Gage's assignment as Abercromby's third in command, encountered similar troubles among his regulars. "I observed this little firing threw our regulars into some kind of consternation," he confided to a colleague. Eyre, however, a veteran of several campaigns along the lakes, was quick to surmise the true nature of the problem.

I observe the fire round them, though at some distance, seemed to alarm them; in the wood where nothing can be seen, but what is near, the men fancy is worse, or the enemy more numerous than they are; our own firing they are apt some times to think is the enemy's our irregulars yelling is believed by those who are not engaged, to be the enemy, in short Sir, I am more than ever convinced that numbers of our people cannot hear a great deal of firing round them coolly. I mean when they hear and do not see.[19]

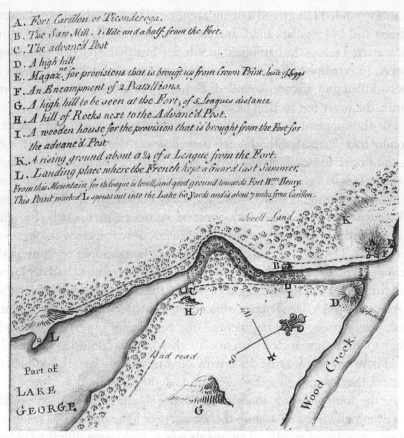

A . Fort Carillon or Ticonderoga.
B . The Saw Mill . 1 Mile and a half from the Fort.
C . The advanced Post
D . A high hill
E . Magaz". for provisions that is brought up from Crown Point, built of loggs
F . An Encampment of 2 Batallions.
G . A high hill to be seen at the Fort; of 5 Leagues distance
H . A hill of Rocks next to the Advanc'd Post.
I . A wooden house for the provision that is brought from the Fort for
    the advanc'd Post
K . A rising ground about a ¼ of a League from the Fort.
L . Landing place where the French kept a Guard last Summer.
From this Mountain for the league is levell, and good ground towards Fort Wm Henry.
This Point marked L spouts out into the Lake 60 Yards and is about 7 miles from Carillon.

Levell Land

K

B
E
F

C
I.
D

H.

L

Part of

LAKE

GEORGE

Bad road

G

Wood Creek.

A map of the proposed flanking march and the area around Fort Carillon by Major Alexander Monypenny. (*Norman B. Leventhal Map & Education Center, Boston Public Library*)

By this point the skirmish had come to a disastrous end for the French. Disorganized, surrounded on three sides, and pinned against the rapids on the fourth, most of Trepezac's remaining men opted to surrender. The rest braved the river, which proved as great a peril as the English. Weighted down by their equipment, dozens were swept away, drowned in the frigid waters, or were picked off by English muskets as they tried to wade across, and those who managed to reach the safety of the opposite shore only did so under the cover fire of a few companies of grenadiers which Montcalm had dispatched at the sound of the approaching gunfire.

An officer in Gage's light infantry claimed that "there were few left to tell the tale." It was not quite as bad as that, but there was little doubt that it was a one-sided contest. About a hundred Frenchmen escaped, among them a wounded Langy and a dying Trepezac. The English captured seven officers and 144 regulars and Canadians. The rest, a little under fifty, were left scattered across the battlefield in a dotted line that led to the cascading waters. In retrospect, British casualties were remarkably light, perhaps a dozen killed and a score wounded. But counted among them was Lord Howe, the heart and tactical head of the army.[20]

For the moment, however, the brigadier's loss changed little. Abercromby had decimated the French detachment before him, and the way was now open to march on and invest Fort Carillon. The problem was that his army was in a state of confusion. What little cohesion it had been able to maintain during its march was completely undone by the skirmish and subsequent pursuit of the enemy. Some of the troops, particularly the light infantry and a number of provincial regiments, were dispersed throughout the woods. The regulars, on the other hand, though more concentrated, were in a worse state. Some toward the head of the columns had deployed into firing lines and now struggled to regain their former formations in the maple-and-spruce-laced maze, while most, located to the rear, were a jumbled, jittery mass. "The regiments," one participant observed, "were all broke to pieces intermixed with one another." It was confusion that easily could have ignited into true chaos with a few mistaken shots. To complicate matters, there were only a few hours of daylight remaining.[21]

At the point of swords and with the hoarse shouts of their officers, order was eventually restored among the regulars, and the march was resumed minus a number of provincial regiments whose ranks were simply too scattered to continue. The army advanced in its former fashion, but because of the nature of the ground it soon divided into two divisions. Around sunset a shot echoed from the front of one of the divisions. The firing soon quickened and was followed by "a loud hideous yell" which collapsed the front of the columns into chaos. "Those in the front," Eyre recalled, "gave way immediately in the greatest disorder." The panic rippled down the length of the columns like a zipper, and "no entreaty could prevail upon the men for some time." Garret Albertson, who had already experienced a hectic day, had yet another close call as buckshot and ball crashed through the foliage into his column. "One poor fellow fell near my side . . . shot across the face." A few minutes later cooler heads realized the mistake, and the cry "All is well! All is well!" echoed through the forest, bringing the firing to a halt. Given what had transpired earlier, it was perhaps to have been expected. It was certainly enough for Abercromby. The two divisions rejoined ranks in the twilight, at which point the general called a halt to the march. Those units with guides were ordered to return to the landing place. The rest were to encamp where they stood.[22]

Several of the British regiments toward the rear were able to make good on the orders and find their way back to the landing place, but others, in more advanced positions, became disoriented and staggered bewildered through the darkened forest. Peter Bond's odyssey that night typified the plight of many of these men. Bond, a private in Whiting's Connecticut Regiment, wandered through the woods for hours with a dozen companions until they were finally fortunate enough to come across an Indian path that led back to the landing site. "We marched toward our boats at ye water side but being dark we made but a stumbling piece of business of it and soon coming among the dead bodies which were strewn quit thick on the ground for some little distance. . . . At length we got to the water just before daylight." For the rest, who chose to encamp for the evening, the difficulties were more psychological in nature but no less difficult. "I do not remember ever to have felt greater distress of mind," Albertson wrote, "than I did that night. I thought the hand of providence was turned against us, in a lonely wilderness." Major Eyre was more direct in his assessment. "I must confess to you," he informed a friend, "that it's my opinion, two or three hundred Indians surrounding us that night, with the apprehensions that some of our people showed must have ended fatally."[23]

It was a dismal state for an army that had started its journey with such hope and high spirits, now scattered up and down the woods from the landing zone to the La Chute River, and more likely to be injured by its own actions than those of the enemy. Remarkably, the evening passed without incident, and with first light those who had spent the night in the woods, which included Abercromby, were able to find their way back to the landing site.

Once they had returned, they went about the task of reorganizing and refreshing themselves, but their spirits were further dampened at the news of Lord Howe's loss. It is not difficult to express the impact the brigadier had made on Abercromby's army. Almost every journal of the expedition, provincial and regular alike, lamented his loss, but Captain Charles Lee's comments perhaps best summarize the army's connection to this dynamic young nobleman, "his only fault was that of not knowing his own value." Still, such realizations did little to change the melancholy mood, and "when his body was brought into camp scarce an eye was free from tears."[24]

THE HEIGHTS OF CARILLON

W HEN THE EXTENT OF THE ENGLISH LANDING BECAME CLEAR, Montcalm ordered in his detachments. Both Captain Germain's and Captain Bernard's volunteers quickly complied and fell back on Montcalm's position near the sawmill, having fired only a few rounds at the advancing barges. Bourlamaque posted, with three regiments at Contoceur's camp followed suit, but his withdrawal did not proceed as smoothly. Montcalm had ordered the baggage and supplies for this detachment removed the night before but later countermanded the order at Bourlamaque's insistence. The colonel was afraid that such an action might discourage his troops. As it turned out, not removing the baggage would discourage them even more. With the English now poised to descend upon his position, Bourlamaque ordered the tents struck and the baggage removed, but there was no time to accomplish either task, and as a result much of the detachment's equipment was either abandoned or put to the torch. By 8 a.m. his force had crossed over the floating bridge, and after waiting a period of time with the rear guard for signs of Trepezac's detachment, Bourlamaque ordered the bridge destroyed and retreated up the portage road to Montcalm's position. Although Bourlamaque had pressed Montcalm to fight, it had never been the marquis' intention to resist the English landing. His forces were simply too weak to conduct such an operation. With the exception of the material losses and a few stragglers, the withdrawal in the face of such a large enemy force went smoothly until around three o'clock when the sound of gunfire was heard echoing across the outlet of Lake George. Trepezac's detachment, which had yet to return, was clearly in trouble. As the gunfire traveled closer, Montcalm dispatched a small force to the banks of the rapids to cover their retreat. There proved little left to cover, as less than half of the original detachment managed to find their way safely across the river. The rest were either dead or English captives. It was not the start that the marquis had hoped for. He was far too short of men to have lost so many in such a senseless one-sided skirmish.[1]

When Bourlamaque reached Montcalm's position, the marquis ordered the bridges near the sawmill broken up and withdrew his forces across the river. His army was now arrayed in a crescent, with Bourlamaque's brigade located on the heights to the northwest of the sawmill and the La Sarre and Royal Roussillon brigades stationed along the edge of the north riverbank. Although it blocked the portage road, the easiest route for Abercromby to move his artillery forward, it was a precarious position. In a council of war, Bourlamaque pushed the marquis to hold this ground, but a pair of senior officers objected. The army was posted in the bottom of the La Chute Valley, dominated by hills to their rear. If the English column that had brushed Trepezac aside arrived on these heights before the army withdrew, they would find themselves pinned between the enemy and the river. The officers' argument was supported by information from Captain Duprat, who informed Montcalm that before he had withdrawn from his post along the La Chute River he had seen an advanced party of the enemy throwing up a bridge over the river in anticipation of their main column. The news settled the matter. Montcalm ordered the sawmill destroyed, and by eight o'clock that evening the army found themselves bivouacked on the heights overlooking Fort Carillon.[2]

As the campfires burned and the sentries made their rounds, Montcalm called together his senior officers to discuss their situation. Brigade-Major Montreuil began the meeting with the state of the army. Their losses thus far had been 188 killed or captured, almost all as the result of the destruction of Trepezac's detachment. These losses, however, had been partially made good by the arrival of 150 Canadians and Marines. The eight weak battalions numbered some 3,400 all told. Added to this were some four hundred Canadians and Marines, and news was that Levis and his men were but a day away with another four hundred reinforcements. There were provisions for five days at the current rate of consumption and ample amounts of powder, shot, and ball.[3]

Next was Ensign Langy, followed by Captains Germain and Bernard, and finally Captain Duprat. The men all told versions of the same story. Twenty to twenty-five thousand English had landed. They had counted at least eight regimental flags from Old England and over a dozen provincial flags. The enemy was busy unloading scores of barges carrying siege guns, provisions, and munitions. It was in every respect the largest army ever as-sembled against the colony. Captain Duprat, however, added something more interesting to the mix. Reports were that the English army had halted before the La Chute. No doubt the failing light and the nature of the terrain before them influenced their decision, but it was also possible that the skir-mish with Trezapec's detachment had left their ranks more confused or more cautious than one might have expected. There was some murmuring among the participants at the thought, no doubt spurred by a need to find some tidings of good fortune in what had otherwise been a depressing day.

Montcalm thanked the men for their reports and turned next to Captain Pontleroy of the Royal Engineers, who had prepared a report on the state of Fort Carillon. Pontleroy painted a disparaging picture of the stronghold and its prospects of withstanding a siege. In the engineer's opinion the fort was poorly laid out and poorly constructed. Although there was only one logical approach toward the fort, that being where they now stood, the structure had been constructed in such a fashion that only two guns could be brought to bear against enemy batteries erected in this position. Not that it mattered, as the ramparts were too narrow on this side, and as a re-sult, there was not sufficient room for the recoil of the cannon. To cover this defect, a pair of demi-lunes had been constructed along the two walls open to attack. Unfortunately, these had been built so high that they screened the embrasures along each of the curtain walls, making firing from these walls nearly impossible. The casemates that would hold the garrison, their food, and their munitions during a siege were too small, damp, and possessed inadequate overhead protection. The parade ground was too small as well, but again, this hardly mattered. The stone barracks were two stories high and overlooked the parapets on the walls. Shot and shell di-rected against these buildings would shower the parade ground and the ramparts with rock splinters, making it impossible for the garrison to appear

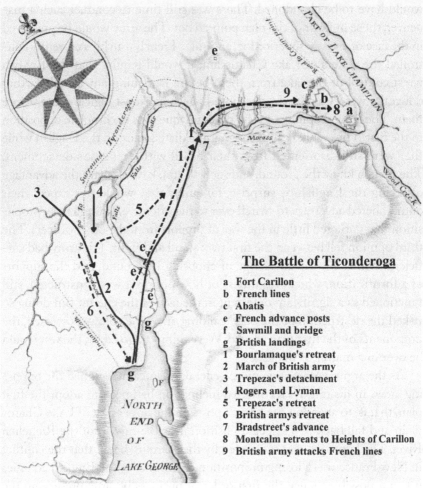

The Battle of Ticonderoga

a   Fort Carillon
b   French lines
c   Abatis
e   French advance posts
f   Sawmill and bridge
g   British landings
1   Bourlamaque's retreat
2   March of British army
3   Trepezac's detachment
4   Rogers and Lyman
5   Trepezac's retreat
6   British armys retreat
7   Bradstreet's advance
8   Montcalm retreats to Heights of Carillon
9   British army attacks French lines

Prelude to the Battle of Ticonderoga, July 6–7, 1758. (*Author*)

in either place. Also, because the fort was too small, much of the garrison's supplies were housed in vulnerable sheds and buildings outside the fort. "Were I entrusted with the siege of it," the engineer finished, "I should require only six mortars and two cannon."[4]

With the reports finished, the topic became the army's next move. The discussion was lively and eventually developed along three lines. The first opinion called for an immediate withdrawal back up the lake to Île aux Noix. Fort St. Frederic would be used as a temporary staging point, but since this position was even more vulnerable than Fort Carillon, it too

would have to be abandoned. There was still time to conduct such a maneuver, those in favor of the plan pointed out. The army would be preserved
in the face of a vastly superior foe, and since French warships currently controlled the waters of Lake Champlain, it would require that the English
wrest control of the lake from them before launching any assault farther
down the waterway. It was clearly the safest and most logical route before
them. The second opinion, led by Bourlamaque, was in complete opposition
to the first. The colonel called for an immediate attack on the English while
they were still disoriented from their brush with Trepezac's detachment.
The French knew the ground, and such an attack would have the advantage
of taking the English by surprise, for surely they would not expect their
outnumbered adversary to switch over to the offensive. It was a risky proposition that garnered little in the way of support from the other officers. The
third opinion fell between the first two: stand and fight. The army had sufficient munitions, the advantage of choosing its ground, and the support
of a fortification, which, regardless of how poorly it was constructed, still
functioned as a significant deterrent in the face of the enemy. But doing so
risked the destruction of the only standing army the colony possessed, the
proponents of the first plan argued. Were things to go badly, the war would
be over in a matter of weeks.[5]

As the argument became more general, Montcalm weighed the oppos-
ing views in his mind. His original inclination had been to adopt the first
plan, that is, to abandon the French posts on the upper part of Lake Champlain and fall back to a selected position near the mouth of the Richelieu
River. The approach was motivated by the marquis' belief that the conflict
in New France was a losing proposition. Victory over the English colonies
was not possible, hence the first order of business became preserving the
core of the French colony for as long as possible in hopes that a peace settlement in Europe would restore what was lost. The only way to accomplish
this, in the marquis' opinion, was to slowly yield frontier territory and maintain an army in being. Ground could be traded for time, and so long as the
colony possessed an army in the field to defend Montreal and Quebec there
was hope.

Eventually, however, his army would run out of options and would be
forced to fight. So, the real question in the general's mind was whether it
should be here and now. The idea of attacking the English was never a serious consideration, but standing his ground? This thought had crossed his
mind. In fact, he had seen it the first time he had laid eyes on Fort Carillon
and the wooded heights to its northwest. A few days before, he had walked

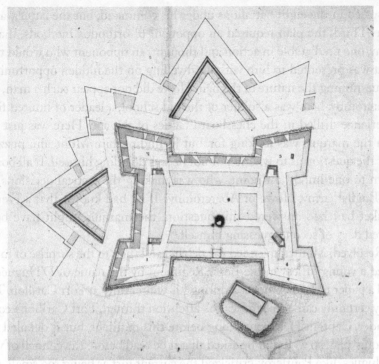

Plan of Fort Carillon showing the western and northern (top) demi-lunes. (*Norman B. Leventhal Map & Education Center, Boston Public Library*)

the ground with his engineers and a number of officers, internally probing the details of his plan, examining the flaws, and weighing the consequences. Lotbiniere, who had chosen not to clear the wooded ridge above Fort Carillon years ago, had glimpsed the possibilities. Certainly, Pontleroy saw the marquis' vision, although he never openly expressed it, and Desandrouins, like Montcalm, a veteran of the Battle of Assietta, perhaps understood it best of all. If the English could be drawn against a barricade of earthworks and defensive obstacles like the French army had been at Assietta in Italy a decade ago, the opportunity existed to not only negate their numerical advantage but to inflict a crushing blow on them as well.

However, as at Assietta, three elements had to align to spring the trap. First, a defensible position which dictated and narrowed the enemy's march had to be found. The heights of Carillon partially served this purpose, its primary flaw being that a determined enemy could push through the woods to the north and outflank the position. Second, the resources and time had to be available to construct the fortifications. The first of these Montcalm possessed in the eight battalions under his command, but the latter was at issue. Third, the plan required an opponent of orthodox methods, that is to say, one predictable in action and thought, an opponent who would take what was presented to him without dwelling on the hidden opportunities or questioning the nature of the bait. Howe did not appear such a man, but Abercromby, here was a soldier of the old school, a leader of limited field experience drilled in the chessboard tactics of the age. Here was just the man the marquis was looking for, but in finding him Montcalm puzzled over the question as to whether or not he was deluding himself. It all boiled down to one important point: who was making the tactical decisions for the English army, Howe or Abercromby? If he had known that a French musket ball had answered this question, the marquis might have been spared days of second guessing himself.[6]

Resolved, Montcalm ended the debate, and then to the surprise of many asked a young officer in the Berry Regiment by the name of D'Hugues to read a paper he had composed during his winter duty at Fort Carillon. The essay certainly came to Montcalm's attention through Fort Carillon's commander, Captain Hebecourt, long before this moment, but it detailed the marquis' plan so well that he asked that it be read before the council of war. D'Hugues, like Pontleroy, criticized the current fort as being too small, and as a result too many vulnerable outworks were required to support it. The peninsula itself, however, was well selected, given that the enemy was only able to open a trench on one side, that being along the heights nine hundred yards to the northwest of the fort. "It is this eminence which 'tis essential to secure," he emphasized,

and a General desirous of preventing a siege, must have a good entrenchment erected on it, which he must even have continued across the plain as far as the Fort Frederic River. That line, 1000 toises in length, forms the base of the angle on which Carillon stands. This entrenchment of trunks of trees to be felled at the moment they are required, must be fraised with dry branches well looped and entangled together; the approach to it ought to be encumbered by that abatis for a distance of 50 toises, observing particularly that no large trunks of trees be piled up at the extremity. . . . This entrenchment, which can be completed in twice twenty-four hours, and well guarded by six thousand men, would cost the party desirous of forcing it, a great many lives, and I even dare assert that, were it well defended, 'twould not be carried by an army three times more numerous than that defending it.[7]

When D'Hugues finished, Montcalm scanned the quiet faces of his officers. Nothing more needed to be said. The army would stand and fight. Pontleroy and Desandrouins had traced out the works earlier that day with the assistance of the men from the 3rd Berry. Tomorrow every available hand would report to the lines to continue the effort.

At daybreak on July 7 Montcalm's troops marched to the works outlined the day before. Pontleroy and Desandrouins were already there, directing each regiment in turn to their section of the line. With regimental flags fluttering down the length of the ridge, work began in earnest around seven o'clock. Behind a defensive screen of grenadiers and volunteers, the day was spent felling trees, stripping branches, digging ditches, and manhandling the timbers into place to form a barricade across the heights. No one was excluded, including Montcalm's officers, who toiled beside their troops throughout the day with axe in hand, each striving "with the greatest ardor to surpass the other." But the works themselves were only part of the task as far as Captain Desandrouins was concerned. Throughout the day the engineer paid particular attention to pull aside small groups of veteran soldiers. He pointed to the strength of the position and the limited approaches available to the enemy and emphasized how narrow the front was they would be asked to defend, knowing full well that, if he could convince these men, his message would find its way to the less experienced elements in the ranks.[8]

Although the works progressed at a furious rate, it was a nerve-wracking day for Montcalm and his staff. The screen of grenadiers and volunteers several hundred yards to the west exchanged sporadic shots with the English scouts throughout the afternoon. In each case, Montcalm and his officers would pause to listen for more shots or an increase in the tempo of the exchange, which might signal a move on his position. Time had become everything at this point. At the moment, his army was in its most vulnerable state. If the English advanced while the works were half complete, they would catch his men strung out on the heights of Carillon with insufficient cover and with no time to reach their boats. Canada's army would be annihilated in a few hours' work and the door to the interior of the colony flung wide open. Although grateful that his enemy had chosen to cooperate with his plans, the marquis' thoughts turned to them throughout the day. Where were they? And what were they waiting for?

Howe's plan, a sweeping march around Montcalm's flank, had its merits as well as its risks. Unfortunately for the Anglo-American army, the risks had become a stark reality. Yet, on the morning of July 7 the plan was still salvageable. The distance involved was not great, and although the march was not easy, it was not impossible. Abercromby's column had stopped just short of the La Chute, at least halfway to its goal. The army, which several witnesses claimed was still in good spirits, could have been summoned to resume their march early that morning. Had they done so and arrived on the heights of Carillon before Montcalm's troops had completed their works, the history of the last French and Indian War might have ended much differently. Such an act, however, would have required the resolve of a decisive leader. In theory, Gage, an experienced officer who had served with Braddock, Shirley, and Loudoun, should have filled the void left by Howe's loss and approached Abercromby with such a plan, but instead the newly appointed brigadier was silent. Nor was the cautious Abercromby such a man. And as such, the moment slipped away.

Abercromby, like many of his men, had spent the night in the forest, and it wasn't until mid-morning that he found himself back at the landing area confronting a new set of problems. He had little in the way of intelligence, several regiments were still missing in the woods to the north, and all were fatigued after having spent the previous night on the water, marching the following morning, and spending another night lying upon their arms. At least this was Abercromby's assessment of the situation. Many of his officers had a different opinion. "Instead of marching the army, and investing the fort immediately and keeping up the surprise the French had been thrown into the day before," one puzzled English officer wrote, "there was talk of resting the troops for four or five hours." A colonial officer saw the same hesitation, and in more of an indictment of his commander than a comment on the loss of Lord Howe, wrote, "I can't but observe since Lord Howe's death business seems a little stagnant." While another noted that, "Upon Lord Howe being slain the whole army were halted, and July 7th, lay still upon the same account. But 18,000 men not able to bring him to life." A third participant agreed, saying, "Never did an army gain more advantage in so little time, whilst the late Lord Howe was alive; but soon after that, we became a confused rabble."[9]

Fortunately for the British, there were men on the general's staff capable of action. With the expedition seemingly stalled, John Bradstreet showed his fiery colors. The floating bridge near Contrecoeur's camp was no sooner repaired than Bradstreet approached Abercromby for permission to advance on the sawmill via the portage road. At first the plan met with opposition, but after pushing forward his argument and with the support of several other officers, Bradstreet finally gained permission to advance with the 44th

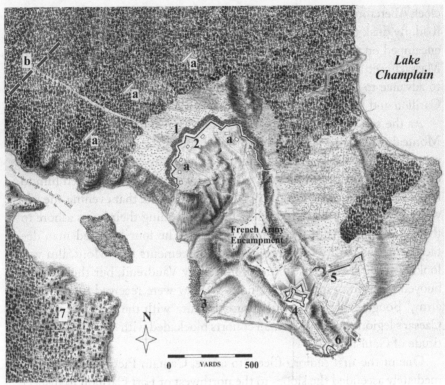

French and British positions on the Ticonderoga peninsula during the evening of July 7, based on a 1759 work by William Brassier of the Ordnance Department. Legend: a. French piquets and sentries; b. advance force of four Massachusetts regiments; 1. abatis; 2. French lines; 3. French battery; 4. Fort Carillon; 5. defensive outworks; 6. docks and landing area; 7. the north shore of Mt. Defiance. (*Author*)

Regiment, the 1st Battalion of Royal Americans, several provincial regiments, two pieces of cannon, and his own regiment of bateaux men. Around eleven that morning Bradstreet led his detachment across the newly constructed bridge and within the space of an hour had reached the destroyed sawmill bridge.

Seeing the lack of opposition and the advantages to be gained, Bradstreet sent a messenger back to Abercromby requesting carpenters to repair the broken bridge and "for leave to proceed and invest the fort." The carpenters were quick in coming, but permission to advance was not. Instead, Bradstreet was ordered to hold his current position. The best he could do for the moment was deploy a handful of scouts on the other side of the river to harass and monitor the movements of the French. Around four o'-

clock Abercromby finally ordered the main army forward along the portage
road. By dusk they had crossed over the recently repaired bridge and were
encamped on the heights near the sawmill. As part of this maneuver, four
Massachusetts Regiments were sent ahead to screen the army, with orders
to advance to within half a mile of the French position on the heights of
Carillon and there entrench themselves for the evening.[10]

As the sun lowered and the mosquitoes descended upon both armies,
Montcalm breathed a small sigh of relief. First, the day's hard work had
created a defensible barrier behind which his army could now stand, and
even better, the English had not interfered with the task or forced him to
make a choice in the matter. Second, a little after six that evening the advanced elements of Levis' detachment began pulling their boats ashore to
the welcoming calls of their tired comrades. The four-hundred-man detachment was hardly the large-scale reinforcements that Montcalm was
looking for and what had been promised by Vaudreuil, but their arrival
buoyed the army's spirits nevertheless. "They were received by our little
army," Bougainville wrote with dramatic flair, "with the same joy as were
Caesar's legions by those Roman cohorts blockaded with Cicero by a mul-
titude of Gauls."[11]

One of the first senior officers to arrive, Captain Pierre Pouchot, immediately ascended the slopes to the northwest of Fort Carillon to inspect
the newly constructed entrenchment. The left of the line, as seen from Fort
Carillon, rested about 150 yards short of the outlet of the La Chute River
on the southern edge of the heights. From here the ground fell off in a
series of sheer drops and brief plateaus to the waters of the river. Even when
cleared of trees it was difficult terrain to navigate. More importantly it was
easily dominated by the left-hand portion of the works and cannon fire
from a redoubt located on a height of land about five hundred yards to the
southeast that protected the piers and docks below the village. From its
southernmost edge, the lines following the contours of the land forming a
crude "C" with the far right terminating on the northern edge of the heights
approximately six hundred yards from the shore of Lake Champlain. In
this area the land was still covered with trees and swamps but exited onto
an open field, which was dominated by the fort and a battery of guns placed
on a shallow ridge just outside the fort's northern wall. The fortifications
themselves consisted of a palisade of tree trunks laid horizontally one upon
the other to a height of six to eight feet. These were backed by a broad
ditch and ample firing ports were notched in the structure, making the defenders almost invisible to an attacker. In addition to this, Pontleroy and

Desandrouins had taken care to lay the barricade out in a jagged fashion so that different portions of the wall could be swept by the fire of nearby parts.

The real strength of the position, however, lay in front of the log wall. The woods in front of the fortifications had been cleared for three hundred yards. While a good portion of this work was used to construct the field fortifications along the length of the heights, the rest was used to create a nearly impassible wooden maze in front of the French lines. For over fifty yards the ground before the entrenchment was choked with felled trees, their branches pointed up and sharpened like spikes, piles of brush, and broken timber. This abatis, or *chevaux-de-frise* as it was known, would make any assault on the wall a slow, and thereby costly, affair.[12]

Pouchot, who had served as an engineer on numerous occasions, was pleased with what he saw. When he encountered Montcalm not long after, the latter asked him his opinion of the fortifications. Pouchot gave an approving nod toward the works and pointed out that, since the English had not forced him off the heights, there was no way for them to know what he had in store for them.[13]

The comments brought a smile to the marquis' face, perhaps the first of the day, and when he returned to his tent later that evening, he took a moment to reflect on his newfound confidence in a short letter to Commissary Andre Doriel in Montreal,

I have opposed to me a formidable army. Nevertheless there is nothing to make me despair. I have good troops. From the movements of the enemy, I see he is vacillating. If by his procrastination, he gives me the time to reach the position I have chosen on the heights of Carillon and to entrench myself, I will vanquish him.[14]

Camped near the sawmill were Abercromby's red coated regulars and over half-a-dozen colonial regiments, their tents and campfires a constant reminder to the French of the size of the force arrayed before them. In one of these thousands of tents Colonel Grant of the 42nd met with a few of his officers. The story from each was the same. A few Highlanders had heard some colonials refer to Fort Carillon as Ticonderoga, its Iroquois name. At first, they had been able to silence the men, but now the rumor had spread within the ranks. Major Campbell must have heard it by now. Grant, who had known that Fort Carillon was on the Ticonderoga Peninsula for some time, shook his head and informed the officers gathered about him that the rumor was true. He halted the murmurs and questions with a raised hand and implored the men not to tell Campbell. They would likely fight tomorrow and he did not need this on the major's mind. They all gave questioning nods to one another and then agreed to convince Campbell that this was not Ticonderoga.[15]

SCARLET AND WOOD

A LITTLE AFTER DAWN ON JULY 8 COLONEL GRANT SUMMONED his officers to go over the state of the regiment before he departed for a council of war with Abercromby and the other brigade commanders. Most of the participants had assembled when Campbell arrived. His haggard look brought a hush over the crowd. "I have seen him!" he shouted out, looking upon those who had spent the evening convincing him that this was not Ticonderoga. He pointed at Grant. "You have deceived me! He came to my tent last night! This is Ticonderoga!" The statement instantly drew the assembly toward him and brought forth a barrage of comments meant to comfort or defuse the situation. Several led Campbell aside to calm him down, but it was not until then that he looked away from Grant.

While the Highlanders dealt with this unusual situation, to the east Captain Stark led a detachment of Rangers to the summit of Mount Defiance. Threading their way up the backside of the mountain was nowhere near as difficult for the Ranger as dealing with his two familiar charges, Lt. Clerk and Captain Abercrombie. Stark's relationship with these British of-

ficers was strained at best, but he was familiar with the spot, which is probably why he was chosen to lead the detachment. He had been here the previous afternoon with the same two men and on several occasions in the
past with his old friend Lord Howe. Situated above and about eight hundred yards to the south of the fort, their location offered a clear view of the
French position on the Ticonderoga Peninsula. Splayed below them was
the fort itself, buffered by numerous redoubts and outworks, and the small
palisade village that had grown up just below it. Certainly, the mass of boats
pulled ashore or tied up at the makeshift piers caught Stark's attention. He
had never seen so many at the fort before. As his gaze swept west, the newly
constructed French lines dotted with white-coated workers and the colorful
regimental flags of Old France were easily discernable. It was this feature
that Clerk and Abercrombie discussed and continually pointed to for the
next forty-five minutes. At one point Stark drifted closer to the men and
commented on the strength of the French works. They gave the Ranger a
quick snub, perturbed at the comments of an untrained colonial in such
matters, and then moved off to carry on their conversation out of earshot.
When the British officers seemed satisfied, Abercrombie motioned to
Stark, and the party descended the heights, arriving back at the main encampment near the sawmills around 8 a.m.[1]

Given all that transpired, Abercromby was determined to be certain of
the information before him; thus he had dispatched the two officers to confirm their earlier report. In addition, the general had dispatched a foreign
engineer from the provincial redoubts to scout the French lines. This officer
had returned earlier that morning, informing the general that he had seen
nothing resembling an entrenchment on the heights above Carillon. After
listening to Captain Abercrombie's and Lt. Clerk's report, which was far
more detailed, the general made up his mind. The army would attack.[2]

The decision was the conjunction of two elements. The first part was
dictated by the favorable reports his engineers had laid before him; an attack
was feasible if carried out before the French had time to solidify their defenses. The second part involved the prisoners he had taken on the sixth,
who were nearly unanimous in saying that the fort was daily expecting
strong reinforcements in the form of several thousand Canadians and Indians. These reports nagged at Abercromby. At this stage he could have
opted to drag his cannon forward and blast the French breastwork to
smithereens, but such matters were time consuming. Although several cannons had already been moved to the advanced provincial redoubts, the
heavy batteries, the twenty-four- and eighteen-pound guns, metal beasts

weighing well over two tons each, were still back at the landing site. In the general's opinion, moving them forward was a week's work, during which time the French would have received several thousand reinforcements, bolstering their numbers to perhaps as many as twelve thousand, according to his current reports. The impending scenario disturbed the British leader. Every day he waited was another day his opponent had to perfect their defenses and become stronger, eventually leaving him with the only option of conducting a conventional siege, a siege where his numerical superiority would be less than two to one, and with an army two-thirds of which were untried provincials. This, coupled with the engineering reports in front of him, tipped the balance of the moment.[3]

The senior officers met at a council of war where Clerk laid a sketch of the French lines before them. According to one English officer, Clerk reported that the French lines were "a slight breastwork of logs, easy to access on the evenness of the ground, and so weakly bound together that it would be easy to push them down," while another stated that the engineer declared "it as his opinion, that it was very practicable to carry them by general storm." It should be pointed out that it is not clear if either of these officers was present at the council of war. Still, the quotes are not far from Abercromby's own words to the prime minister. Clerk, however, had another element to his plan. He pointed to his sketch, which showed a glen on the northern side of Mount Defiance. The location flanked the French lines from across the La Chute River some eight hundred yards away. Three brass six-pound cannons and a five-and-a-half-inch mortar, he followed, would be transported by raft to this site before the attack. Once in place, these guns would be able to rake the French entrenchment. Combined with the frontal attack, Montcalm's position would be untenable.[4]

Clerk scanned the faces about him for a comment, only to notice that more than one senior officer had turned to look at Major Eyre, the acting commander of the 44th Regiment. It was not lost on anyone present that Clerk was but a young lieutenant serving in his first command as chief engineer. Nor was it lost on those present that the job really belonged to Eyre. With Colonel Montressor not accompanying the expedition, the next senior engineer was Eyre, but with Gage's appointment to Abercromby's staff, it fell on Eyre to command the 44th Regiment. Thus, there was an apparent conflict, given that Eyre held parallel commissions in both the regular army and the Royal Engineers. For the major's part, he did not see an issue and informed Abercromby that he could both command the engineering detachment and see to his duties as acting commander of the 44th.[5]

Abercromby, however, perhaps as some have stated, for political reasons associated with Clerk, demanded that Eyre choose between his two duties. "This department devolved upon me by Colonel Montressor being ill and not able to act," Eyre wrote of the incident, "but, I was told if I did not give up the command of ye regiment I must have nothing to do with it; to this I answered, I could not do voluntarily, as there was no field officer to the regiment but myself, but was very willing if the general was pleased to order me, or allow me to act as Major and I would do my utmost in directing and supervising the (engineering) brigade, and carrying on that service; this I was sensible I could do in the most important parts of it, but it was not complied with, and from that time I was never asked or spoke to in relation to that branch."[6]

Now was Eyre's moment to express his professional opinion or perhaps vent his frustration by critiquing the plan in front of him, but he did neither. The plan, if the information on the French entrenchments was correct, was sound. And even if the information on the French works was mistaken, Clerk's positioning of cannons to enfilade the French lines would quickly undermine Montcalm's defenses.

Instead, the major asked how the troops would be deployed for the attack, in column or line. He favored the former. It would concentrate the attack against specific points on the French line and in his opinion was the most practical way to navigate the abatis before the breastwork. The idea was quickly dismissed, claiming that it would cause too much confusion to attack in such a manner and that there was no time to waste in debating the specifics of which points along the French line should be targeted. The regiments would deploy in line and attack along the entire length of the French works simultaneously. A piquet of volunteers drawn from the battalions would have the honor of leading the attack on the right, supported by the grenadiers. The Rangers, light infantry, and Bradstreet's men would advance first and form a skirmish line at the edge of the abatis. They in turn would be followed by half a dozen provincial regiments who would form up a hundred yards behind them and act as a screen should the regulars be forced to retire or have to reform their ranks. The remaining provincials would be held in reserve.

"When?" came the question from one of the senior officers. Abercromby turned to Clerk. The rafts for the artillery would not be completed until noon, the engineer replied. "Noon then," the general answered. "Sir William," he followed, as the other officers began looking at their pocket watches. William Johnson, who had arrived late on the seventh with four hundred Mohawks, stiffened a little at the words. Abercromby pointed to Clerk's map. "Sir William, at your earliest convenience, would you be pleased to take your detachment over to Sugarloaf Mountain to cover the landing of the artillery." Johnson nodded at the request, and with the remaining details agreed upon, the council broke up around nine o'clock.[7]

For Montcalm the morning hours brought a pleasant surprise. Around daylight a somewhat haggard but cheerful Levis climbed the hill to the general's tent. Montcalm was delighted to see his executive officer and Lt. Colonel Etienne Senezergues, the commandant of the La Sarre Regiment. "Gentlemen," he pronounced as he shook hands with his senior officers, "it seems you are just in time." After a few minutes of pleasantries, Montcalm briefed the two men on the current situation and then led the pair on a tour of the lines. The marquis informed Colonel Senezergues that he would take command of his regiment posted on the French left while Levis would take command of a brigade of three regiments holding the right wing. When he had finished his tour and left the two officers to see to their respective commands, Montcalm, like any general placed in such a position, began to have second thoughts as to his strategy. Was there still time to retreat and avoid the upcoming engagement? For a moment he considered sending two officers to Fort St. Frederic to oversee preparations for the arrival of the main army. As he pondered the possibilities, he encountered Captain Pouchot and stopped to ask the veteran if he thought the enemy would attack today. Pouchot removed his hat to wipe his forehead and nodded. "Sir, I believe they will," he answered. "The enemy cannot know about the preparations you have made," he continued, placing himself in the shoes of the English commander for a moment.

They will imagine that they have only to exert pressure on the units which occupy the heights. They sense that if they dislodge you from them, they will be masters of everything. But your trench works are immune from assault, sir. Should they attempt it, you have high hopes of repelling them. If they don't do it today, they will no longer be able to in two or three days, because they will have to open up roads to bring in their artillery. In that case, your position would change and you would have time to make up your mind on the best course to take.[8]

The advice, remarkably close to Abercromby's reasoning as it turned out, suppressed any second thoughts the marquis was experiencing. Montcalm thanked Pouchot and turned his attention back to the matters at hand.

True to his assignment, Johnson and his Mohawk detachment were in position less than an hour later. From their new vantage point, they let loose a stream of war whoops and shouts to announce their presence to the French working five hundred yards away. Not content with this, they turned to amusing themselves by launching a useless fusillade on the French lines. The firing caused work on the entrenchments to pause for a moment, but as the distance was too great, "We did not amuse ourselves by answering them," Montcalm noted in his report.[9]

Around 11 a.m. Abercromby gave the order for the first lines to advance. The vanguard consisting of Rogers' Rangers pushed into the woods before the French lines. About five hundred yards from the fortifications they were fired upon by the French advance guard. As soon as they started taking fire Rogers deployed his men into a skirmish line and shifted his march to the right to advance on the French sentries. The latter exchanged shots with the Rangers for some time, darting from tree to tree, slowly giving ground as they did so. Even when Gage's light infantry began probing forward on Rogers' right and Bradstreet's bateaux men entered the fray on Rogers' left, the French pickets coolly held to their assignment. "They withdrew in good order and held up the enemy for a long time," Captain Pouchot noted of their conduct.[10]

With the numbers clearly against them and their task complete, the last of the sentries covering the French center and left entered the safety of their lines around 11:30. Within a few minutes of their departure, a ribbon of skirmishers emerged from the woods onto the open ground some 250 yards from the abatis. Whatever momentum Abercromby's advanced guard had generated was quickly stymied when they reached the abatis. "We drove in the French pickets and came into the open where the trees were felled tops towards us in a mighty abatis as though blown down by the wind," one of Rogers' men recalled. "It was all we could undertake to make our way through the mass."[11]

Rogers', Bradstreet's, and Gage's men soon settled in at the outer edge of the abatis and occupied themselves with sniping at any sign of movement along the log wall. Behind them but unheard over the scattered musketry were the echoed calls of the officers of the first line of the provincial regiments, five Massachusetts Regiments and the 1st Battalion of the New York Regiment. With the way now cleared before them, the six colonial regiments threaded their way through the broad-leafed maples, ferns, and looming elms, clearing the edge of the woods before coming to a halt a hundred yards later. That is, all but the New York Regiment on the far left.

When Rogers had steered right to engage the French sentries, he had inadvertently shifted the entire skirmish line to the right. The French guard in front of Rogers had retired before the assault, but those on the French right, having encountered no one, had remained in place. The New Yorkers, thinking the way before them was clear, now blundered into these troops, who promptly greeted them with several sharp volleys. The fire halted the advance, but the New Yorkers soon recovered and returned fire. For nearly half an hour a sharp firefight raged amongst the trees on the English left. The French were not the only threat, as one soldier recalled, noting that, beyond the damage inflicted by the enemy, "our friends in the rear did us considerable damage by firing at random." Hard-pressed by the English numbers and their task complete, the French piquets retired through the abatis into their entrenchment.[12]

Along the French lines, the opening gunfire brought an immediate response. Troops threw aside their picks and shovels, snatched up their arms, and raced to their stations long before the signal cannon was fired as a call to arms. As the initial shuffling died down, the support crews came forward carrying powder, cases of shot, casks of water for both the troops and to put out fires, as well as spare flints and spare muskets to be distributed among the different regiments. Montcalm, stationed in the center of the lines, took a moment to peer out of a loophole and then turned to meet briefly with his staff. One by one the runners and couriers reported the regiments ready as the popping musketry edged closer. The general nodded at the reports and made a final review of the arrangements. Levis would command the French right with the regiment of La Reine anchoring this wing, followed in succession by Bearn and Guyenne, whose position ended along the right-hand half of a redan that jutted forward from the lines. Montcalm would personally direct the center with Royal Roussillon stationed on his right along the return half of the previous redan up through the right-hand portion of a second redan. This was followed by five piquets from Levis' recently arrived detachment, who occupied the return portion of the redan. The 2nd Battalion of Berry to the left of the piquets completed the center defenses up to the salient angle of a third redan. Languedoc, under Bourlamaque's command, covered the left-hand portion of the redan up to La Sarre, who guarded the line up to the southern crest. The grenadier company of the 3rd Battalion of Berry completed the alignment with the task of defending the far-left wing. Each regiment was allotted a hundred paces of the line, and behind each was stationed their respective grenadier companies and a company of volunteers to act as local reserves and plug any

A sketch of the opening stages of the Battle of Ticonderoga based on a 1759 work by William Brassier of the Ordnance Department. The precarious state of Montcalm's right is readily seen in the map. **French Forces**: 1. La Reine; 2. Bearn; 3. Guyenne; 4. Royal Roussillon; 5. Piquets and 2nd Berry; 6. Languedoc; 7. La Sarre; 8. Gren. Co. 3rd Berry; 9. Duprat's and Bernard's Volunteers; 10. Marines and Canadians; 11. 3rd Berry; 12. French Battery; 13. Fort Carillon; 14. Position of British flotilla when fired upon by Fort Carillon.

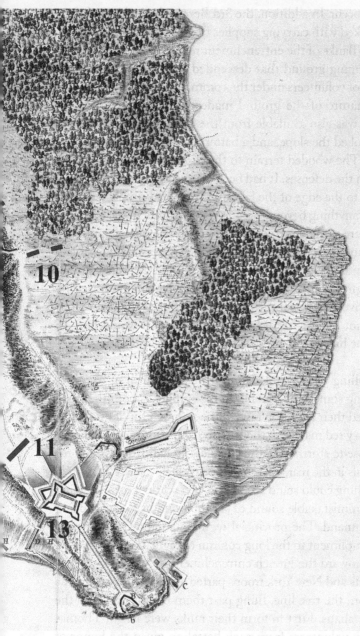

British and Colonial Forces: a. 80th; b. Rogers' Rangers; c. Bradstreet's Bateaux men; 1. Proby (Piquets) and Haldimand (Grenadiers); 2. Haviland's Brigade; 3. Donaldson's Brigade; 4. Grant's Brigade; d. Glazier (1st New York); e. Bagley; f. Williams; g. Partridge; h. Doty; i. Ruggles (note: part of this regiment was sent to the rear at the start of the engagement to set up aid stations); j. Preble; k. Johnston (New Jersey); l. Babcock (Rhode Island); m. Fitch; n. Wooster. (*Author*)

breaches that might occur. In addition, the 3rd Berry, who had been left to man the fort, was tasked with carrying supplies forward during the battle.[13]

The forces on the flanks of the entrenchment reported ready as well. To the left along the sloping ground that descended to the La Chute River were two companies of volunteers under the command of Captains DuPrat and Bernard. The nature of the ground made this position inherently strong. Support fire was also available from the far left of the entrenchments, which overlooked the slope, and a battery of six cannon posted behind the volunteers. The wooded terrain to the right of the entrenchment was the weak point in the defenses. It had been planned to extend the works through this ground to the edge of the lake, but there had simply not been enough time to erect anything beyond a crude two-foot wall in the foremost section. Nor were there sufficient troops to guard this avenue of approach, which extended almost five hundred yards to the western bank of Lake Champlain. Four hundred Canadians and Marines under Marine Captain Raymond were assigned this ground. If the reinforcements promised by the governor had arrived, Montcalm would have stationed them here, but such promises had not materialized. Instead, the marquis would have to make do with what he had and count on the English not attempting to exploit this gap.[14]

Around noon, rolling drums and the unmistakable shrill of bagpipes crept forward, creating something of a lull in the sniping as both the English and French turned their attention toward the sound. "Out of the woods behind us issued heavy red masses of the British troops advancing in battle array with the purpose to storm with the bayonet," one of Rogers' men recalled. To the colonials in the rear, unaccustomed to such warfare, it seemed impossible that anything could stand before the neat scarlet ranks, a feeling accentuated by the unmistakable sound of six thousand bayonets clicking into place upon command. The provincial regiments removed their hats, paying a military compliment to the long column of regulars as they passed through their ranks toward the French entrenchments.[15]

The Massachusetts and New York troops parted as the regular regiments began to emerge from the tree line, filing past them one by one onto the open area before the abatis. First to form their ranks were Major Thomas Proby's piquets, fifty volunteers from each battalion given the honor of leading the attack on the French left. Behind them, Colonel Frederick Haldimand arranged his detachment of four hundred grenadiers, the elite soldiers of the army, eighteenth-century shock troops made up of the biggest and strongest men in the battalions and easily discerned on any battlefield by their tall mitre caps bearing the insignia of King George. Haldimand's task was to support the piquet's advance, and if possible, exploit any breach they made in the French lines. Behind and slightly to the left of the grenadiers, Colonel William Haviland's brigade, consisting of the 27th Regiment and the 1st and 4th Battalions of the Royal Americans, began forming on the open ground, and to his left, Colonel John Donaldson's brigade of the 44th and 55th Regiments began doing likewise. Colonel Grant's brigade, made up of the 46th Regiment and the 42nd Highlanders, were to form to the left of Donaldson, but at the moment they had barely begun to exit from the woods.

The plan, at least as envisioned, was for Major Proby's piquets to lead the attack supported by the grenadiers who would, in turn, be supported by the rest of the regiments: "the whole were ordered to march up briskly, rush upon the enemy's fire and not give theirs until they were within the enemy breastworks." In essence it would be a simultaneous bayonet assault along a broad front of the French works, a moving wall of "cold steel" that would simply overwhelm the French defenses and defenders.[16]

Unfortunately for the British, such a plan never materialized. "The attack was made, I am sorry to say, not in the most regular manner," Major Eyre recalled, "some of the regiments beginning before the others were formed." Captain Abercrombie, who had accompanied Clerk earlier in the day on the reconnaissance of the French lines, was more specific. "The piquets who were supported by the Grenadiers and they by the whole line, rushed on to the attack before any of the Army was formed . . . and as the regiments came up they joined piecemeal in the attack."[17]

Whether a deliberate breach of orders, as one English officer claimed, a simple misunderstanding, or as one author has theorized, a lapse in judgment brought about by sheer exhaustion, Major Proby ordered the piquets to attack before the rest of the regiments had finished forming. Colonel Haldimand, seeing the piquets advance, ordered his men forward to support their effort. Haviland followed suit with his brigade a few moments later, and Donaldson, caught off guard by the maneuver, saw little choice but to order his men forward as well, whether they had finished arranging their ranks or not. Grant, who had just cleared the woods, faced a similar problem, and after spending a few frustrating minutes trying to organize his forces, he gave up and signaled his men to advance.[18]

The net result was that the four columns of British regulars advanced in a haphazard echelon left formation. Proby steered his men toward the depression running along the left-hand side of the La Sarre Regiment in

an obvious attempt to flank the French position. Haldimand, true to his
orders, followed close behind, prepared to make the most of any success
the piquets might achieve. Haviland's brigade, a few dozen yards to the rear
of Haldimand, held to the higher ground on the French left, opposite the
Languedoc and 2nd Berry Regiments, in order to draw their fire and provide support for the piquets and grenadiers. Donaldson's brigade, although
later in starting its attack, quickly made up ground and directed its march
toward the center of the French lines, while Grant, a good distance behind,
carried his attack farther left toward the redan guarded by La Reine and
Bearn.

On the French left, Bourlamaque peered out of a loophole at the on-
coming British columns, although doing so was hazardous, given, as Desandrouins noted, that "a very great quantity of fire from good marksmen,
Scottish and American, hidden behind the stumps and tree trunks, was
coming from the space between the attacking columns." Montcalm had
foreseen that the English might attempt to draw his fire and expend his
ammunition in this fashion, and in response he had assigned a handful of
marksmen in each regiment to deal with the threat. Thus far this was the
only fire coming from the log wall, leaving the casual observer with the impression that the French defenses were nearly abandoned, but every British
soldier approaching the works knew better and inwardly braced for the inevitable storm.[19]

When Proby's and Haldimand's columns reached the outer edge of the
abatis, Bourlamaque stepped back from his vantage point, and standing behind the triple ranks of anxious soldiers, shouted "Ready!" which was echoed
down the length of the La Sarre and Languedoc Regiments. There was a
shuffled rush as the first rank of French soldiers stepped forward and thrust
their muskets through the waiting firing ports. "Aim!" the colonel bellowed,
which brought forth a pulse of cricket-like clicks as two hundred muskets
were cocked in unison. And then, after a pause that seemed far too long
for those hanging upon the next word, the command "Fire!" rang down the
line.

The left side of the French line erupted in yellow flashes and puffs of
blue-white smoke. The soldiers in the first line stepped back as the command "Second line!" was issued from their officers over the bark of a number of small swivel and wall guns that now added their notes to the deadly
chorus. The second rank of regulars stepped forward and took aim. "Fire!"
rang out, and another sheet of smoke and flames rippled down the left wing
of the French lines. "Third line!" was the call as the soldiers in the second

line moved to the back of the firing queue and those behind them stepped forward to take their place. And after a brief pause, the command "Fire!" propagated down the line, launching yet another volley toward the attackers.

By now a dense white pall hung over the entrenchment, threatening to engulf those within. Clearly, the initial rate of fire could not be sustained, not only because the shroud it created threatened to obscure the enemy, making any continued firing ineffective, but because it consumed ammunition far faster than it could be brought up. As with the skirmishers, Montcalm had foreseen this problem as well. "The soldiers cannot be too strictly warned that the great fault of the regulars lies in hasty firing without aim; the result is ammunition is speedily exhausted," he spelled out in his battle orders. "The officers will see to this important matter, which cannot be too often repeated. They will see to it the soldier fires slowly and they must urge him to take good aim." In keeping with the directive, the command "Fire at will!" was repeated down the line as regimental officers paced behind their sections of the wall, urging their men to take careful aim and pick out their targets before firing.[20]

Although whole files were struck down by the opening volleys, Proby's and Haviland's columns doggedly pressed forward into the abatis. Here, whatever order they had hoped to maintain in their ranks quickly disintegrated as they found themselves floundering amongst the brush. Ensnared on sharpened branches and toppling over jumbled trees, the advance slowed to a crawl as men attempted to carry each other forward, all while being subjected to a barrage from an enemy who was only occasionally seen snatching a quick glimpse over the top of the breastworks. "We were so entangled in the branches of the felled trees that we could not possibly advance," one English officer described his predicament. "The enemy were sensible of this, and remained steady at their breastworks, repeating their fire, which from their numbers, was very weighty."[21]

Remarkably, Major Proby waded through the obstacles and enemy fire to lead the head of his detachment to within a few yards of the breastwork before he was cut down and the attack faltered. Haldimand's grenadiers fared no better, and like a wave that had crested, the two British columns on the French left began to recede. As Proby's and Haviland's men fell back, Donaldson's brigade weaved its way into the wooded curtain and was greeted in a similar fashion by the guns of 2nd Berry, Royal Roussillon, and the five companies of Levis' recently arrived piquets. As these British troops struggled forward, breaking themselves against the barricade, a runner brought alarming news to Montcalm. At least twenty English barges had been spotted near the mouth of the La Chute River. The English, it seemed, were attempting to land an expeditionary force behind his left flank in order to unhinge his position on the heights. Not wasting any time, Montcalm summoned Captain Medard Poularies, in command of the nearby grenadier company of the Royal Roussillon Regiment. The marquis, cupping his hands to his mouth to be heard over the gunfire, shouted to the veteran officer for him to take his company and the company of volunteers and immediately reinforce Duprat and Bernard.

The English boats were not carrying a landing force, as Montcalm supposed, but the cannon that Lt. Clerk had arranged to be landed at the base of Mount Defiance. In this sense they were a far greater threat than Montcalm had first perceived, for once situated, they would rake his lines with six-pound shot, placing his entire position on the heights into question. The plan had been for the artillery to be in place before the attack commenced, but Major Proby had started early, and loading the artillery onto the rafts had taken longer than expected. Regardless of the timing, the battle now hinged on Clerk's rough sketch and the interpretation of this sketch by an officer of the Royal Artillery. A little before one o'clock, twenty whaleboats slowly towed the two artillery rafts down the outlet of the La Chute River as gunfire echoed along the heights to the north. Their commanding officer searched the south shore for "an open place described by the engineer" but found neither himself nor anyone in his crew was able to locate the position. Not realizing that they had passed the intended spot and believing the sketch to be in error, the commanding officer gave the order for the flotilla to turn around, but by now it was too late.

When the lead vessels rounded a small point of land, they came within range of Lt. M. de Louvicourt's three-gun battery on the southwest bastion of Fort Carillon. The colonial artillery officer gave the order, and one after another the dull thumps and puffs of white smoke as seen from the English vessels translated into nearby geysers. The boat crews pulled hard on their oars, but the French, having had ample opportunity to range their guns in on this location, rained havoc among their ranks. One of the rafts and one of the whaleboats were swamped, and the rest were sent scurrying back, hurried along their way by a few parting shots from Duprat's and Poularies' men. For the moment, fortune had favored Montcalm.[22]

As Donaldson's column stalled before the breastworks, Colonel Grant's brigade advanced on the French right. The Highlanders of the Black Watch, intended to be held in reserve, proved too impatient and flung themselves at the abatis with such a fury that one observer likened it to "roaring lions breaking from their chains." Regardless of their ardor, the Highlanders found, as had the other brigades, that the abatis "put it entirely out of our power to advance briskly, which gave the enemy (an) abundance of time to mow us down like a field of corn." But it would take more than brush, branches, and ball to break the Scots' resolve. Urging each other on, they pushed forward, many casting aside their muskets and drawing their broadswords in an effort to hack their way through to the French entrenchments. Musket balls shattered wood and bone about them while the deadly bark of a swivel gun issued a cloud of lead that ripped through their ranks. Still, they pushed forward, the entangled wounded calling on the able-bodied to press home the attack. Perhaps the regiment's commander, Colonel Grant, typified the spirit of the charge. Standing at their head, he rained Gaelic insults upon the French with one breath and words of encouragement to his men with the next as he swung his broadsword in wild arcs at the knotted brush before him. He ignored the musket ball that tore through his bonnet, but it was quickly followed by a spent ball that struck him in the head, knocking him senseless. Dazed, the commander was helped to his feet, only to push away those who wished to lead him to the rear, and undaunted, he once again joined the attack.[23]

One witness from the Rhode Island Regiment was surprised by the Highlanders' resolve. "They even went up to the Breast-work," he wrote of their advance, "but were knocked down so fast, that it was very difficult for those behind to get over the Dead and Wounded." Somehow through this maelstrom a handful of Scots led by Captain John Campbell managed to reach the log wall. Without scaling ladders, they stood on each other's shoulders or drove their bayonets into the wall to serve as steps as their comrades discharged their muskets into nearby firing ports. For a brief moment Campbell and his men could be seen standing on the top of the wall, which brought a loud "huzzah" from the provincial regiments in the rear, before in the next instant disappearing over to the other side.

For Abercromby, nothing had gone as planned. The general had come forward with the 42nd Regiment at the rear of the British column and was shocked with what he found. Up until now he had assumed that the irregulars and perhaps a few of the provincial regiments were responsible for the firing. Instead, he found that the attack had not only started but had been committed to wholesale by the regulars. As the Highlanders streamed left, Abercromby and his aides moved right to position themselves on a small hill half a cannon shot from the French left. It only took a few moments from their new vantage point before the general began barraging his aides with questions. Where was Clerk's artillery? Why had the attack started before the guns were in place? Why were the regiments not formed before the signal was given to advance? Who gave the signal? Someone get Clerk! And get an update from the field commanders!

Runners were dispatched as Abercromby examined the scene unfolding before him. The piquets and grenadiers were falling back, as was Haviland's brigade. Donaldson's men were wavering, and farther north the 46th and the 42nd were advancing, but from his vantage point at the southern end of the French lines it was difficult to see what headway they were making. The general was no tactical genius, but it did not take one to realize what was occurring. The disjointed advance had left the French with the opportunity to shift their resources to meet each threat as it presented itself. Regiments had committed themselves to the attack without any regard to the overall plan or the actions of the units around them. Essentially, the battle had become a series of localized conflicts with no one in control.

It did not take long before he had seen enough. Until the artillery was in place, be it Clerk's guns or ones dragged forward from the provincial redoubts, the attack would have to be suspended. Abercromby was on the verge of issuing the recall, when a loud "huzzah" was heard emanating from the far right of the French lines. The first impression was that Grant's brigade had entered the French lines, but it was impossible to tell from his location. He questioned his aides as to their opinion, and runners were sent to ascertain the nature of the cheer. A short time later one returned with a report that the 42nd had breached the enemy's lines. With the news, Abercromby set aside his previous opinion and made a fateful decision to continue on with the attack.[24]

Whatever success Abercromby or the provincial troops perceived was short-lived. Severely outnumbered and unsupported, Captain Campbell's men fell victim to scores of bayonets the moment they crossed the log wall. Like the rest of the regulars, the hail of buckshot and ball proved too great, and the remainder of the Highlanders began falling back a short time later. As the regular officers struggled to reform their ranks, the order came for the provincial troops to advance to the abatis and cover the regulars' retreat.[25]

Around one o'clock the Massachusetts Regiments, the New Jersey "Blues," the Rhode Islanders, the New Yorkers, and a pair of Connecticut Regiments advanced along a broad front to the edge of the abatis. After what they had witnessed, it was a harrowing prospect for men who a few months before had been farmers, merchants, and tradesmen. Garret Albertson, a private in the Jersey "Blues," vividly remembered the scene years later. "When we came near the field of battle, and the bullets began to whistle round us, I felt a tremor or panic of fear, and I strove to conquer it but in vain." Although some officers endeavored to keep their men out of harm's way, most pushed their troops to the edge of the abatis and, beside the British skirmishers already there, began fusillading the French lines from behind whatever cover they could find. For a time, the engagement became something akin to what had occurred at the head of Lake George a few years before, a duel of hide and shoot, a contest where the French held a distinct advantage given that the English troops saw nothing "but their hats and the end of their muskets."[26]

Albertson, having managed to put aside his initial fear, found himself behind a large pine log along with several other members of his regiment. "We would drop and load, then rise and fire over the log, until our ammunition was almost spent; my firelock at length got so hot I could not handle it." Not far away, David Perry of Prebble's regiment was undergoing a similar experience. The sixteen-year-old, who thought he was too small to pass muster, found himself pinned down behind a white oak stump, "the balls striking the ground within a hand's breath of me every moment. A man could not stand erect without being hit any more than he could stand out in a shower, without having drops of rain fall upon him," he recalled nearly sixty years later. During a lull in the firing, Perry darted to the cover of a felled tree where several of his comrades had taken shelter, but he found his new position little better. "The balls here came as thick as ever. One of the men raised his head a little above the log, and a ball struck him in the center of the forehead."[27]

The provincials, however, had accomplished their task. A little after two o'clock, the scarlet columns to the rear began advancing once again. As they passed through the provincial positions, the separation between the units became blurred, and the orderly advance mutated into knots of men beating themselves against a maze of timber, firing on the French, and cursing their plight. "It was so very bad," one British officer claimed, "that after we were within gun shot the enemy might easily fire 10 rounds before we got up to the length of their entrenchments." Again, the attack bogged down under the defenders' fire, although some, particularly the stubborn Highlanders, reached the base of the wall before meeting their end.

"If the abatis held up a little the advance of the enemy columns," Pouchot commented, "they also contributed to saving them a lot of men, because they provided cover." As one scanned the battlefield, they would have had a difficult time agreeing with the Frenchman's statement. Hanging on branches like roses growing in a thorny hedge were hundreds of fallen regulars, and clustered about them, attempting to crawl out of the wooded web or lying bewildered by their fate, were hundreds more wounded. "The dead men and the wounded lay on the ground," one provincial officer would later write in a shaking hand. "Having some of them their legs, their arms, and other limbs broken; others shot through the body and very mortally wounded. To hear their cries and see their bodies lay in blood, and the earth tremble with the fire of the small arms, was as mournful (an) hour as ever I saw."[28]

Around three o'clock there occurred an odd incident recorded by chroniclers on both sides. As the English columns were retreating, Captain Jean Bassignac of the Royal Roussillon Regiment apparently tied a red handkerchief to the barrel of his musket and, standing atop the breastworks, began waving it in an act of defiance. The act brought the head of a nearby English column to a stop. The reason was simple. In the military etiquette of the day a parley or a surrender was signaled by showing the enemy's colors. Believing that the French wished to surrender, a few hundred Englishmen advanced on the location, holding their muskets up with both hands, shouting "Quarter!" The event brought a brief stop to the firing and more French troops to the top of the wall. Thinking that the English wished to surrender, the Frenchmen beckoned them forward, all the time calling upon them, "Put down your arms! Put down your arms!" It was a bizarre situation, a terrible miscommunication brought about by a foolish act of bravado. Both sides believed that the other wished to surrender, when in reality, neither wished to do so. As the English, still in possession of their arms, came closer, it became apparent to Captain Pouchot that something was amiss. "Fire, Fire!" he screamed at the troops on the wall. "Can't you see that they are going to overrun your position?" But it proved an unnecessary command. Captain Poularies, in command of the Royal Roussillon grenadiers, had already come to the same conclusion and ordered his men to fire, which felled a score of Englishmen and sent the rest scurrying back in confusion.[29]

The regulars did not take long to return. Haviland's brigade, along with Haldimand's column, consisting of what was left of the grenadiers and piquets, renewed their efforts against the French left, while Donaldson's and Grant's brigades, led forward by the martial wailing of bagpipes, converged on a point between the flags of Bearn and Guyenne. Again the provincials and skirmishers responded by pelting the log wall with musket balls in sup-

The Battle of Ticonderoga by Frederic Remington. (*New York Public Library*)

port of the advance, firing at the tops of hats, loopholes, or anything else that looked promising. Although the attack once again fizzled, there was a moment of concern for the French. The 2nd Berry was considered by Montcalm and many of his officers a questionable unit, given that most of troops had never been under fire. For this reason, Montcalm placed them directly under his command to keep a close eye on their conduct. It proved a wise choice. After hours of fighting, a handful of men in the unit panicked and bolted for the rear. The action had a ripple effect, and within a few minutes it appeared that the entire regiment was on the verge of abandoning its position, but the frantic calls of their officers and the lowered bayonets of the grenadier companies behind them convinced them to return to their posts "so promptly, that the enemy did not perceive it."[30]

There were other problems as well. At the start of the engagement, Lt. Colonel Marie Joseph de Trecesson, in command of the fort, found himself forced to fire on a large number of Canadian militia who had abandoned their post and were attempting to reach the boats. The tactic worked, and all but one, who was wounded in the exchange, returned to their position on the far right of the entrenchment. Once here, however, they had done little beyond taking occasional long-range shots at the enemy. Given that this force of four hundred Canadians and Marines had not been attacked, Levis, who had already had his hat knocked off his head by a musket ball, sent an officer with orders for them to fall on the flank of the English column attacking the French right. Although these troops had been recently reinforced by 250 men under Lt. Francois Duplessis, they showed little interest in following the brigadier's orders. Twice their commander, Captain Raymond, called on them to advance. The first time a handful of men advanced, only to scatter at the first shots fired at them, and the second time they left Raymond cursing their conduct after only one officer stood to join him.[31]

Overall, Montcalm's regulars behaved quite well. Desandrouins, whose engineering duties concluded once the battle started, acted as aide-de-camp to the marquis. Throughout the day he raced from one end of the line to the other, gathering information, gauging the morale of the men, and questioning them on what they needed. In each case he found the troops in good spirits and lacking nothing. The engineer was quick to hand out the praise he felt was due to the troops. It was "impossible to describe the sang-froid and bravery our soldiers showed that day," he wrote of their conduct. "I noticed that none fired without aiming at his target first, and most were waiting often quite long to see or look for a skirmisher posted behind a stump so as not to miss, although the hail of musket balls was dense."[32]

Just before the battle started Abercromby ordered Colonel Ruggles to set up aid stations at the rear of the army. The Massachusetts troops had barely taken to the task when the regulars advanced on the French lines. Soon wounded began appearing and in numbers far beyond what the surgeons could handle, meaning many soldiers died before their wounds could even be looked at. "The guns did roar like thunder and from about noon till about sunn sett there was a steady fire," one Massachusetts soldier stationed at the post recalled, "and the groans of the wounded there were continually sounding in our ears."[33]

A little after five o'clock the English gathered for one last effort as small fires smoldering throughout the abatis added their embers to the drifting haze. Haviland and Haldimand once again pressed on the French left while Grant's and Donaldson's brigades, the latter minus their colonel, who now lay among the fallen, shifted their focus to a section of the wall guarded by Royal Roussillon and 2nd Berry. The attack, like those before it, never stood a chance. The troops were exhausted and most were low on ammunition, but remarkably their spirit remained unbroken, although, as one English officer commented, "it was not in the power of courage or even chance to bestow success."[34]

By now the futility had become obvious to all, including Abercromby who, after making the decision to continue the attack, was strangely silent.

Even when Clerk, who now lay mortally wounded in the field hospital, informed him that his artillery had been forced back and damaged by French guns, Abercromby took no action. Now, as the fourth attack in as many hours began to falter, the general gave the order to retreat. The drums furiously beat out the recall, and after several attempts the regulars finally broke off the engagement and fell back behind the provincials, who in turn retreated into the woods towards the sawmill. Entangled and ensnarled within the abatis it proved impossible to carry off all the wounded. "We got away the wounded of our company," Perry recalled, "but left a great many crying for help; which we were unable to afford them." The skirmishers, led by Rogers, covered the retreat and exchanged shots with the French until dusk, and then they, too, pulled back, effectively bringing an end to the battle.

Part of the army was immediately ordered to the landing area, while the rest gathered about the sawmill and the provincial redoubts. The engagement had been a costly one, but the army was convinced, almost to a man, that siege operations would start the next morning. There was no reason to believe otherwise. They had a clear line of communications behind them, ample supplies, control of the high ground about the fort, and even after their casualties, nearly fourteen thousand men fit for duty, not to mention an impressive train of artillery just waiting to be hauled forward. The French had not stirred out of their entrenchment, and although they had prevented the English from seizing these works, they had neither altered the numerical superiority the latter possessed nor denied them the freedom of movement they required to conduct siege operations. Fort Carillon, it seemed, would not fall in a day but in a week, perhaps two at the most.[35]

Montcalm was of the same opinion. He had won the day and punished Abercromby's army in the process, but at best, all he had done was buy time. If he was fortunate, the English would foolishly continue their attack on his lines the next morning, but such thoughts were wishful thinking. It was far more likely that the enemy would begin hauling their heavy cannons forward, and within a few days, they would be in position to reduce his entrenchment to splinters; that is, if they didn't put a few pieces on Mount Defiance first, which would undermine his defenses even faster. Beyond doubt, the marquis had saved his army. They could easily slip away in the next few days while the English conducted their siege operations, but as far as Fort Carillon was concerned, its fate was still very much up in the air.

9

"VERY FINE LIMBS, BUT NO HEAD"

A T DUSK THE TROOPS ENCAMPED ABOUT THE SAWMILL RECEIVED orders to immediately return to the landing place and prepare to embark. The directive was greeted with shock and bewilderment. "I believe no men ever received any orders with more surprise, nor executed them with more reluctancy," one senior British officer observed, while the wounded Captain Charles Lee, never shy in expressing his opinion, was more direct, referring to the command (and the person who had issued it) as "dishonorable and infamous," with "strong symptoms of cowardice." Among the provincials there was a similar level of disbelief. "To my great surprise," Colonel Babcock wrote to the governor of Rhode Island, "the whole army was ordered to return to the bateaux, to the great mortification of (the) chief of officers."[1]

The order, which several officers attempted to dissuade Abercromby from issuing, set off a wave of confusion. The portage road soon became clogged with men stumbling over one another in the darkness, dragging supply carts, wounded, and artillery on a path that was so muddy that, in many places, they sank up to their knees. At times the procession slowed to such a point that exhausted men fell out of the ranks to catch a few hours' sleep, while others, tired of their burden, freely cast aside supplies and nonessentials to ease their plight. Guards had to be posted at the bridge over the La Chute River to control the exodus and prevent the withdrawal from becoming a panicked retreat, which only served to slow the march down even further.[2]

Many provincial troops located in the redoubts to the east of the sawmill did not receive the order to fall back until hours after it was issued, or in some cases, never received it at all. To their astonishment, Colonels Partridge and Williams only realized that the army was retiring when they heard the commotion to their rear around midnight. Others, such as Lt. Archelaus Fuller, fell asleep only to awaken and find "that the army (was) chiefly gone." Several companies of Colonel Wooster's regiment had a similar problem. Posted toward Fort Carillon, they did not discover the retreat until the next morning, when upon returning to the sawmill they found the place nearly deserted.[3]

Around mid-morning the order was given for the army to embark. One colonial soldier referred to it as "a sea of confusion" as men attempted to locate their regiment's boats, and when they could not find them, board the closest available vessels. The artillery and wounded were successfully loaded aboard the boats, but in the chaos much of the supplies were simply abandoned or destroyed to expedite the process. Colonel Bradstreet, at the center of the commotion, attempted to head off the chaos but with limited success. Vessels not carrying their quota were ordered ashore to take on more men, while other vessels were ordered to delay embarking to ease the congestion. With time, Bradstreet might have established an orderly withdrawal, but around ten o'clock Wooster's and Rogers' men suddenly appeared upon the scene and were mistaken for the enemy. The confusion now turned to panic as the cries of "push off! push off!" echoed down the beach. Fortunately, no shots were fired, and the error was realized a few minutes later, but by then the inertia of the retreat was too much to overcome. The outlet of Lake George soon became an entwined mass of vessels, each looking to outpace the other up the length of the lake.[4]

For Montcalm, the morning of July 9 was as anxious as that of the previous morning. Although he did not seriously expect another frontal assault, his troops had spent the evening preparing for one. More importantly, the morning would bring an important decision upon him, namely, whether the English would start bringing forward their heavy guns, leaving him with no option but to preserve his army and abandon Fort Carillon. At daybreak the drums beat the troops to their posts. From here they nervously scanned the tree line for some sign of activity. Less than an hour had passed when it became clear to the marquis that something was wrong. With no indications of the English before him, patrols were sent out to secure the battlefield "who dispatched some of the wounded who wished to defend themselves, and brought within the lines those who did not resist."[5]

While this task continued, Captain Bernard pushed forward with a party of volunteers and by mid-morning sent a report that the enemy had abandoned the sawmill, a fact easily corroborated by the thick column of smoke that could be seen rising from the area. Later in the day Bernard's men probed farther south along the portage road, noting the signs of retreat everywhere. A few stragglers rounded up in the woods claimed the English had left, and that evening Lt. Wolf and his detachment, released by Abercromby earlier that morning, appeared before the French lines to confirm the suspicions. Levis settled the matter the next day by taking possession of the portage with a large detachment. What he found astounded him. Hundreds of barrels of flour caved in or floating aimlessly in the lake, scores of shoes left stuck in the mud as if abandoned in terror by their owners, burned pontoons and wrecked boats scattered along the shoreline, hats, knapsacks, and all manner of flotsam and jetsam drifting about; and large caches of entrenching tools and provisions simply abandoned for the taking. The signs were telltale. It had not been a retreat but a panicked flight.[6]

Montcalm and his men celebrated the news. The marquis had achieved a stunning victory, and in the process his losses had been reasonable, some 572 casualties in all, with a good part of these having occurred amongst Trepezac's detachment on July 6. His decision to stand on the heights of Carillon has been praised throughout history, as successful ventures typically are, but in the light of the moment it was an incredibly risky proposition. The marquis offered battle under the assumption that the English would accept the trap he had set and batter themselves against his prepared position, but even though they took the bait, a dozen things could have gone wrong.

While Montcalm succeeded, a good deal of the credit belonged to the British. Had Clerk's guns come into action on Mount Defiance, Montcalm would have had a much different day. Had the English attacked in column against specific sections of the line, as Eyre had recommended, and penetrated his defenses in numbers, the marquis, with no place to go, would have had a disaster on his hands. Had the English, during their frontal assault, probed left with several regiments and found the woods to his right guarded by only a handful of Canadians, they might have quickly out-flanked him, leading to yet another disaster. And had Howe not been killed on the first day, the likelihood is good that the marquis would have found himself invested or perhaps even cut off at the sawmill before he had time to extricate his forces.

In many ways Montcalm had gambled his army and the fate of Canada on low odds. Low, because even if he did defeat the English before his en-trenchments, he did not have the resources available to contest a conven-tional siege, which could have only one logical conclusion. Low, because outnumbered four to one it was unfathomable that the English, in control of everything but the Ticonderoga Peninsula itself, would abandon the entire campaign, even if they did suffer a setback before his entrenchments. Low, because even if he won, he could have suffered devastating losses, losses al-most impossible to make up with English control of the shipping lanes from France. This being said, all Montcalm needed to justify his actions was point to the outcome. "It was the affair of L'Assiette renewed," Desandrouins wrote in his journal. Precisely what Montcalm had wagered on.[7]

For Abercromby there were far more questions as his demoralized army hauled their boats ashore near the ruins of Fort William Henry. How things that had started so promising had turned out so badly is difficult to com-prehend. It is true that the campaign was late in starting. As we have seen, had the English moved forward even a month sooner Fort Carillon and Fort St. Frederic would have never stood a chance, but putting this strategic planning matter aside, much of the blame for the tactical failures of the campaign must be placed squarely on the shoulders of the general and his staff. Howe's loss was clearly the crucial blow in the campaign. Certainly the young nobleman, as noted by other English officers, "exposed himself too much," and thus he bears his own share in the campaign's failure. But the matter goes deeper. Why did Abercromby not delay a few more days to allow Johnson's Mohawks to arrive and perhaps even the New Hamp-shire Regiment, recognized by almost everyone for their woodland skills? Why indeed, if the army proposed a sweeping flanking maneuver through the woods to the north of the landing area? These forces would have seemed ideally suited for such an operation. With Johnson's Mohawks in the lead (or Rogers' men for that matter), would Howe have fallen? Would the encounter between Trepezac's troops, mostly volunteer regulars, have occurred in any fashion close to what actually transpired?

There are three possibilities here. First, Howe never informed Aber-cromby of his intentions to march along the western edge of the rapids and invest the fort. This seems difficult to believe. Second, Abercromby simply became frustrated with the delays and let his emotions get the better part of his judgment and decided to proceed without these troops. This has some merit and seems plausible, particularly when one considers that the general was worried about the French reinforcing Fort Carillon during the series of delays. Third, an unfounded confidence had been placed in Gage's light infantry, which made the skills possessed by Johnson's Mohawks, the New Hampshire troops, and even Rogers' men irrelevant. This was probably the case and the driving factor.

Even with Howe's loss the campaign was far from settled. The first question to be asked after the brigadier's death is who took his place? It seems Abercromby, but this should not have been the case. Gage was the logical man to fill Howe's role as tactical leader. He had rank and experience and was viewed as something of an expert in North American warfare. Yet Gage was oddly silent. Nowhere does one see his opinions, his council, or even mention of him being present among the numerous journals and letters pertaining to the actions of July 7, 8, or 9. Instead, John Bradstreet seems to have been the figure to step forward, but only in a limited fashion, and his opinions were only enacted upon when vigorously defended by other officers. Who then was acting as tactical advisor to Abercromby? Two figures that come to the forefront are Captain James Abercrombie and Lt. Mathew Clerk. The first was an aide to the general and the second was the chief engineer for the expedition. Both men had firsthand experience with the terrain, having been on previous scouts of the area, and in their current positions both had direct access to the general.

The latter of these two men, Clerk, has traditionally been the scapegoat of Abercromby's failure and became a focal point of criticism. Beyond doubt, the general went out of his way to have Clerk appointed chief engineer for the campaign, first, by knowing full well that Montressor's ailing condition made his actual participation unlikely, and second, by snubbing Eyre's seniority and placing the major in a command entanglement that for all practical purposes existed only in the general's mind. Should Abercromby have consulted Eyre on the French defenses? Should he have sent him to the top of Mount Defiance to view the enemy works? Of course. Eyre had more practical engineering experience, combat experience, and knowledge of warfare in North America than almost any man on the continent, a fact borne out by his later appointment to the post of chief engineer in North America and his promotion to lieutenant colonel and command of a regiment. Would it have made a difference? Perhaps Eyre, who had participated in the Battle of Lake George, who had built Fort Edward and Fort William Henry, and defended the latter from a French attack, might have had a better appreciation of the strength of the French lines, or more importantly, the viability of landing artillery at the site Clerk had selected.

Did the fact that Eyre was not consulted call Clerk's plan into question? Not necessarily. However, it is clear is that Clerk underestimated the strength of the French entrenchments, a fact that can easily be explained by his lack of experience, but his plan to enfilade the French works with cannon from Mount Defiance was sound—sound, that is, on paper. The criticisms that can be made of Clerk deal more with the execution of his plan than the plan itself. Foremost among these criticisms was the site he chose for his artillery. The officer in charge of the artillery boats and his crew could not locate the site. Given that Clerk had selected the location from atop Mount Defiance, it begs the question as to whether or not it was accessible from the river. The engineer does not seem to have conducted a reconnaissance from the water level to verify his choice, nor did he accompany the boats to direct them firsthand to the landing zone, which seems odd given the role these cannons were to play in the attack. Furthermore, when the attempt to land the artillery failed, we do not see Clerk personally leading a second attempt, even though this mission was absolutely crucial to the plan of attack. For that matter, why was there no second attempt to land the artillery? Although the artillery boats progressed too far and came under fire from the French, British accounts do not mention the loss of any vessels or their cannons. Further, there is no mention of any loss of artillery at all during the campaign. Why, then, was no second attempt made?[8]

The answer is probably to be found in the criticism directed toward Abercromby on how he handled himself both during and after the battle. To be fair to the general, the attack started before the forces involved were prepared. Major Proby has been almost universally blamed for this, and given the evidence it seems to have been a just conclusion. The early start seems to have agitated the general and certainly unbalanced his vision of how the assault would proceed, but the critical moment came near the conclusion of the first attempt on the French entrenchments. Up to this point nothing had gone as planned. There was no word of Clerk's artillery, the regiments had attacked piecemeal instead of as a unit, and half of them were in retreat. It was clear that the plan of attack had gone awry. A retreat should have been sounded at this point, the troops reorganized, and if need be, artillery dragged forward to deal with the French defenses. Abercromby was on the verge of doing just this when a cheer from the provincials at the opposite side of the line, coupled with sketchy reports that the 42nd had entered the French lines, caused him to alter his decision and press forward with the attack.

It was an odd choice and one out of character for such a methodical man. A few days before, he had held the army at the landing site because, as he claimed, he lacked sufficient intelligence to make a decision on how to move forward. On the morning of the attack he had sent Lt. Clerk and Captain Abercrombie back to Mount Defiance to confirm their observations from the day before, determined to be certain of the information before him before proceeding. And although the army was prepared to march earlier that morning, he delayed the attack until noon to allow Clerk to place his batteries across the La Chute River, a logical delay taken to improve the odds of the attack succeeding. Yet now in the midst of a battle, one in which he did not have a clear picture of his forces, their progress, their losses, and the location or status of the supporting artillery, he chose to set aside his initial judgment and press forward? This leads one to wonder if the tide of the moment did not prove too much for the aging Scot or if others about him did not influence the decision. Along these latter lines, there was an enticing motive—the opportunity to destroy the standing army of Canada in an afternoon. After all, how many occasions like this would present themselves? If the general halted the attack and shifted to siege operations, the French army would escape, but if the attack succeeded Montcalm would be crushed, New France left defenseless, and the war possibly over by the end of the year. Whatever the case, Abercromby chose not to intervene in the uncoordinated assault and, by doing so, quickly relegated himself to the role of spectator.

Just as much, if not more, criticism was leveled against Abercromby's decision to retreat and how the retreat was conducted. Several officers attempted to talk the general out of his decision. Colonial legend has it that William Johnson went so far as calling the general a coward to his face and reached for his sword before being restrained. The story seems quite unlikely, but it does say something about how the provincials viewed the two leaders. Captain Abercrombie put his opinion forward that siege operations should start immediately but noted that "others who have not seen half the service, and whose nerves are not quite braced for war, advised the contrary." Most never understood the reasoning behind the retreat, and Captain Loring even questioned the use of the term, writing, "In short it appeared we

Run away from our selves and not from the Enemy, and can in no shape be called a Retreat, as no Enemy ever attempted to follow us."[9]

The general was slow in justifying his decision. In a letter to his son nearly a month after the battle he laid out his reasoning. The bulk of his argument revolved around the belief that huge French reinforcements were on the way to the fort. In this the general was correct. But whereas Abercromby envisioned Montcalm's numbers at ten or twelve thousand by the time the British siege guns opened fire, the reality of the matter was that it was not until July 31 that the French army on the Ticonderoga Peninsula peaked at numbers just over seven thousand men. The imagined French strength was used to justify the rest of his arguments, which ranged from the inadequacies of the provincials and the vulnerability of his army during a siege to the perceived month-long task of hauling the cannon up from the portage. As to the nature of the retreat, the general was quick to blame the colonials, who he claimed retired to the landing place in great disorder once the battle had concluded.[10]

Abercromby's arguments did little to help his cause. To believe that Canada could have so quickly sent six to eight thousand men to the aid of Fort Carillon, especially when being pressed on its flanks at Louisbourg and Fort Duquesne, demonstrated a perceptible lack of understanding as to his enemy's abilities. The questioning of his provincial troops' abilities and the vulnerability of his army during the siege is another subject of debate. In an open battle Abercromby would have been justified in questioning his contingent of untried militia, but a siege was quite a different matter. Early on, Loudoun had recognized that provincial troops possessed exactly the skills desired for such operations, pointing out that one provincial soldier was worth two regulars in such circumstances. The reasons were simple. Provincials were tradesmen by nature, used to the labor so necessary in guaranteeing the success behind this type of military operation. Thus, one must ask the question of how well Abercromby understood the provincials he seemed to despise commanding. His fear was that he would be forced to depend on his regulars to defend the siege lines, leaving his rear to the uncertain defense of colonial regiments. Yet among these colonial troops were a number of good regiments, all of whom would have the advantage of defending fixed positions. Given this, and the degree at which the siege works would have progressed with at least six thousand colonials working daily on them, one has to question the general's belief in the vulnerability of his army.

The matter of the time to bring his cannon forward, however, is perhaps the most difficult of his arguments to reconcile. By the afternoon of the battle, at least six brass cannons and three mortars were already on the Ticonderoga Peninsula, and several larger ones were on the portage road a few hours away from joining them. How long then, with fourteen thousand men at his disposal, could it have taken to bring the rest forward? Lastly, it was easy to blame the confused retreat on the provincials. Given that they were not professional soldiers, few would question such a statement. Undoubtedly, a good number of colonial troops panicked when Wooster's and Rogers' men appeared at the beachhead, but the withdrawal was poorly coordinated from the start, which when combined with the anxiety projected by the army's leaders, eventually boiled over into terror.[11]

And so Abercromby now found himself back at the head of Lake George attempting to explain his actions and his casualty list of nearly two thousand men to William Pitt, the governors of the different colonies, and his army superiors. To his men there was little to explain. Few had anything good to say of their commander, who with an army still strong enough "to have marched through any part of Canada," was now requesting reinforcements from General Amherst at Louisbourg. "The provincials are now most openly calling our commander Mrs. Nabbycromby, since he thinks of nothing but fortifying himself," Colonel Williams informed his uncle a few days after the army's return. "What with fatigue, want of sleep, exercise of mind, and leaving the place we went to capture, the best part of the army is unhinged. I have told enough to make you sick, if the relation acts on you as the facts have on me." A wounded Captain Lee lying in an Albany hospital was one of Abercromby's harshest critics. How could such a person be appointed to command the army, he fumed in a letter directed for open circulation in England, "who is so utterly destitute of all accomplishments necessary for that high station." Not that it mattered anymore, given that "the troops have too mean an opinion of his qualifications as General (both in point of courage and capacity) to act with any sort of spirit under his auspices." But perhaps the best assessment came from a Mohawk sachem who, after informing the general that his men were leaving, is reported to have told him "that the English army had very fine limbs but no head."[12]

For the moment the army was abuzz with talk as to what was next. Many believed that Montcalm might actually advance up Lake George to pay them a visit. This was supported by a rumor that the general was sending a pair of twenty-four-pound cannon and a number of artillery supplies back to Albany, as if fearful that they might end up being used against their current owners. It seemed certain then that the army would abandon their camp on Lake George and retreat to make a stand at Fort Edward. This

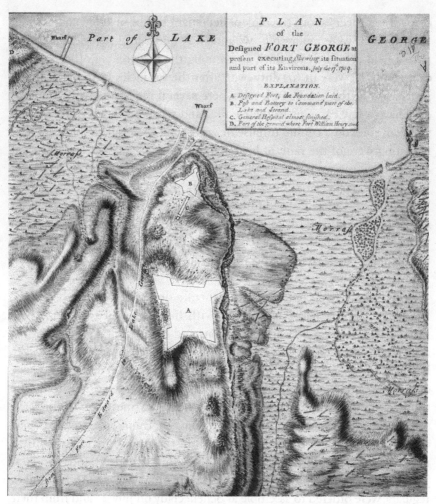

British defensive works at the head of Lake George in July 1759. Much of this work was started by Abercromby's army after the retreat from Ticonderoga. Work would continue on Fort George (A), but was never finished. (*Norman B. Leventhal Map & Education Center, Boston Public Library*)

was soon supplanted with talk that the army would reembark to make another attempt on Fort Carillon, which in itself was replaced by news that the regiments would be ordered to Albany and there board vessels bound for a siege of Quebec.[13]

None were the case. Abercromby viewed his army as too shattered and too demoralized to do anything beyond act defensively. Of greatest concern were the losses suffered by the regulars, particularly among their officer corps. Ten officers above the rank of lieutenant had been killed and another twenty-seven were reported as wounded. A number of regiments did not have a field officer fit for duty, and among the twelve field officers in the camp, only six were fit for duty even after the vacancies were filled. It was just as bad at the company level, where several regiments were found to only have a few captains in their ranks, and when a general court martial was convened on a capital offense, it was found that half the officers participating were of the rank of lieutenant or below. Lt. Clerk had died and Major Eyre was wounded, leaving Abercromby with only the services of Lt. George Garth, a recent graduate of the Royal Engineers Academy at Woolwich, and a few untried foreign engineers in the Royal Americans to rely upon should he wish to make another attempt on Fort Carillon. Not that he ever seriously considered returning to Carillon. For the moment his plan was to fortify his position, secure his supply lines, and await Amherst's reinforcements.[14]

There was one exception to the general's defensive policy. On July 12 Bradstreet approached Abercromby with his former plan to seize Fort Frontenac. Based on his earlier opinions and the current condition of the army, Abercromby was at first opposed to the plan. Bradstreet, however, having gained some measure of credit with the general by means of his conduct at Ticonderoga, pressed on him to convene a council of war to debate the matter. Abercromby agreed, and after "the warmest opposition," the scheme was "reluctantly approved." The next morning orders were issued, drafting nearly three thousand troops from the ranks for the expedition, mostly colonials from Massachusetts, New York, Rhode Island, and New Jersey. These men, along with a detachment of artillery and a handful of regulars, were ordered to assemble at Schenectady on July 24 and from there proceed up the Mohawk River under Bradstreet's command. Although Abercromby certainly second-guessed himself in regard to releasing so many troops, it proved to be the best decision he made as commander in chief in North America.[15]

As Abercromby's troops worked on their defenses and constructing vessels to assure naval superiority over Lake George, French and Indian war parties struck at the supply convoys traveling from Fort Edward to Lake George. Looking to interdict these raids, on August 2 Major Robert Rogers led a detachment of eighty Rangers, three hundred Connecticut Rangers under the command of Major Israel Putnam, ninety Massachusetts troops under Captain Giddings, and sixty Regulars from the 44th and 80th under Captain James Dalyell, in a sweep of South Bay and the surrounding area.

Having waited in ambush at South Bay for several days, only to give away their positions through the inexperienced actions of several of the colonials, Rogers sent 170 of his detachment back to Fort Edward and camped with the remainder near the ruins of Fort Anne on the night of August 6.

Early the next morning while Rogers and his men ate breakfast, a debate broke out in regard to the marksmanship of Ensign William Irwin of the light infantry. Several declared his aim better than that of Rogers, who at least unofficially was viewed as reigning English champion. Rogers was not of the character to allow such talk to pass unnoticed. After a few moments of speculative conversation, the Ranger leader challenged Irwin to a match, which he quickly accepted. It was a foolish mistake and a violation of his own ranging rules, but at the moment pride overcame judgment, not just for Rogers and Irwin but for those men around them who urged the contest on.[16]

About a mile away a detachment of three hundred French and Indians under Marine Lieutenant Joseph Marin looked up from their morning meals. The war party, which had left Fort Carillon only two days before, listened as the next several shots placed the source up the trail toward old Fort Anne. Marin, a veteran partisan, began issuing orders as the echo of another shot reached them, although it was not necessary. Men tossed aside their meals, stuffed their equipment into their packs, and snatched up their firearms. Marin correctly surmised that the shots were from an enemy patrol and that, if he hurried, there was time to arrange an ambush along the trail leading to Fort Edward.[17]

With the shooting debate apparently settled, Rogers' detachment broke camp and pressed on toward Fort Edward. Major Putnam led the way with his Connecticut troops followed by Dalyell's light infantry, Gidding's Massachusetts troops, and finally Rogers, whose men were still buzzing over the results of the contest. The rude Indian trail leading to Fort Edward was nothing more than a narrow corridor of trampled brush, which forced the detachment to advance single file through the damp maze of broadleaf trees and tall thickets. An hour later, around seven that morning, Putnam and several of his men emerged from the woods into a small clearing. Instantly they were beset by French Indians. Putnam raised his musket at the nearest attacker, but his weapon misfired, and before he had time to do anything else, he and four of his men were dragged away under the threat of a dozen muskets. A moment later a volley rang out which threw the trailing Connecticut troops into disorder, followed by another, which splattered among the leaves or concluded in a dull thump when a ball found its mark. The stunned Connecticut troops fell back, seeking cover wherever they could find it, as Marin's forces rushed forward, tomahawk in hand, to press their advantage. The fighting quickly became hand to hand as small clusters of men vied with each other amidst the tangled foliage. Flashes of muskets, individual war whoops, and the sound of musket balls tearing through the brush became the order of the moment.

Because of their single-file march, Rogers' column was strung out for nearly half a mile, which hindered any immediate response. Dalyell, who was closest to the action, pushed forward with his regulars, which threw the attackers off balance and stalled their advance. Rogers, with a detachment of Partridge's light infantry, pushed through the woods to the right of Dalyell, while Giddings and the Massachusetts' troops moved to take up positions on his left. In the meantime, a number of the scattered Connecticut troops were rallied by one of their wounded officers and threw themselves back into the fray in support of Dalyell. For a time, the battle swirled about a large fallen tree in the English center. Here a huge native sachem waged a one-man war against the English. He leapt upon the tree, quickly dispatched two regulars with his hatchet, and then bellowed in defiance at those around him. An officer of the 80th, using his musket as a club, struck him, but it accomplished little more than making himself a target. The enraged war chief knocked down the Englishman and was about to dispatch him when a well-aimed shot from one of Dalyell's men toppled him from his perch.

Marin extended his left in an attempt to outflank the English position, only to find a strong firing line held by Rogers and his men. He attacked here several times, but each time he found he could make no inroads. The tables were slowly turning as the more numerous English began taking the offensive. When firing started to Marin's right it became clear to him that he had badly underestimated the size of the enemy detachment. With a number of his Canadians having already fled, and on the verge of being enveloped, Marin pulled a trick from Rogers' book. He broke his men up into small detachments and ordered them to make their way as best they could to an agreed rendezvous north of Fort Anne. The tactic worked, and Rogers chose not to pursue.[18]

While Rogers' victory buoyed the morale of Abercromby's army all thoughts of it soon fell to the wayside when two important pieces of information reached the camp. The first, arriving in late August, was confirmation that Louisbourg had fallen. To celebrate, the troops were paraded out. The newly launched sloop the *Earl of Halifax* began the festivities by firing a salute, followed in turn by one from the Royal Artillery and a volley from each of the regiments. The firing, which lasted almost twenty minutes, circled the camp twice more before ending with three "huzzahs." For Abercromby the news had a double blessing. It meant that Amherst would soon be on his way to join him with six regular regiments. The general dispatched orders to the governors of Massachusetts and New York in anticipation of Amherst's arrival and ordered all preparations put in place to expedite their march to Lake George. With any luck, there would still be time to make another effort against Fort Carillon.[19]

The second piece of news was just as important as the first, and a little sweeter as far as Abercromby was concerned given that it directly involved his command. On September 8 a post rider delivered a letter from Bradstreet reporting that his detachment had captured Fort Frontenac. Bradstreet's expedition had gone almost exactly as he had planned. In an impressive display of boatmanship, his detachment ascended the Mohawk River, ported over to Wood Creek, crossed Lake Oneida, and descended the Onondaga River, arriving undetected at the ruins of Oswego on the night of August 21. The next morning the detachment set sail onto Lake Ontario, and on the evening of the twenty-fifth landed without opposition about half a mile from the fort. Bradstreet's artillery train put ashore the next morning, and by evening two batteries of cannons and mortars had been positioned within a few hundred yards of the old stone fort. At dawn Bradstreet gave the order to open fire on both the fort and a pair of French brigs in the harbor. A few hours later the two vessels had been hulled and run aground by their crews, the fort's walls had been breached, its guns dismounted and silenced, and the powder magazine damaged. At eight o'clock the French commander ordered a red flag run up to announce his surrender.

Bradstreet's capture of Fort Frontenac at the cost of a handful of wounded yielded an enormous booty. One hundred and ten prisoners, sixty cannon ranging from four to twelve-pounders, sixteen mortars, nine vessels including a sixteen-gun brig, vast military and naval stores, provisions for twenty thousand men for six months, and Indian goods destined for the Great Lakes nations computed at a value of eight hundred thousand livres. Fort Frontenac, the grand magazine for the western garrisons, was in English hands, and with it went French naval superiority on Lake Ontario. Bradstreet tossed the cannon into the lake, loaded what supplies he could into the two largest vessels, and burned everything else, including the fort, before setting sail for Oswego the next day.[20]

The news of Louisburg and Fort Frontenac, coupled with the reports that Forbes was advancing on Fort Duquesne, which could not possibly hold out now that the former fort had fallen, brought about a shift in colonial spirits. It appeared that almost every target of the year's campaign would fall into English hands. All that remained was Fort Carillon, and with reports that Amherst had left Louisburg on August 30 with six regiments, eyes once again began turning toward the French bastion on Lake Champlain. "There begins some talk about returning to Carillon," one of Rogers' men wrote to a colleague. "Some expect it, others desire it, and many are afraid of it."[21]

10

VICTORY, DIVISION,
AND RECALL

A S THE ACTUAL FIGHTING SETTLED INTO INFREQUENT SKIRMISHING between small patrols, another was escalating between the French field commander and his superior. The dispute between the two men on how to best prosecute the war, which had erupted after the fall of Fort William Henry, had cooled slightly during the winter only to flare up again over the orders the governor issued to Montcalm upon the latter's departure for Fort Carillon in June. With the surprising victory of July 8 the differences once again resurfaced, this time at a level that placed the French court in a difficult position. The quarrel came in two forms: the role played by the Canadians, Marines, and native allies in the defense of Fort Carillon, and the familiar argument of how best to follow up the victory.

Strangely, the first of these disputes came not from either of the two leaders but from their supporters, who by now had become so thoroughly polarized that they viewed even the smallest matters of inter-service rivalry as an opportunity to sharpen their pens. Montcalm had not been pleased with the governor's efforts to reinforce him before the outbreak of the battle, nor had he been enamored with the conduct of his Canadian contingent during the engagement. Both were legitimate points. Levis and his men, shifted from the Mohawk Valley expedition, had managed to reach him before the battle, but the Canadians and Marines who were to accompany Levis on this mission could not? He also expressed his displeasure at there being so few Indians scouts at Carillon. Where were they? He had asked the governor to call out the nations weeks before, yet few if any had found their way to him before the battle. There was also the matter of the few hundred Canadians at the battle who behaved poorly in the marquis' opinion. Several had fled at the start of the engagement, and when ordered to launch a sortie against the enemy's flank, most had outright refused. Still, to Montcalm's credit, in the interest of a united front he praised his Canadian contingent in his official report on the battle, writing to the governor the day after the engagement that "[t]he Colonial troops and Canadians have caused us to regret that they were not in greater number. Chevalier Levis, under whose eyes they fought, speaks highly of them."[1]

Had it been left at this, the matter might have never become a point of contention. Everyone understood that the lion's share of the victory belonged to the troops of the line, to their officers, and in particular to Montcalm. Had the marquis been gracious enough to dole out a small piece of the glory to his colonial partners, all would have been happy and unity maintained. Such, however, was not the case. Privately Montcalm wrote to Commissary Doriel in Quebec that "the Colonial troops and the Canadians have behaved very indifferently" and that he had only praised them in the published narrative "for the good of the service." Montcalm knew full well that this ardent supporter would quickly disseminate the news, and true to the cause, Doriel forwarded the letter on to the new Minister of War, Louis-Charles-Auguste Fouquet, Comte de Belle-Isle, with the comments, "As we have reason to suspect that the bureau of the Marine will endeavor to vaunt the glory of four hundred men belonging to the troops of the Militia and the Colony, who were in this action, and perhaps to diminish those of the troops of the line, I must inform you, my Lord, of what the Marquis de Montcalm has written me."[2]

Clearly, such a statement was bound to reach Vaudreuil's ears. As to be expected, the governor penned a stern response to Montcalm, but as the original accusation had been directed toward the Minister of War, Vaudreuil felt no choice but to direct his response to the Minister of the Marine as well. The recriminations flew between the two men for the next few months. To no real purpose letters were sent, only to be returned with comments and points of contention scribbled in the margins. To these, addendums were attached and more letters sent and copies of everything forwarded on to whatever minister in Paris the sender thought might be sympathetic to his cause.[3]

While this argument played itself out, a second, on how best to exploit the victory, took form. The promised reinforcements, several thousand Canadian militia and native auxiliaries from half-a-dozen nations, flooded into Fort Carillon in the days following the battle, and with them came a letter from the governor. In the letter Vaudreuil pressed upon Montcalm the need to prevent the English from reforming and renewing their plans toward Fort Carillon. There was still time to capitalize on the terror of the English retreat by launching forays against them to keep them on the defensive, but such actions had to be accomplished before the Canadians had to return for the harvest. "I send you all the militia belonging to the government that are fit for duty, to execute such movements as you will deem proper," he wrote the marquis.

'Tis of importance, Sir, that we always have strong detachments both on the lake and at the head of the bay. They could not be too numerous, so as to harass our enemies constantly, cut off their communication with old Fort George, and intercept their convoys. No better maneuver is in our power to force them to abandon their position, bateaux, artillery, campaign train, provisions, etc. 'Twill oblige them to retire, and thereby deprive them forever of all hope of renewing their attempt.[4]

Montcalm exploded at the letter. In a reply to the governor a few days later, which eventually found its way into the hands of the king's ministers, he claimed that the directive had "been written only with a view to make the Marquis de Montcalm responsible for all the events that may arise." He followed this by summarizing the superior strength of the British forces even after their defeat and then chided the governor by pointing to the fact that "a superior enemy force is not compelled to abandon a position by simple detachments." The English might choose to abandon their posts for their own reasons, but that would not be determined by anything he was capable of doing. Not content with this, he then launched into a direct attack on Vaudreuil.

'Tis always astonishing that the Marquis de Vaudreuil considers himself qualified at a distance of fifty leagues to determine on operations of war in a country that he has never seen, and where the best Generals, after having seen it, would have been embarrassed. . . . Were I so fortune, Sir, as that your important occupations would permit you to be at the head of the army, you would see everything yourself, and I should have the satisfaction to receive clearer and less embarrassing orders.[5]

As with the dispute on the conduct of the colonial forces during the battle, the recriminations only escalated from this point. Montcalm claimed that the governor did not understand the nature of the war, which was not like those previously fought with the English colonies, and that more confidence should be placed in him. Why, after three years of campaigning, was the governor still dictating senseless details to him that he would "blush to prescribe to a lowest captain?" The men who advised him were whispering poison into his ears at the expense of the general and his troops. Vaudreuil in turn claimed that Montcalm had purposely misinterpreted his orders, thoughtlessly alienated the Indian nations, and continually denigrated the contribution of the colonial troops to expound those of his regulars. He wrote to the Minister of the Marine that Montcalm's victory on July 8 had gone to his head such that "he lost sight of the moderation he owed to himself." Their supporters only aggravated matters. Doriel, in a letter to the Minister of War, bluntly stated that that for the public good the government should be handed over to Montcalm, for although Vaudreuil possessed administrative talents, he had "one original drawback—he is Canadian."[6]

After weeks of arguing, the two men did agree on one thing. Montcalm wrote letters home to petition his recall and asked the governor to do the same on his behalf. Vaudreuil was more than happy to comply, and in early August he wrote to the Minister of the Marine to petition the king for Montcalm's recall. "So far from thinking of injuring him, I consider, my Lord, that he deserves to be promoted to the rank of lieutenant-general," he began his request.

No person renders more justice than I do to his excellent qualities, but he does not possess those which are required for war in this country; 'tis necessary to have great deal of suavity and patience to command the Canadians and Indians. The King having confided the colony to me, I cannot avoid anticipating the unfortunate consequences which the Marquis de Montcalm's longer sojourn might produce.[7]

When news of the dispute reached the New York newspapers, some efforts were made toward reconciliation, if for no other purpose than to promote the king's interests. Montcalm wrote Vaudreuil in early August, suggesting that they agree to disagree for the moment. "We do not think ourselves wrong, neither the one nor the other of us. It is to be supposed, then, that we are both so, and that some change must be applied to our mode of proceeding." To emphasize his point, the marquis sent Bougainville, one of his most trusted aides, to speak personally with Vaudreuil in order "to smother" the discord between the two men. Bigot attempted to moderate the conflict as well but with limited success, conceding to the Minister of the Marine that the two men's attitudes were too opposed to expect more. Bougainville's and Bigot's efforts, however, did make some inroads. Both men, at least for the moment, were more careful in selecting their arguments, and the dispute between the two slowly subsided to the point that Montcalm reconsidered his request to be recalled. In September he wrote Belle-Isle asking that it be set aside, basing his change of heart on his commitment to his duty and the deteriorating state of the colony.[8]

Traditionally, blame for the split, the polarization of the colony's defenders, and just about everything but Canada's weather has been placed on Vaudreuil, in part because Montcalm's advocates were more vocal and far more efficient in making their case. In reality, a good deal of the blame falls on Montcalm. The physical rigors of three wilderness campaigns, the confounding, confusing, and corrupting mechanisms of the Canadian government, the draining experience of coercing and cajoling Canadians and native troops to accept his directions, the financial consequences of his assignment, and his inability to assert his will over the direction of the colony's defense had left him thoroughly embittered. Vaudreuil's assessment was correct—the marquis no longer had the patience for his assignment. He was no fool and understood quite well that the governor wished to employ the old philosophy of "*petite guerre*" in an attempt to switch the English from a proactive to a reactive stance. What is more, it took little to follow through with this approach, and in reality, whether it worked or not, there were few options but to pursue this path after the victory at Carillon. Yet he feigned ignorance and acted contrary, when doing so would accomplish nothing but to antagonize the situation. His remarks directed toward Vaudreuil, his superior, bordered on insubordination and might have led to his immediate removal had a man like Frontenac occupied the office at the time. In regard to the controversy surrounding the contribution of the colonial troops on July 8, Montcalm's activities bordered more on ego than "the good of the king's service," which he continually claimed to be his motive. There was more than enough glory to go around after the victory, but even passing a small amount of this on seemed beyond his or his supporters' ability.

And the governor? Certainly Vaudreuil played a willing part in this drama. After Dieskau's capture at the Battle of Lake George in 1755, Vaudreuil had informed the French Court that in his opinion a general officer from France was not required to see to the war effort. The conflict in North America was so different from those in Europe that such an officer would be at a severe disadvantage in dealing with the colonial forces. Thus, it can be asserted that Vaudreuil was biased against Montcalm from the start, a prejudice that only deepened once he had a taste of the marquis' character. He could be as headstrong as Montcalm when he wished, and although he repeatedly claimed to have attempted to defuse his disputes with Montcalm whenever they arose, he clearly did not do all that was within his power to ensure this was the case. Another criticism is that he did not take Montcalm into his confidence. This can be supposed to be a consequence of the first point, but it does not absolve Vaudreuil from the mistake. In fact, the governor, once he had seen Montcalm's character, should have made an even more concerted effort to make the general a part of his inner circle. Doing so, whether he abided by the marquis' opinions or not, would have done much to sooth Montcalm's easily bruised ego and promote cooperation between the colonial and regular forces. There was also validity in Montcalm's claim that the governor viewed the prosecution of the current conflict along the lines of those in the past, when in actuality it was much different. In this Vaudreuil probably made his greatest mistake. At the onset of the conflict the governor had a clear vision of how the conflict should be pursued, and to his credit, it proved mostly successful. But as the war ground forward and shifted more toward a European-style conflict, his experience, based on his early days in the colony under his father, became less relevant and Montcalm's more so. His failure to recognize and accept this fact accounted for much of the friction between the two men. The graft in the Canadian government was also to blame. Montcalm and his supporters were worn down by the corruption which seemed to eat away at their efforts like a cancer. Here Vaudreuil did little to sway their opinion, and to the contrary, even enriched himself by these means. For all these failings, however, an important difference between the two men should be noted. Montcalm was a Frenchman, fighting for his king and the glory of French arms, while Vaudreuil was a Canadian, fighting for his king and, more importantly, his home.

For Canada the schism was devastating. "Too much jealousy has already spread among the different corps," Bigot informed the Minister of the Marine. The colony, outnumbered, besieged on land and by sea, and barely able to sustain itself could ill afford a division of leadership, one of the few advantages it possessed over its enemy. Every resource, be it Canadian, Marine, native ally, or French regular was needed if Canada was to survive. Thus, for the sake of the colony, one of the two men had to go, but neither did. Montcalm was promoted and the division between the two men temporarily patched over, but in the end this lack of trust would play an important role in the loss of Quebec the following year.[9]

To the south, at the head of Lake George, matters were much different. There was no division of leadership, just a feeling that none existed. News of Bradstreet's success and Amherst's expected arrival had invigorated preparations for a second attempt against Fort Carillon. The sick were sent back to Albany and a pair of heavy siege cannon were hauled up to the lake from Fort Edward along with provisions sufficient to sustain an army in the field. All the tools needed for a siege were collected and inventoried. The boats at the lake were ordered re-caulked and repaired, and more were brought forward. A pair of row galleries were nearing completion, as was a radeau, a square-sailed flat-bottomed vessel named the *Tortuous*, which along with the fourteen-gun sloop *Earl of Halifax*, would guarantee naval superiority on the waterway.

Rogers and his men were bringing back favorable reports as well. Montcalm still possessed a sizable force around Fort Carillon, but his numbers had clearly diminished, undoubtedly because he had to release much of his militia to tend to the harvest. As the leaves began to take on their autumn hues, all signs pointed toward another assault on the French fort, but the spirits of an army are not as quickly changed as the foliage. Few had any confidence in their general, and even fewer knew anything about the soon-to-arrive General Amherst. "These days here is a great deal of talk of our going to Ticonderoga again," one provincial noted in his diary, "but 'tis little regarded." General Lyman wrote to the governor of Connecticut along the same line. "We are yet in hopes of another attack this fall . . . but I can't say I am very confident that we shall attempt it."[10]

On October 5 Amherst arrived at Lake George to consult with Abercromby. He had been late, but his six regiments were now at Albany. For the troops living in tents and bark huts along the water's edge, the visit was a climax to all the rumors. By the end of the day they would know: Ticonderoga, winter quarters, or home. The army was paraded, and Abercromby,

Amherst, and Gage reviewed them for almost two hours before retiring to discuss the matter. The question, of course, became whether or not to proceed against Montcalm. There were no issues in regard to boats, supplies, troops, or artillery. All were present in sufficient number. Indeed, with the inclusion of the six Louisbourg regiments, the army now totaled in the vicinity of eighteen thousand men, at least half of whom were regulars. Instead, the decision revolved around French numbers and the failing weather.

Although Montcalm's strength had dipped slightly in September, it had increased again with the passing of the harvest. Estimates were that he now commanded eight thousand men at Fort Carillon and that at least as many Canadians were being held in reserve farther down the lake at Fort St. Jean. In addition, the French had perfected their defenses along the heights of Carillon and about the fort itself. After reviewing the intelligence, the three generals agreed that if they went forward, the only practical approach would be a formal siege. The problem was that formal siege operations were time consuming, and time was something that they did not appear to have. Since mid-September the troops had been waking up to ice in their water buckets, and on September 26 the autumn skies began spitting snowflakes. Although the cold fall rains had yet to appear, it was only a matter of weeks, perhaps even days before they arrived, turning the paths and trails to Albany and Fort Edward into a nearly impassable quagmire. Given that the army would not be able to move forward until mid-October at the earliest, which realistically meant late October, and that a siege before the French post might last weeks, the decision was simple. There would be no second attempt on Fort Carillon.[11]

With the matter resolved, it now only became a waiting game to see which army broke camp first. By late October, with news that Montcalm was departing, Abercromby completed his assignment of a winter garrison for Fort Edward: he sank, hid, or buried his boats, filled in the field fortifications at the camp on Lake George, and marched his army off to Albany and winter quarters. From here the colonial troops were thanked for their service and dismissed, and "thus," wrote one of these men of his experience, "ended the most ridiculous campaign ever heard of."[12]

Technically, Pitt would bring an official end to the campaign. As he reviewed a map of North America in his office, the first minister nodded in satisfaction as he placed a small symbol of a British flag over Louisbourg, Fort Frontenac, and Fort Duquesne. The capture of the first of these would allow for an attack on Quebec in the spring, while the last two had crippled French power in the west, leaving the last major French stronghold in the

General Jeffery Amherst. After successfully capturing Louisbourg, in late 1758 Amherst would be appointed to replace Abercromby as Commander-in-Chief in North America. Amherst would take a much different approach toward Fort Carillon in 1759, capturing the French stronghold after a brief siege at the cost of less than seventy casualties. (*Anne S. K. Brown Military Collection, Brown University Library*)

region, Fort Niagara, another target for the campaign of 1759. Pitt's eye then fell upon the French flag at Ticonderoga and Crown Point. He sighed and shook his head, realizing that he would have to send another expedition against the French stronghold as well. After a few moments the rain splattering against his office window caught his attention. He glanced out at the approaching storm before returning to his desk and composing a pair of letters. The first was addressed to Abercromby, relieving him of command in North America, while the second was addressed to the new commander in chief in North America, General Jeffery Amherst.

For Major Duncan Campbell none of this mattered. Badly wounded in the attack on the French lines, there at first appeared hope that his foretold tale of gloom might not come to fruition. Struck in the arm, he was helped off the battlefield and transported back to the camp at Lake George before being forwarded to Fort Edward. Here, however, doctors determined the wounds too severe and elected to amputate the major's arm. He died not long after the operation on August 17. The next day the Black Watch buried their major to the rustling of a cool summer breeze and the sound of the bagpipes. For those that knew him well, long before there was any thought of a French fort named Carillon, there was a strange sense of sadness bound

with closure. Sadness over the loss of their friend and comrade and closure
with the realization that he was no longer forced to live with this foretold
appointment with fate. For those that never believed his story, who scoffed
at the talk, or who joked at the self-imposed gloom, there was a realization
as well, that the name Ticonderoga would always speak to something far
more than a battle—to a time when this world touched the next.

APPENDICES

A. The Armies

BRITISH ARMY		
Major General James Abercromby		
Brigadier General Augustus Howe		
Brigadier General Thomas Gage		
STRENGTH		
Regulars	6,367	
Provincials	9,024	
ORGANIZATION		
BRITISH REGULARS		
1st Brigade (Haviland)	2nd Brigade (Grant)	3rd Brigade (Donaldson)
27th	42nd	55th
1/60th	46th	44th
4/60th		
	Eng. Brigade (Clerk)	
	Royal Artillery (Ord)	
PROVINCIALS		**RANGERS AND BOATMEN**
Left Wing (Lyman)	Right Wing (Preble)	80th Lt. Infantry
1st Brigade	1st Brigade	Rogers Rangers
Lyman (Conn.)	Preble (Mass.)	Bradstreet's Boatmen
Fitch (Conn.)	Williams (Mass.)	Johnson's Mohawks
2nd Brigade	2nd Brigade	Partridge (Mass.)
Whiting (Conn.)	Ruggles (Mass.)	Doty (Mass.)
Wooster (Conn.)	Bagley (Mass.)	
3rd Brigade	3rd Brigade	
Johnston (NJ)	Glazier (NY)	
Babcock (RI)	Woolsey (NY)	
FRENCH ARMY		
Major-General the Marquis de Montcalm		
Brigadier General Francois-Gaston Levis		
Colonel Charles Bourlamaque		
STRENGTH		
Regulars	3,411	
Colonials	415	
ORGANIZATION		
REGULARS		
Bourlamaque	Montcalm	Levis
Languedoc	Royal Roussillon	La Reine
La Sarre	5 Co. Piquets	Bearn
Gren. Co. 3rd Berry	2nd Berry	Guyenne
		Marines/Militia
RESERVES (FT. CARILLON)		
3rd Berry		

B. Casualty Returns

Major General Abercromby's Army, Returns of Action on July 6–8, 1758 (Compiled from the *Boston News-Letter* July 27, 1758.)

Regulars	Officers & NCOs			Rank & File			by
Unit	K	W	M	K	W	M	Regiment
27th Regiment	9	0	0	21	92	3	125
42nd Regiment	13	33	0	190	265	0	501
44th Regiment	3	18	0	40	135	9	205
46th Regiment	13	10	0	55	131	12	221
55th Regiment	6	10	0	35	116	3	170
1/60th Regiment	2	15	0	21	82	0	120
4/60th Regiment	2	13	0	25	120	0	160
80th Regiment	1	1	0	3	15	0	20
Rangers	0	3	2	17	16	0	38
Battoemen (Bradstreet)	0	0	0	17	33	0	50
Engineers	1	0	0	0	0	0	1
Totals:	50	103	2	424	1005	27	1611
Provincials	Officers & NCOs			Rank & File			by
Unit	K	W	M	K	W	M	Regiment
Prebble (Mass.)	0	6	0	7	13	1	27
Bagley (Mass.)	2	1	0	4	10	0	17
Ruggles (Mass.)	0	0	0	0	2	0	2
William Williams (Mass.)	0	2	0	4	11	0	17
Doty (Mass.)	0	0	0	0	5	0	5
DeLancy (N.Y.)	3	10	0	25	51	0	89
Johnston (N.J.)	1	3	0	10	44	2	60
Babcock (R.I.)	3	7	0	15	45	0	70
Fitch (Conn.)	1	1	1	4	15	2	24
Wooster (Conn.)	1	1	0	3	14	0	19
Partridge (Mass.)	2	2	0	3	6	2	15
Totals:	13	33	1	75	216	7	345
Total British Casualties	K	W	M	K	W	M	Totals
Regulars	50	103	2	424	1005	27	1611
Provincials	13	33	1	75	216	7	345
Totals:	63	136	3	499	1221	34	1956

Another account currently in the Fort Ticonderoga Museum is in agreement with the above with the exception that twenty-three provincials are mysteriously added to the total line. A British account gives ten killed and six wounded during the skirmish on July 6, with an unspecified number of colonial casualties, which were likely on the same order as the regulars.

Marechal de Camp Montcalm's Army, Returns of Action on July 6–8
*(Levis Papers: Relations et Journaux de différentes expeditions, 162-163; NY
Col. Doc., X, 750-751; RAPQ 1931-1932, 83.)*

July 6th	
Officers and NCOs	**Total Casualties**
Regulars	9
Colonials	1
Rank & File	
La Reine	42
La Sarre	6
Royal Roussillon	6
Languedoc	6
Guyenne	33
Bearn	44
2 Btns Berry	5
Marines/Militia	45
Totals:	197
Reported Prisoner by Abercromby	
Officers	7
Rank & File	144
Totals:	151

July 8th							
Unit	Officers & NCOs			Rank & File			by
	K	W	M	K	W	M	Regiment
La Reine	1	4	0	7	45	0	57
La Sarre	3	2	0	7	31	0	43
Royal Roussillon	1	0	0	2	18	0	21
Languedoc	2	6	0	9	35	0	52
Guyenne	1	3	0	24	36	0	64
Bearn	2	3	0	11	36	0	52
2nd Berry	2	3	0	16	28	0	49
3rd Berry	0	0	0	6	8	0	14
Marines/Militia	0	2	0	10	11	0	23
Totals:	12	23	0	92	248	0	375
July 6th	10			187			197
July 8th	35			340			375
Total French Casualties	45			527			572

La Pause lists five officers captured on the sixth which is in accordance
with Abercromby's later letter to Montcalm where he informs the marquis
that he has taken a captain, four lieutenants, two cadets, and 144 soldiers
prisoner. Montcalm, in a letter to his mother on July 14, states that his
losses on the sixth were eight officers killed or captured and 183 soldiers
either killed or captured. ("Montcalm's Correspondence," 73).

C. Eyewitness Accounts

While it would be impractical to print all of the accounts of the Battle of Ticonderoga, several have been included for the reader's perusal. These eyewitness accounts fall into three categories: colonial American (Spicer), British regulars (Loring and Eyre), and French regulars (Malartic). I have edited the spelling in many cases to make the documents more readable, while trying to keep some of the old-style flavor intact. The originals and additional firsthand accounts of the campaign can be found by consulting the bibliography or the given reference.

Abel Spicer

Abel Spicer was a native of North Groton, Connecticut. He enlisted in Colonel Nathan Whiting's regiment in the spring of 1758 and would not only serve throughout the remainder of the French and Indian War but would be present at the Battle of Bunker Hill and the Siege of Boston. He would later command a company of Connecticut troops, and near the end of the Revolutionary War he would be appointed to the state's inspector-general's staff.[1]

The Diary of Abel Spicer, July 5-9, 1758[2]

Wednesday, July 5—We was all rallied by the beat of the drum and ordered for to pack up our things and strike our tents and carry them aboard of the bateaux. And we was ordered to prayers by sunrise and then to the bateaux. And about 9 o'clock we all got going. We carried two floating batteries and the men in general seemed for to go on very cheerfully. Yesterday here was 20 Frenchman that had been in a flag of truce to Fort Edward and desired that General Abercrombie would guard them. And he told them that tomorrow he would guard them with twenty thousand men, and they was taken along with the army. And we came on with all speed and made no halt but rode all night.

Thursday, July 6—About 10 o'clock we landed on the west shore and just as we landed here was 3 Frenchmen and a woman taken by the regulars and one Frenchman and an Indian taken by our Provincials. And the French that were encamped there struck their tents and put off as fast as possible. And we marched on as fast as we could towards the fort and before we had got a third part of the way we heard a firing at a distance, for the regulars, some of them, were before us, and Lord Howe was before, who was killed at the first shot from the enemy, and the skirmish lasted about three hours and the fire ceased. And there was a great number of prisoners brought in and guns and lashed hats, but how many killed it was not known, but there was a great many seen to lie in the woods killed and wounded. The regiment was very much broken to pieces and some came in and some was lost in the woods, and came in the next morning.

Friday, July 7—After the men had generally got in, we marched again and marched about a mile and was ordered in again. There is prisoners brought in every hour, almost, but how many of our men was killed or taken is not known, but it was supposed there was not many. The chief that was killed was regulars and Jersey Blues. About sunset we marched again and the regulars marched about two hours before and we took two brass cannon with us and we marched as far as the Ticonderoga Mills about two miles from the fort and there encamped.

Saturday, July 8—In the morning there was a number of men sent after some more of the cannon and the whale boats and artillery stores and provisions and such stores and at the same time the engineer went with a guard upon a mountain against the fort for to look and see if he could spy a good place for to plant the artillery and he came back again about 8 o'clock. And when we came in we was ordered for to stay there awhile and rest ourselves and the chief of Colonel Whiting's regiment was sent about 3 miles back after the artillery stores and provisions. And while they was gone Major Rogers fired on the French sentry and then our regulars was marching to the fort and they had two brass cannon on a floating battery and the rest was not got to the lake but came very soon. But the regulars pushed on as fast as possible and marched up to the breast works ten deep and fired volleys at the breast works, which was as high as the enemies heads, and they had holes between the logs to fire through, and the regulars ventured very near the breast works and they fell like pigeons. And the highlanders fired a few volleys and rushed on upon the breast works with their swords and bayonets and killed some of the French in the trench, and the French fired upon them with grape shot from the fort, which killed almost all that had got into the trench, and them that was left of them was forced to retreat. And before that they had done this the chief of the other forces came up and fired and the French set up their hats just above the top of the breast work for to deceive the soldiers and hoisted English colors for a deception and the regulars marched up to go in and take possession and they fired on them and killed a great number of them. And them that was left behind and had not been in the fight was ordered to build a breast work and after it was built they was ordered for to carry back their cannon. And after all the men had got within the breast work, about midnight, we was ordered to take our packs and go down to the bateaux and we rallied all and marched off and it was very dark and the way miry which made a very tedious march but we arrived to our bateaux just as the day broke.

Sunday, July 9—We was rallied before we could get any refreshment, for we was exceedingly beat out, and when we had got off we was ordered for to wait for the captain of the artillery and he waited for the regulars, and it was ten o'clock before they could get off, for they had their wounded men to take care of. And while they was waiting they was gathered in a large body they was alarmed by the rangers which wanted to get into some of the bateaux for to come with us, but they did suppose it to be enemies, and if it had been undoubtedly they would have killed a great number of men. But it was not three minutes before that it was known that it was friends and they cried "All is well," and they took them in and we came to the head of the lake about sunset and unloaded the artillery the same night.

[Later in the diary Spicer gives a more detailed account of the battle.]

July 8 A. Dom. 1758. Saturday—This morning after a tedious nights march Captain John Stanton with about half of his men and as many more from other companies that was a mind for to go with him went with the engineer to the top of a mountain against the fort for to view it and for to see if he could find any place for to plant their artillery to advantage. And we went and stayed on the side of the mountain next to the fort where we had a fair prospect at the fort and the men at work. And we see them drum off their guard and while we was there the Mohawks fired upon them and we see them run into the fort and within their breast work. And after a small space of time they ventured out to work again and after the engineer had viewed the fort he ordered them all for to return back again. And we got to our encampment at 9 o'clock in the morning and at the same time there was a number of men sent to the place where we landed our stores after cannon and artillery stores and whale boats. And they came back before that the engineer [was ready] and was sent back again for more stores. And when he got back the guard that went with him was ordered for to tarry there till further orders. And the chief of Colonel Whiting's regiment was sent after stores and the Mohawks went upon the same mountain after we came down and fired and shouted for to alarm the French and then came down and went to the fort and fired on the enemy. And the rangers fired on them which alarmed the French and this was before that our artillery had got up except six small brass cannon and 3 cohorns [*Also known as a Coehorn mortar. These were not the large siege mortars of the day but lighter and more portable infantry mortars.] which was brought up the night before and they had them on a floating battery. And then the rangers began to fire and then the regulars and Jersey Blues marched on as fast as possible and they had not above a mile and a half for to go before they came to the breast work. And while they was going the French fired on the floating battery from the fort but did no harm to it. The regulars marched on and was ordered not for to fire till they had orders and the French fired on them and killed a great many of them, but the regulars was not yet ordered for to fire and the French loaded and fired on them again before they had orders which killed the chief of the officers belonging to the regiment that was in the front for they had nothing to shelter them but the open air. And they was ordered for to march ten deep and the enemy had a breast work for to defend them. And in the height of action the rest of the artillery stores was brought up to the place where we encamped and there was a guard set over it. And the provincials marched after them but did not venture so near and they had a small wood for to cover them and there was but a few of them killed. Some regiments did not go to the field of battle but was ordered to build breast works for fear the enemy would drive them back again and they should have no place to defend themselves. But the battle continued with a continual fire from 1 o'- clock in the afternoon till night and the wounded was carried along, them that could not travel, and them that could travel went along back again, to the place where we landed. The streets was almost full all the time of the fight. And in the evening after the battle here there lay men, some dead, some wounded that could not go. The roads was so full that a man could hardly walk without tread- ing on them. And after the fire ceased the men that was left came within the breast works that we had built, but I left before they came in. There was orders for to carry back the stores and artillery and put them aboard of the bateaux. And after they had got all within the breastwork we was all rallied and ordered for to march off as fast as possible and we had but very little sleep for two nights before. The night being cloudy and in the woods which made it very dark so that a man could not see by the man that was before him and the path was very miry so that it would take a man in half leg. And every regiment was scattered amongst other they being rallied in the night, but they got down to the place where they was ordered next morning. The number of the killed and wounded was about 4065 and wounded about 1730, and a great many of them was mortally wounded.

[See Appendix B for reported casualties on both sides.]

Captain Joshua Loring

Loring, a native of Roxbury, Massachusetts, went to sea when he was twenty-one, and by his mid-twenties he was a captain of a New England merchant vessel. When news of King George's War arrived in Massachusetts, Governor William Shirley issued Loring a Letter of Marque. Loring's career as a privateer was short, being captured two months later off the coast of Louisbourg. When he was released that fall his information regarding the French fortress and its garrison proved invaluable to Shirley, who used this to launch an expedition against the French fortress on Cape Breton Island in 1745. For his part in the successful venture, Loring was made a lieutenant in the Royal Navy and commanded a schooner during the campaign. With the reduction of the navy upon the conclusion of the conflict Loring went on half-pay and returned to Roxbury. On March 13, 1756, Loring was reactivated, promoted to commander, and given command of the fourteen-gun brigantine *Loudoun* which had been constructed at Oswego on Lake Ontario the year before. Loring would never see this vessel as the fort was captured by the French a few days after he arrived at New York City. Loring was then sent to Lake George to oversee a small fleet that had been built to secure naval control over these waters. The next year Loring would command a small dispatch vessel in Loudoun's failed expedition against Louisbourg. In December 1757 he was given command of the HMS *Squirrel*, but this seems to have been done to give him the rank of post captain as he would not serve on the vessel. Instead, he would return to Lake George in the summer of 1758 to begin construction of a fourteen-gun sloop and a number of smaller armed vessels. He would accompany Abercromby on the Ticonderoga campaign but more in an advisory role as the warships he had started were not complete. The next year Loring would accompany Amherst, and after Fort Carillon and Fort St. Frederic were captured, he would oversee the construction of a pair of warships to challenge the French for control of Lake Champlain. While Loring successfully captured the bulk of the French navy on the lake, the season was so late that Amherst was forced to call off the campaign. Loring would serve with Amherst the following year in the latter's advance down the St. Lawrence to Montreal and was badly wounded engaging Fort Levis in the twenty-two-gun *Onondaga*. Loring would continue in his role as commandant of the lakes until retiring in 1767. A few years later, not long after the Battle of Lexington, Loring abandoned his Roxbury estate and traveled to Boston. A loyalist, he left the city for England, were he died in 1781.[3]

Captain Joshua Loring to —-, Lake George 19 Aug, 1758.[4]
Sir,
    I take this opportunity to transmit you a kind of Journal of what has happened in this Army from the 5th of July to this day.

July 5—In the morning the Army embarked with the Artillery Stores etc. consisting about Sixteen Thousand Eight Hundred Men on Board about Eight hundred Battoes, and One hundred and Sixty five Whale Boats—In short we had so fine an Army that the General thought proper not to wait for the New Hampshire Regiment which was a very fine one, and Sir William Johnson with about three hundred Indians which were within Six hours March of us— We left the place where Fort William Henry stood at Eight a clock in the morning, and at three in the afternoon encamped upon Point Pleasant which is Twenty Two Miles. Remained their till Eleven at Night when we embarked and proceeded down the Lake.

July 6—At five in the Morning we was in Sight of the French Advance Guards—At Twenty Minutes after Nine Landed Our Troops without any Opposition within four Miles of Ticonderoga.

Lord Howe Landed at the Head of the Grenadiers, the Light Infantry and the Rangers on the right, Coll Bradstreet with the Batteau Men and a detachment from the Provincial Troops, went about a Mile further down the Lake, and took possession of an advantageous post which the French had to Gard a Bridge that was thrown over a Narrow part of the Lake—Which post the French Abandoned with the utmost precipitation, Leaving their Money, Cloths, Papers, and in short everything behind them. Thus far we had got without the Loss of a single Person.

At Twelve General Abercromby and Lord Howe Marched with the Main Body to take possession of the Ground between the Bridge and the Saw Mill, but his Lordship very anxious to get forward, Left the Main Body and Marched on with the Light Infantry, part of the 44th, and some Provincials, but soon after fell in with near Five Hundred French & Indians which had been sent out to Reconnoiter our Army. All this party was cut to pieces or taken, not Ten of them got off.

General Lyman who commanded the Connecticut Troops (and who has behaved extremely well) Fell in with a party of French killed many and took One Hundred and Seven Prisoners.

But this piece of Advantage we paid very Dear for, for here we met with a Loss, by much too great, a Loss that was soon felt in the most Sensible manner by the whole Army. Lord Howe, who fell in the first of the Action Dead on the spot, so far things had been properly Conducted and with Spirit, But no sooner was his Lordship Dead, then everything took a different turn, and finally ended in Confusion and disgrace. The Army instead of being Marched on to the Fort which might have been done with the utmost ease, was Suffered to Wander about the Woods till Night, when part of them Returned to the place where we first Landed, the others Lay upon their Arms Scattered up and Down in the Woods.

July 7—At Eight in the morning the General Returned to the place where we first Landed, with Two or Three Regiments with him, and Instead of Marching the Army, and Investing the Fort Immediately and keeping up the Surprise the French had been thrown into the Day before, there was Talk of resting the Troops for four or five hours, But Coll Bradstreet went to the General and begged he would give him the Command of Four or Five Thousand Men, that he would go Immediately and take possession of the Saw Mill a very advantageous post, About one Mile and a half from the Fort, and after Soliciting the thing for a Long time and being Backed by Several of the Officers in the Army he was at Last permitted to go, and Immediately Marched with the 44th Regiment, Six Companies of the first battalion of the Royal Americans and three Regiments of the Provincials, and took possession of that post with the utmost ease, the French abandoning it at their first approach Leaving Everything behind them. As soon as this was over Col. Bradstreet wrote Immediately to the General for Leave to proceed and Invest the Fort which was not taken the Least Notice of. At Four the General Marched with the Rest of the Army to the [sawmill] Mills and joined Col. Bradstreet where he Lay that Night, three of the New England Regiments was Marched on about a mile further, which Brought them within Seven hundred Yards of the French Lines, where they encamped on a Rising Ground, and Entrenched themselves, and lay very quick that night, the French not attempting to disturb them.

July 8—In the morning the army marched from the Mills to the place where the New England regiments lay, when they were ordered to halt and remained there about three hours, during which time the French lines were said to be reconnoitered, and reported to be a slight breastwork of logs, easy to access on the evenness of the ground, and so weakly bound together that it would be easy to push them down by the Light Infantry.

Upon which orders were immediately given to attack the lines with the utmost dispatch, but without guns howitzers, mortars or any kind of assistance from the artillery, though they lay very contiguous at the landing place, and could very easily have been brought up long before the attack had they been ordered, and I think we had the finest train for attacking of lines that was ever in America. Having –

4—Iron 18-pounders
6—Light Brass 12-pounders
6—Light Brass 6-pounders
1—13-inch Iron Mortar

2—10-inch Iron Mortar

8—Brass Royals

9—8-inch Howitzers

4—5-inch Howitzers

With 200 rounds of shot and shells for each gun and mortar, this attack was carried on with the utmost bravery for near five hours, but to no purpose the situation of the enemy being quite different from what was reported; having a regular breastwork made of large square timber, raised seven feet above the ground and on an eminence about 500 yards from the fort between the uppermost log and that next to it was but full of loop holes which they fired through, so that the enemy were covered six inches above their heads, and from these lines they had fallen trees for about fifty yards from the breastwork outward which rendered our approach almost impossible. After many unsuccessful attempts in which many of our troops sustained great loss, and finding their efforts of no effect, and being left without any orders how to act they acted entirely by their own discretion, and made a slow and orderly retreat to the Saw Mill which was very easily done as the French never offered to stir out of their lines or fort.

Part of the army was ordered immediately down to where we first landed, the rest lay that night between the Saw Mills and the French lines, some of them within half a mile, where they lay without being disturbed in any shape, supposing the attack would have been renewed again the next morning by investing the fort in a regular manner with the assistance of the artillery, our army being full fourteen thousand strong and the men eager for the attack not withstanding, the loss we had sustained.

No sort of panic having seized the army but on the contrary, everybody was eager for renewing the attack the next morning, as the strength of the enemy was well known to us, by the numbers of prisoners we had taken, the two days before, and thus ended the eight day.

July 9—A day which seems to be remarkable in America was one of the most unhappy days I ever saw, and I think Braddock's affair may be reckoned a piece of prudence good conduct and bravery to this. At nine in the morning there was orders given to all the regiments then remaining between that and the French lines to march immediately to the place where the boats lay, and to embark their troops as fast as possible they could, and I believe no men ever received any orders with more surprise, nor executed them with more reluctancy, in short some of the regiments lay there till five o'clock in the morning, thinking there must have been some mistake in the orders, and two companies of Col. Wooster's Regiment did not come down to the boats until half past ten, when all the rest of the army had embarked and got a long way from the shore, and it is very certain by several of our people who have got in since we arrived, that lay within a few yards of the French lines all night, being much fatigued, and overslept themselves, that the French never stirred out of their fort or lines till late in the morning, and then but a few yards from the breast-work, and by three deserters that came into our camp two days ago we are informed that the French had got all their boats ready expecting we should have renewed the attack early the next morning, and with cannon, and that as soon as ever we carried the lines, which must have soon been the case, with the train of artillery we had with us, to have gone off with the main body of their army to Fort St. Jean at the lower end of the lake leaving a small garrison in the fort, just to have amused us in order to have the better secured their retreat. In short it appeared we ran away from ourselves and not from the enemy, and can in no shape be called a retreat, as no enemy ever attempted to follow us.

We had every advantage that we could possibly wish for till that rash mad and inconsiderate attack was made upon their lines, and even after that with all the loss we had sustained, we had strength enough left to have marched through any part of Canada. Tis publicly said that there was no such thing as any general consultation of officers, General Lyman who was then laying within a mile of the French lines, sent for entrenching tools, and to the General desiring he might have leave to throw up a breastwork, that he could very easily maintain the ground should the French attempt to come out but all would not do he was ordered to march.

Accordingly all marched to the boats, and began to embark at six in the morning, and at half past ten the last boats left the French shore with a fair wind and pleasant weather, and arrived at the place where Fort William Henry stood at six in the afternoon, and this ended the most unhappy day which ever happened in America.

Since which I have been employed in building a large sloop of sixteen guns, four pounders, but what use is to be made of (it) I am a stranger too, we have now here about seven thousand troops, several regiments having been sent up the Mohawk River, I suspect we shall tarry here till very late in the fall in Order to protect the vessel and boats which are intended to be sunk as soon as the ice begins to make, I am extremely sorry we failed in this part of the plan especially as everything was so much in our favor, but if ever we attempt Quebec which I hope in God will be next spring, it may be by the river St. Lawrence and Kennebec.

I have the honor to be, your most obedient and humble servant,

Joshua Loring

Lt. Colonel William Eyre

William Eyre was one of the early Royal Engineering graduates of the Woolwich Academy in England. Eyre, who held both an engineering warrant and the army rank of captain, served throughout the war of Austrian Succession. He was present at the defeat of Bonnie Prince Charlie's army at the Battle of Culloden Moor, participated in the Battle of Laufeldt, and was part of the doomed defense of Bergen op Zoom. He would come to America with Braddock in 1755 and was the only redcoat present at the Battle of Lake George later that year. While Abercromby questioned Eyre's abilities to command both a regiment and the engineering brigade, Amherst did not, and the following year he appointed Eyre chief engineer in the successful campaign against Fort Carillon and Fort St. Frederic. Eyre would serve with Amherst the next year and was present at the surrender of the French colony on September 8, 1760. He would later be appointed chief engineer in North America and, unfortunately, was drowned in a shipwreck off the Irish coast while attempting to return to Britain in 1764.[5]

Major William Eyre to Robert Napier, Lake George, 10th July 1758.[6]

Dear Sir,

I cannot help taking the most early opportunity of acquainting you of an unhappy affair we have very lately been engaged in, this is the Attack of the French Intrenchment before Tyunderoga [Ticonderoga] the 8th Inst: We embarked from hence the 5th And the next morning arrived in sight of the Enemy's advanced Post, where they had about 3 or 4 hundred men; We were in Number about Sixteen Thousand Men, five thousand Regulars, & the rest Provincials, light Armed Troops, Ranger, & batteau Men; we landed without opposition the Enemy retired a Cross the Carrying Place to the Saw Mill: & in two or three hours after we got Ashore We proceeded on our March towards the Fort. We were about four Mile & a half to go close to the falls leaving it on ye Right Hand, & about Six Miles if we kept further from the falls, which was the Way We intended to go, & only three Miles to go by the Carrying Place: this last, would be difficult if the Enemy Opposed the Passage of the River at the Saw Mill, on Account of the advantage of the Ground. We proceeded the Other Way, (that of Six Miles) being the most Secure but before we got much more than A Mile our advanced Party's were Attacked, or fell in with near 300 of the Enemy, which were almost [all] killed And taken Prisoners, all Regulars: in this first Skirmish the Gallant and good Lord Howe fell, killed Upon the Spot, greatly lamented (And that with great Justice) by the Army. I observed this little firing threw our Regulars in to some kind of a Consternation, which, though ended Soon, And luckily, Struck me, and gave me some uneasiness. I observed the fire round them, though at some distance, seemed to Alarm them; in the Wood, where nothing can be Seen, but what is near, the men fancy is worse, or the Enemy more Numerous than they Are; our own fire they Are Apt some times to think is the Enemy's Our Irregulars Yelling is believed by those who Are not engaged, to be the Enemy; in short Sir, I am more than ever convinced that numbers of our People cannot hear a great deal of firing round them coolly. I mean when they hear & do not See: these Are A few Observations I made during this little Scramble, however we continued our March on towards the Fort; this Affair I think happened about 3 or 4 o'clock in the Afternoon, & about Sun set or a little after, as the Heads of the Columns were descending a low ground. A fire Was heard in the front; We Marched, I think in three Columns, I mean the Regulars the Other Troops were Upon Our flanks and Front, as it was intended they should; the firing grew quicker, & it was followed by a loud hideous Yell those in the front gave Way immediately in the greatest Disorder, and it ran down for two or three hundred Yards along each Column, as it appeared to me; no entreaty could prevail with the men for some time, but in about an hour's time after this, we found out, the fire that began this Confusion in the front was from Our Selves, & by all I could learn Since not a Single shot was fired against us by the Enemy; by this time it was almost Dark, we were separated & had some difficulty to Join Afterwards; but in a very irregular Way, the Regiments intermixed with each Other, And as it appeared to me in a most wretched situation: I must confess to you, that it's my opinion, two or three hundred Indians surrounding us that night, with the Apprehensions that some of Our people Shewed, must have Ended fatally; believe me Dear Sir, I do not Exaggerate this affair, I cannot describe as it appeared to me, without making you think I carry it further than it really was. however, time will inform you better of it. We remained there All Night, I must observe to You, all the Army was not at this Place, part of ye 55th & the 42d had returned to the Landing place before night, having lost the rest of the Army, during the Skirmish, with a great Number of the Provincials. I must confess the Colony Troops behaved extremely Well, were in great Spirits & was Willing to do Anything they Were desired, however next Morning we got some Guides to shew us the Way back to the Landing Place, R: there the Army Joined in one Body, not long after this, the 44th, Six Companies of the Royal Americans, & four Regiments of Provincials marched to take possession of the Saw Mill, this As I observed to You before was the nearest Way to the Fort; Upon Our Arrival there we found it Abandoned, & the Enemy fled likewise from the Other Side of the River, And retreated to their Breast Works before the Fort. Our Rangers And light Armed Troops with some of the Provincials pursued them to that place, where they continued all night the Enemy not daring to sally out: Upon this the whole Army followed And crossed the River and Encamped opposite the Saw mill, this Place is one Mile and A half from ye Enemy's Fort, the Carrying Place is also one Mile a half A Cross, the next Morning it was resolved to Attack the Intrenchment, & in consequence of it all the Commanding officers of Regts were called together; as I had the honor to be at the head of the 44th Was one of the Number: I remember it was asked whether We should Attack three or four deep, it was carry 'd for three, the next question if the Grenadiers & Pickets of the Regulars should attack at the Same time or support each Other, it was agreed to support each Other, there was a Plan of the Ground, & the Intrenchmt given in by Mr. Clerk Who had the Direction of the Brigade: This Department devolved Upon Me by Col. Montresor being ill & not Able to Act, but, I was told if I did not give Up the Command of ye Regt I must have nothing to do with it; to this, I answered, I could not do Voluntarily, As there was no field Officer to the Regt but myself, but was very Willing if the General was pleased to order me, or allow me to Act as Major And I would do my utmost in directing & Superintending the Brigade, and carrying on that Service; this, I was Sensible I could do in the most Important Parts of it, but it was not complied with, & from that time, I was never Asked or spoke to, in relation to that Branch, Until I arrived at this Place after our Retreat. I beg pardon for dwelling Upon this Article, but I fancied you might Ask how it come about I was not employed or consulted before the Attack of the intrenchment was made, as you know I have been Generally in time of Service employed in that Branch of the Service, however the Attack was made, I am Sorry to Say not in the most Regular Manner, some of the Regts beginning before the Others were formed, particularly the Brigade — I think to the Rt which consisted of the 27th Regt & two Battalions of the Royal Americans,— that of the left was the 42nd & 46th the Center the 44th & 55th Col Holiman [Haldimand], commanded the Grenadiers which Supported the Pickets, that were under Major Proby who began the Attack. Unhappy for us we presently found it a most Formidable Intrenchmt & not to be forced by the Method we were Upon, for upwards of one hundred Yards in front of it, Trees were fell down in Such Manner that it Broke our Battalions before we got near the Breastwork, as we marched a Battalion in Front three Deep; I was of opinion we should attack it in Column, each Regt picking one, or two to Support each Other, As we could more easily force Our Way through the fell Trees than by making so large A Front, but it was said this would cause confusion; in short, it was said, we must

Attack Any Way, and not be losing time in talking or consulting how. Attack we did, but it's hard to describe which way, The Pickets and Grenadiers with the Regt to the Rt, began the Attack before the Center Brigade had formed: we Marched from ye Rt, the Center Brigade followed, the Left brought Up ye Rear, We formed to the left when we came Upon Our Ground; this I know, the Regt upon My Rt & left did, so, Apprehend the Others did the Same. I found the Attack had been began some time before I could form Our Regt this being done, all was left for each Commanding Officer of a Regt to do, was to support & march up as quick as they could get Upon their Ground And so on to the Intrenchment, after it was found that this Scheme would not do, we remained some time before We had any order to do Anything; I cannot tell how Matters were going on in the whole, but it was plain, something should be undertaken; We had at last orders to draw off the Regulars, & some Provincial Regts were ordered Up; we retreated to two Breastworks that were made between this Place & the Saw Mills, And After that, (towards Evening) All the Troops filed off by the Saw mill A Cross the River, & so continued their March to the Landing Place that night Where we embarked next Morning in Our Batteau, & the Same Evening arrived at this Place. Great faults are found with the Method of the attack the little knowledge we had of the Strength of the Enemy's Works, & the Sudden Retreat to this Ground. Col. Donaldson, Col. Bever, Major Proby, Major Campbell & Major Rutherford, killed; Major Browning, Major Tullikens [*Lt. Col. John Donaldson, 55th; Lt. Col. Samuel Beaver, 46th; Major Thomas Proby, 55th; Major Duncan Campbell, 42nd; Major John Rutherford, 60th, Major William Browning, 46th; Major John Tullikens, 60th.] & myself Wounded, Mine is only A flesh Wound through the Side of My face, the Jaw-Bone I hope has escaped. I believe we may have lost near Two thousand Men killed And Wounded, I fancy about fifteen or Sixteen hundred of them Regulars.

I hope Sir, You will excuse the rough Manner I send this Account to You, I Am pretty Sure the facts I have related are exact, tho not properly digested And put in order, but this, I presume you will be so good As to pardon On Account of the hurry I Am in to Send you the most early Notice by the fust Messenger that goes from hence. I have done my Endeavour to get a Strong Fort built this Campaign at the Onida Carrying Place at the head of the Mohawk River, this is almost one hundred Miles from Albany; A Place I think has been long neglected, & yet I fear there will be nothing very respectable built there; I offered to undertake to build one in three Months with two thousand Men & finish it so far before the Winter as to be out of Danger of Any Insult, there are near five thousand Men going Up there, what they will do is more than I can say; some Diversion may be made On lake Ontario If whale Boats are carried there.

There is some talk of re building Fort William Henry, but this I Apprehend will not be carried into Execution; what we shall do now, or how we are to proceed, heaven knows; surely we are the most unfortunate People that ever met together. A few Days Ago everything looked cheerful, now the Contrary. I understand Col. Gage's light Armed Troops is approved of; I hope I shall be Appointed to Succeed him in the Regt, there is but three Majors in America Older than Me; there Are Several Lieut Colonelcy's Vacant, this I hope will give me a better title to Succeed in our Regt, for should I be removed into a New Regt & it reduced, by being An Engr I am not entitled to half Pay. We hear the Siege of Louisbourg is going on successfully, may heaven grant them More Success in the End, than us, though it's impossible that they could have a better Appearance upon Landing on ye Island of Cape Breton than we had on that at ye Advanced Guard.

I hope His Royal Highness the Duke is in health and Spirits, long may He live, be happy, & Prosperous, is, and always are my Constant Wishes.

My best Compliments to Mrs. Napier. I am Dear Sir, Your Much Obliged and Most Obedient humble Servant.

William Eyre

Major Gabriel de Maurès de Malartic

Born in Montauban, France July 3, 1730, Malartic would enter the French Army as an ensign in the La Sarre Regiment in 1745. A year later he would be appointed second lieutenant in the Bearn Regiment, and a few months after that was made captain. Malartic would campaign in Flanders under Count Saxe and in Italy during the War of Austrian Succession. His professionalism seems to have attracted attention, as a year after the conclusion of the conflict he was promoted to major. Malartic would arrive in Canada along with the Bearn Regiment in June 1755. The next year he would be involved in the siege of Oswego, winning acclaim from Montcalm in the process. He would be present for the siege and surrender of Fort William Henry in 1757, the Battle of Ticonderoga in 1758, and would retreat with the French army to Montreal after the Battle of the Plains of Abraham in September 13, 1759. Malartic was wounded at the Battle of St. Foy the following spring and was present at Montreal when Governor Vaudreuil surrendered the colony. After returning to France with his regiment, in June 1763 Malartic was made Colonel of the Régiment de Vermandois. He would serve as commander of this unit, primarily in the Caribbean, for almost twenty years. Malartic would continue to rise through the ranks, being made brigadier general in 1770 and major general in 1780. In 1792 he was promoted to lieutenant general and appointed governor of Ile de France, a post he would serve in until his death in 1800.[7]

Excerpts from the Journal of Military Operations before Ticonderoga by Major Gabriel de Maurès de Malartic, Bearn Regiment.[8]

[July] 5th Service as usual. Transported the artillery furniture; began baking in the three ovens. At two o'clock in the afternoon, heard a shot from the mountain to the left of the Beam camp, and a white flag was seen hoisted and lowered, which is the signal furnished to the Lieutenant who was detached thither, signifying that he discovers some barges or bateaux on the lake. One hour afterwards, a part of M. de Langy's detachment returned to report that, having started in the morning from the Bay of Ganaouské, [Northwest Bay] he had been seen from Fort George, whence 60 barges were sent in pursuit, which followed pretty closely for awhile and then fell off; that Messrs de Langy and La Roche had remained with their canoe three leagues from this to watch them. M. de Bourlamaque immediately detached Captain de Trepezec, of the Bearn regiment, with three pickets of 51 men each, some volunteers and Militia, the whole numbering 300, to the Bald Mountain to observe the enemy's movements and to oppose their landing. M. de Langy, who arrived at the moment, assured that the enemy was approaching close after him. Captain de Germain, of the regiment of La Reine, was sent at 5 o'clock with three pickets between the mountains and the lake to support our advanced guards and to prevent the enemy establishing themselves there. All our troops had orders to be on the alert, and ready at the first call.

On the 6th, at one o'clock in the morning, a dozen shots were heard in the direction of our advanced posts. The brigade rushed to arms; a quarter of an hour afterwards, it received orders to dismiss. We learned that the English had fired on a corporal and the relief; that they had collared the corporal and one of the sentinels, supposing them prisoners, but the latter had freed themselves, repulsing them with the bayonet, and that the shots the others had fired, forced them to retire. At daylight the flag was seen to be frequently lowered and hoisted; many barges were discovered crossing from the north to the south and appearing in search of a place fit for landing. The scouting barge returned with word that it had perceived over 1,500 of them. At 7 o'clock M. Germain's detachment came back. M. de Bourlamaque gave orders that the baggage be removed, the tents struck, and the march commenced at 8 o'clock. He remained with the rear guard, with the companies of grenadiers and volunteers, in order to receive news from M. de Trepezec. Receiving none, he had some shots fired at the barges which were approaching, and then followed us without our being troubled in our retreat. On arriving at the Falls, the Marquis de Montcalm posted us on the right of the La Sarre brigade at the foot of the heights, withdrew the brigade of R. Roussillon from the right bank, caused the bridges to be broken up and ordered a halt. Sent to Carillon for some bateaux to embark the baggage, which was embarrassing the soldiers. At 3 o'clock M. de Raymond, Messrs St. Ours and Lanodiere passed in front with a detachment of the Marine and Canadians. At four o'clock we heard several shots which we judged were fired at M. de Trepezec's detachment. A quarter of an hour afterwards we saw some soldiers wading, and M. de Trepezec arrive mortally wounded; he told us that he had lost his way through the fault of his guide, and that wishing to reach the Falls, he had got into the midst of a considerable party of the enemy; that after having defended himself some time, 50 or 60 men escaped; that the remainder were killed, taken or drowned. At ½ past 5 we took up our march to Carillon; at 7, arrived at the entrance of the clearing, where we arranged ourselves in the order of battle, and passed the night in bivouac.

7th The drum beat *la generale* at daybreak; some soldiers took provisions; the three brigades posted themselves at 7 o'clock at the entrance of the wood where they commenced an abatis at which they vigorously continued the entire day, encouraged by the presence of the Generals.

This abatis embraces the whole of the ground between the River of the Falls and the ravine which borders on the reserved timber that stands on the margin of Lake Champlain. At 5 o'clock in the evening, the ground was equally divided between each wheelbarrow; it made 127 paces for each. Permission was given to erect some tents and to boil the soup behind the abatis. We had orders to sleep in bivouac; the guards, to line the abatis, to patrol frequently outside and to keep the fires burning. The troops of the Marine and the Militia were posted at the opening. At 5 and 7 o'clock the detachments designed for the expedition to Korlak, [Corlar (Schenectady, N.Y.)] arrived and encamped in the rear of the three brigades together with the volunteers.

8th The *generale* was beat long before day. M. de Levis arrived with M. de Senezergues. At 5 o'clock, each battalion set to work to strengthen the abatis, 150 paces in front of which the guard were posted, to protect the workmen. At 9 o'clock, a body of troops was discovered on the summit and at the foot of the mountain, on the right of the River of the Falls, whence they were examining our position, and fired a few shots at us. Bernard's volunteers gave them a few shots in answer. Chev. D'Arenes, Lieutenant of that company, had his arm broken on that occasion. Our Generals made a tour of inspection of the abatis, which they found in a pretty good condition and made arrangements for the defence. At ½ past 12, the regiment of La Reine and Beam were going to construct some epaulements to protect themselves from the heights, when a heavy firing was heard on the left; a moment after at the center, and next at the right. The discharge of a cannon from the fort, announcing the arrival of the enemy, brought every man to his post. The companies of grenadiers and guards came in again without losing a single man. The battalions lined the abatis, three deep, having their grenadier companies and pickets in line of battle in their rear, ready to march wherever needed. La Sarre's brigade, commanded by M. de Bourlamaque, responded by some effective firing, to a column that had shewed itself; the R. Roussillon and Guyenne regiments, to two which attacked the center, where the M. de Montcalm was posted; and those of La Reine, and Bearn, to a fourth which had an anxiety to attempt the right commanded by Chev. de Levis. Several barges deployed from the river of the Falls, to come and land some people and to turn our left; M. de Poularies with his grenadier company and Bernard's volunteers, went down to the bank of the river to fire at them. A few cannon shot were fired from the fort, which, after sinking two, made the others retreat up the river whence they made no further appearance. The fire was pretty brisk on each side, though a little more active on ours. The attack and defence was sustained with incredible valor. The enemy's columns, though refreshed by the reinforcements they were continually receiving, and often combining to make common efforts, to attempt the right, the center and the left, were not making any progress and experienced everywhere an obstinate resistance, sustained by the bravery of the troops and the attention of the Generals to send the grenadiers and pickets to the exposed points. Chev. de Levis posted himself apropos with the regiment of La Reine behind that of Guyenne, where the enemy in force was appearing desirous of making an impression; he checked them and sent out some soldiers of the Marine and Militia, who went to fire on the enemy's left flank. At 8 o'clock, the fire began to slacken; some soldiers were allowed to go out who took some prisoners; at 6 o'clock, the enemy made a new attempt with no better success than the first. Perceiving at 7 o'clock that they had not made any progress, they bethought them of a retreat, leaving their best marksmen to cover it. Fatigue and our small numbers, prevented us offering any opposition. Firing was forbidden, because 'twas perceived that the fire we were receiving, proceeded only from a few men in ambush behind some trees, who were waiting for nightfall to retreat. The loss of the enemy is estimated at five or six thousand men, in killed or wounded; and ours at 300, including 38 officers. The Mis de Montcalm had wine and beer conveyed to the field of battle, to refresh the troops who stood in great need of it; he and Chev. de Levis passed in front of all the battalions and expressed how pleased they felt at their conduct. This memorable victory is due to the goodness of the Almighty, who has manifested Himself so often and so visibly the defender of the country; to the prudence of the General's arrangements and their attention in watching the enemy's movements; to the activity generally of all the officers; to the bravery and intrepidity of the soldiers, all of whom have manifested incredible ardor, thinking only of taking good aim, and sighting everything that shewed itself from behind trees or stumps. The night was spent in cleaning the arms; in raising some epaulements on the left, as a cover from the damage to which we were exposed from the musketry, being seen in reverse. The troops bivouacked through the night, along the abatis, very alert and wishing for the return of the enemy on the morrow.

9th The *generale* was beat an hour before day; the troops lined the abatis, anxiously waiting the arrival of the enemy. At 5 o'clock some soldiers were sent out, who dispatched some of the wounded that wished to defend themselves, and brought within the lines those who did not resist. A very thick smoke was perceived at the Falls, which led to the supposition that the English were abandoning that place, and were occupying themselves only with their retreat. M. de Bernard went scouting with his company, and sent word to the Marquis de Montcalm that on the road to the Falls was an intrenchment which he could set on fire. That General immediately sent him the orders to do so, which he executed at once. Some Indians, who had gone ahead to plunder, came to give notice that the enemy were thinking only of embarking. Buried all our dead. At 8 o'clock in the evening, M. Wolf arrived with his detachment, reported to the M. de Montcalm that he found no one at Fort George on his landing, but two leagues from that fort fell, unawares, on a considerable party, commanded by Major-General Lord Howe who has been killed by M. de Trepezec's detachment, and encamped in a hollow square, with all the barges, bateaux, artillery and ammunition in the center; that the General had demanded his orders, had shewn him a great deal of civility, and had him forwarded next morning to Fort Lydius [Fort Edward], where General Abercrombie received him politely and detained him, telling him that the M. de Vaudreuil's letters required an answer which could not be given him for some days. That he was well aware that he was detained to prevent him coming to inform us of their maneuvers; that the General had asked him news of one of their parties, commanded by Captain Rogers, which had met with a misfortune; that on being answered, the General had scolded the Captain very severely, and reproached him with having ran away the moment his troop was engaged; that they had conducted him back to Fort George, on the assembling of their army there, which he believes consisted of 22 or 25,000 men; that there were nearly 2,000 barges or bateaux, 1,500 of which have been employed in transporting troops, and 500 in coming and going; that this army had been embarked in an instant, and had taken the portage route, marching thither as to a certain conquest; that he had been brought along and when their troops had arrived at the Falls, was taken to the Bald Mountain, where he had been three days, very dissatisfied with the little attention paid to his detachment; that Colonel Johnson arrived the 7th with 400 Indians belonging to the Five Nations or *Loups;* that a courier was sent off that same day who proclaimed, everywhere, that Cape Breton was taken; that on the 8th at night, he had seen a great number of barges file off, loaded, apparently, with wounded; that the officer who was guarding him, hailed many of them, and discontinued, expressing great regret; that on the morning of the 9th the whole army had, without making much noise, taken up the march to Fort George, whither he was conducted, and having complained of it to the Major-General, the officer in whose hands he was placed, received orders to land him at his canoe, in which he repaired to the Portage and thence here, himself and his detachment exhausted by hunger and fatigue. The troops still bivouacked along the abatis. The prisoners were sent to Montreal. The Mis de Montcalm dispatched M. de La Roche to the Governor-General to announce to him the retreat of the enemy.

10th Chevalier de Levis went to the Portage with the grenadier companies and pickets; found some intrenchments on both sides of the Falls, at the Portage and the Burnt camp; had 200 barrels of flour brought back; saw a great many which had been thrown into the water, after having had the heads stove in; also considerable other stores. The soldiers and Canadians returned loaded with plunder and with an immense quantity of shoes with their buckles.

NOTES

The following abbreviations have been used for frequently cited sources.

C.O.5   Colonial Office Records, American and West Indies, London

CWS   Lincoln, *The Correspondence of William Shirley, Governor of Massachusetts and Military Commander in America, 1731-1760*

DCB   *Dictionary of Canadian Biography*

DHSNY   O'Callaghan, *Documentary History of the State of New York*

EIHC   *Essex Institute Historical Collections*

FTMB   *Fort Ticonderoga Museum Bulletin*

HL   Huntington Library and Art Gallery, San Marino, CA

LO   Loudoun Papers, Huntington Library, San Marino, CA

JP   Sullivan, *The Papers of Sir William Johnson*

NAC   National Archives of Canada, Ottawa

NEHGR   *New England Historical and Genealogical Register*

NY Col. Doc. O'Callaghan, *Documents Relative to the Colonial History of the State of New York*

NYHSC   *New-York Historical Society Collections*

RAPQ   *Rapport de l'Archiviste de la Province de Quebec*

W.O.   War Office Records, London

INTRODUCTION

1. Richards, *The Black Watch at Ticonderoga*, 43-45; Stewart, *Highlanders of Scotland*, I, 279-284, 295-296.

2. Bascom, "The Legend of Duncan Campbell," 33-36.

3. Stewart, *Highlanders of Scotland*, I, 295-296. Campbell purchased a majority in the regiment on December 17, 1755. (Ford, *British Officers*, 23.)

CHAPTER 1: THE FRENCH AND INDIAN WAR IN THE MOHAWK AND CHAMPLAIN VALLEYS

1. Ambler, *George Washington and the West*, 63-91; Clayton, "The Duke of Newcastle, the Earl of Halifax, and the American Origins of the Seven Years' War," 571-603; Higonnet, "The Origins of the Seven Years' War," 57-90; Riker, "The Politics behind Braddock's Expedition," 742-752.

2. *NY Col. Doc.*, X, 275-278. The French Foreign Minister Rouille wrote of the situation, "We see with regret that war alone can end our differences." (Pease, *Anglo-French Boundary Disputes in the West*, 161.)

3. "Pierre de Rigaud, Marquis de Vaudreuil," DCB, IV.

4. Gipson, *The Years of Defeat*, 103-105. The vessels destined for Canada under Comte DuBois de la Motte's command were; armed *en flute*: *Defenseur* (22), *Dauphin Royal* (22), *Algonquin* (22), *Espérance* (22), *Actif* (22), *Illustre* (22), *Opiniâtre* (22), *Lys* (22), *Léopard* (22), *Apollon* (22), *Aquillon* (22); armed *en guerre*: *Entreprenant* (74), *Alcide* (64), *Bizzare* (64); frigates: *Sirenne* (30), *Comète* (24) ("La Pause Papers," *RAPQ 1931-32*, 4.) The frigates *Diane* (30) and *Fidéle* (30), were to leave in late March, collect river pilots at Quebec, and then rendezvous with the fleet near the Gaspé peninsula in order to guide them up the St. Lawrence. (*N.Y. Col. Doc.*, X, 277, 299.)

5. Minutes from the Alexandria Council Meeting, 14 April, 1755, C.O. 5/46; Braddock to Robinson, 19 April, 1755, Craig, *Olden Times*, II, May 1847, 230-233.

6. Corbett, *England in the Seven Years' War*, I, 40-43; Gipson, *The Years of Defeat*, 101. Also see Minutes of April 10th Cabinet Meeting in Pease, *Anglo-French Boundary Disputes in the West*, 206-207.

7. Gipson, *The Years of Defeat*, 125-126; Corbett, *England in the Seven Years' War*, I, 57-58. A firsthand French account of the capture of the *Lys* and *Alcide* can be found in Craig, *Olden Times*, II, May 1847, 275-277. On board the *Alcide* was the new governor of Three Rivers, all three of Dieskau's engineers, one of his aide-de-camps, one of his two commissaries of war, and his second in command, Colonel Rostaing, who was killed in the engagement. (*N.Y. Col. Doc.*, X, 357.) (Corbett, *England in the Seven Years' War*, I, 58.)

8. Kopperman, *Braddock at the Monongahela*, 50-92. Sargent, *The History of an Expedition Against Fort Du Quesne*, 353-357, 384-389; CWS, II, 217-221; Gipson, VI, 127-150.

9. CWS, II, 158-166; *NY Col. Doc.*, X, 306-313, 327-328, 338-344; JP, I, 892-894, II, 7-17; *La Campagne de 1755*, 52-53; Relation de Combat du lac Saint-Sacrement, NAC, MG 1 F3 vol. 14, 184-185.

10. Perry, *Origins in Williamstown*, 344-347; O'Callaghan, *Documentary History of New York*, 689-690; Blodget, *The Battle near Lake George in 1755*, 1-5: Relation de Combat du lac Saint-Sacrement, NAC, MG 1 F3 vol. 14, 185-186; *N.Y. Col. Doc.*, VI, 1000-1007, X, 316-344; JP, II, 16-28; Fowler, *The History of Durham, Connecticut*. Hartford, 137-138; DeForest, *The Journals and Papers of Seth Pomeroy*, 110-115.

11. "Vaudreuil to Lotbiniere, Sept 20, 1755," FTMB, (Jan 1928); Lotbiniere to Minister, 31 Oct., 1756, MG1-C11A, vol 101, fols. 333-334.

12. Mount Independence was referred to as Pointe au Diamant at the time, while Rattlesnake Mountain was a literal translation from the French *Serpent a Sonnette*.

13. Lotbiniere to Minister, 31 Oct., 1756, MG1-C11A, vol. 101, fols. 333-334.

14. "Michel Chartier de Lotbiniere the Engineer of Carillon," NYHM (1934) 32; Lotbiniere to Minister, 31 Oct., 1756, MG1-C11A, vol. 101, fols. 333-334; *NY Col. Doc.*, X, 493-494; Rogers, *Journals*, 8-9.

15. Pell, "Montcalm: Origins and First Steps," *FTMB* #4 (1949), 131-159; Montcalm, *DCB*, IV; "Montcalm's Correspondence," *Report of the Public Archives (Canada) for the Year 1929*, 32; *NY Col. Doc.*, X, 393-395, 414; Casgrain, *Lettres de la Cour de Versailles*, 26-27. Montcalm's instructions can be found in ibid., 39-43.

16. "Montcalm's Correspondence," 36.

17. Louis-Antoine Bougainville, *DCB*, IV; Casgrain, *Montcalm's Journal*, 20.

18. François-Gaston Levis, *DCB*, IV; Casgrain, *Montcalm's Journal*, 18.

19. "Montcalm's Correspondence," 38; Montcalm, DCB, IV; Casgrain, *Montcalm's Journal*, 22; *NY Col. Doc*, X, 491.

20. *NY Col. Doc.*, X, 403-406, 420-426, 441; *CWS*, II, 343-350, 423-424; *N.H. Provincial Papers*, VI, 460-467. Secretary Fox's letter informing the northern governors of the change in command is in *NY Col. Doc.*, VII, 75-76.

21. Pargellis, *Lord Loudoun*, 83, 89; *Correspondence of the Colonial Governors of Rhode Island*, 1723-1775, II, 222; *JP*, IX, 484; "The Correspondence of Dr. Thomas Williams. . .," 214-15; Council of War held at Albany, 16 July, 1756, C.O.5/47.

22. Anderson, "Why did Colonial New Englanders Make Such Bad Soldiers?", 395-417; Provincial Field Officers to Loudoun, 12 Aug, 1756, C.O.5/47; Loudoun to Fox, 19 Aug, 1756, C.O. 5/47; *CWS*, II, 495-510, 521-530. Dr. Thomas Williams, a member of Winslow's army, wrote his wife that if Loudoun forced a union of the provincial and regular troops that "it would knock the expedition in the head, at least for this year." (Williams Correspondence, 215).

23. "Dr. A.R. Cutter's Journal," *A History of the Cutter Family*, 64-65; "Williams Correspondence," 215-216; *JP*, II, 549.

24. Pargellis, *Lord Loudoun*, 164-165; *JP*, II, 554-559; *Mante*, 65.

CHAPTER 2: THE FALL OF FORT WILLIAM HENRY

1. Rouville, *William Pitt, Earl of Chatham*, II, 45-86; Williams, *Life of Pitt*, I, 146-148, 279-285.

2. Lecky, *A History of England in the Eighteenth Century*, II, 508-531; Pargellis, *Lord Loudoun*, 229-230; Hotblack, *Chatham's Colonial Policy*, 44-53; Gipson, *Years of Defeat*, 378-379.

3. Kimball, *Pitt Correspondence*, I, 15, 53; Pargellis, *Lord Loudoun*, 232.

4. Kimball, *Pitt Correspondence*, I, 18, 39-40, 74; Pargellis, *Lord Loudoun*, 234-235; *Colden Papers*, V, 156. General James Abercromby, Loudoun's second in command, accompanied the expedition in the event Loudoun was disabled or could no longer exercise command.

5. Hamilton, *Bougainville Journals*, 108-109, 112; "Journal de Marche du Detachment Commande par M Rigaud de Vaudreuil," RAPQ (1932-33), 338-341; Casgrain, *Relations et Journaux*, 77-86; Eyre to Loudoun, 20, 24, 25, 28 March and 6 April, 1757, CO5/48; Journal of an Attack made on Fort William Henry, WO34/10; "Relation de M Poularies,"*La Pause Papers*, RAPQ (1931-32), 47-48.

6. *NY Col. Doc.*, X, 497-498, 565-567; Hamilton, *Bougainville Journals*, 104, 108-109.

7. *NY Col. Doc*, X, 499-518; Hamilton, *Bougainville Journals*, 113-117; *Pouchot Memoirs*, 113; Hunt, *The Wars of the Iroquois*, 47, 109.

8. *NY Col. Doc*, X, 584-586, 627; Hamilton, *Bougainville Journals*, 119.

9. Webb to Loudoun, 1 Aug, 1757, C.O.5/48.

10. Casgrain, *Levis Journal*, 87; Webb to Loudoun, 1 Aug, 1757, C.O.5/48; Loudoun to Holdernesse, 16 Aug, 1757, C.O.5/48.

11. Monro to Webb, 3 Aug, 1757, (three letters) C.O.5/48.

12. Gabriel, *Desandrouins*, 87-88; Hamilton, *Bougainville Journals*, 160-161.

13. Gabriel, *Desandrouins*, 89; Hamilton, *Bougainville Journals*, 161-162; "Bartman Letters," 419; "Frye Journal," 349; "A Journal Kept During the Siege of Fort William Henry," 147; The Journal of Adam Williamson, Williamson Family Papers, NAC A-573. The bulk of the cannon mounted at Fort William Henry had been left there by Winslow's troops after their abortive campaign the year before. The quality of such guns, which likely sat idle in colonial armories for dozens of years, was certainly suspect. Johnson noted that many of their guns that he had been issued in 1755 were honeycombed with rust from years of neglect. This, combined with the thermal and mechanical stresses of continued firing, and the poor iron working practices of the time (that is, the use of poor grade high sulfur or high phosphor content iron ore) often lead to metal fatigue which resulted in split and cracked barrels, rendering the gun useless.

14. "Bartman Letters," 419; *Montresor Journal*, 26, 38; Webb to Loudoun 5 Aug, 1757, C.O.5/48. La Chesnaye was apparently surprised while killing one of the garrison's cattle in the woods near the Fort Edward road.

15. "Relation of M Poularies," *RAPQ*, 1931-1932, 59; Hamilton, *Bougainville Journals*, 162-163; "Bartman Letters," 420-421.

16. *NY Col. Doc.*, X, 602; Hamilton, *Bougainville Journals*, 162; Gabriel, *Desandrouins*, 89-90.

17. "Frye Journal," 349; "Relation of M Poularies," *RAPQ*, 1931-1932, 59; Hamilton, *Bougainville Journals*, 162-163; "Bartman Letters," 420-421.

18. Gabriel, *Desandrouins*, 90; "Relation of M Poularies," 59; Hamilton, *Bougainville Journals*, 165-166; *NY Col. Doc.*, X, 603.

19. "Frye Journal," 349-350; "A Journal Kept During the Siege of Fort William Henry," 147.

20. "Frye Journal," 350; Monro to Webb, 6 Aug, 1757, LO 4041A; Transactions at Fort William Henry During its Siege in August 1757, LO 6660.

21. *Montresor Journal*, 38-39; *N.H. Provincial Papers*, VI, 603-605; "Bartman Letters," 421-422. In keeping with Webb's resolve to abandon Fort Edward Bartman directed Christie on August 5 to send nothing but empty wagons up to the fort at this point. ("Bartman Letters," 421).

22. "Bartman Letters," 422-423; *Montresor Journal*, 26-27; *Gridley's Diary*, 47.

23. Hamilton, *Bougainville Journals*, 166-167; "A Message to Fort William Henry...," *Huntington Library Quarterly*, #16, 377.

24. "A Journal Kept During the Siege of Fort William Henry," 148-149; *NY Col. Doc.*, X, 603, 613; "Frye Journal," 351; Lt. Thomas Collins Remarks, LO 4394.

25. Gabriel, *Desandrouins*, 92; "Relation of M Poularies," *RAPQ*, 1931-1932, 59; Hamilton, *Bougainville Journals*, 167-168; *NY Col. Doc.*, X, 604, 614.

26. "A Journal Kept During the Siege of Fort William Henry," 148; *NY Col. Doc.*, X, 604, 614; Hamilton, *Bougainville Journals*, 168-169; Monro to Webb, 8 Aug, 1757, LO 4041.

The rumors of a relief force proved to be false and no relief force was ever dispatched from Fort Edward. In a later narrative, Jedediah Stickney of Frye's Massachusetts' troops expounded on a colorful rumor that William Johnson had started his march only to be called back by Webb. The two men were then said to have had heated words whereupon Johnson drew his sword and had to be physically restrained from running the general through. Although the account is pure fiction it does show the regard in which Johnson was held as compared to Webb, as well as attempting to address the belief that the garrison had been purposely abandoned to their fate. ("Massacre at Fort William Henry," *Essex Institute Historical Collections*, 3, (1861), 81.

27. "Bartman Letters," 422-423; *Montresor Journal*, 26-27; *Gridley's Diary*, 47.

28. Gabriel, *Desandrouins*, 93; "Relation of M Poularies," 60; *NY Col. Doc.*, X, 604; "A Journal Kept During the Siege of Fort William Henry," 149.

29. "Frye Journal," 356; "Roubaud's Letter," 179; Hamilton, *Bougainville Journal*, 172; *NY Col. Doc.*, X, 618-619, 633; Mante, *The History of the Late War in North America*, 95-96. Mante's accusation that the melee was instigated by a French partisan is partially supported by Captain Pouchot who speculated that the French interpreters, annoyed at not having obtained any booty, put their charges up to the affair. (Pouchot, *Memoirs*, 120.)

30. *Montresor Journal*, 28; Carver, *Travels*, 324; *Pennsylvania Gazette, 25 Aug, 1757*; "Fitch Diary," *Mayflower Descendent*, V, 252.

31. Steele, *Betrayals*, 133-139, 143-144; LO 4313; "Roubaud's Letter," 181. The camp followers in particular are impossible to account for. One account for instance states that the number of women and children was reduced from about eighty to ten in the incident. (*Pennsylvania Gazette, 18 Aug, 1757*. This statement, however, does not clarify whether they were killed, captured, or taken into custody by the French. Steele in his analysis of the casualties states that perhaps twenty-seven camp followers never returned from the campaign.

CHAPTER 3: RANGERS AND PARTISANS

1. Hamilton, *Bougainville Journal*, 178-180, 187; *NY Col. Doc*, X, 669, 836-837; Casgrain, *Levis Journal*, 103-105, 109-110.

2. Loescher, *The History of Rogers Rangers*, I, 63-65. Rogers' commission from Shirley, dated March 24, 1756, can be found in W.O.34/76.

3. *Montresor Journal*, 41-48; Rogers, *Journals, 56-59*; Loescher, *The History of Rogers Rangers*, I, 184-185. The Cadet company of fifty-five volunteers was officially disbanded seven weeks later. Several of the cadets, however, stayed with Rogers, twelve of whom later became officers in the Rangers. (Loescher, *The History of Rogers Rangers*, I, 185.

4. Loescher, *The History of Rogers Rangers*, I, 193-194. It seems far more likely that the sentries saw Clerk and let him pass without giving way their positions.

5. Ibid., 194-197; *Montresor Journal*, 50; *NY Col. Doc*, X, 836-837. Abercrombie's report of the scout is in LO 4915.

6. Loescher, *The History of Rogers Rangers*, I, 202-207; The Proceedings of Rogers Court of Inquiry (LO 4969) are printed in Appendix II of this text (304-309).

7. Loescher, *The History of Rogers Rangers*, I, 208-209 and Haviland to Abercromby, 16 Dec, 1757," (LO 6859) printed in Appendix II (309-311).

8. Rogers. *Journals*, 71-75; "Joshua Goodnough's Old Letter," *Harper's Magazine*, Nov. 1897, 878-889; *NY Col Doc*, X, 703, 837.

9. Loescher, *The History of Rogers Rangers*, I, 358-359; *NY Col. Doc*, X, 703, 837; Casgrain, *Lettres du Marquis de Montcalm*, 122.

10. Rogers, *Journals*, 75; Kimball, *Pitt Correspondence*, II, 191; Loescher, *The History of Rogers Rangers*, I, 213-218, 431-432.

11. Ibid., 218-221; Rogers, *Journals*, 75-78.

12. Loescher, *The History of Rogers Rangers*, I, 222-223. Rogers' plan is outlined in a January 13 letter to Loudoun (LO 5398).

13. Gipson, *The Victorious Years*, 150; Kimball, *Pitt Correspondence*, I, 193-194; Pargellis, *Military Affairs in North America*, 400-402; Instructions to Lord Howe, 2 Feb, 1758, W.O. 34/76.

14. *NY Col. Doc*, X, 691, 693, 697, 703, 837; "Fitch Diary," *Mayflower Descendent*, X, 187, XI, 145, 147; Loescher, *The History of Rogers Rangers*, I, 229-231.

15. "Fitch Diary," *Mayflower Descendent*, IX, 213, XI, 145-147; Loescher, *The History of Rogers Rangers*, I, 232-233. *NY Col. Doc*, X, 837.

16. Loescher, *The History of Rogers Rangers*, I, 233-237; Pargellis, *Lord Loudoun in North America*, 348-349; Kimball, *Pitt Correspondence*, I, 194; "Fitch Diary," *Mayflower Descendent*, XI, 221-222. Officially, Loudoun claimed that the expedition was called off because "the frost has at last set in so very hard that it will be impossible to erect batteries." (Kimball, *Pitt Correspondence*, I, 194)

17. Rogers, *Journals*, 79-80. Fitch identifies the Putnam's missing Ranger as John Robens. ("Fitch Diary," *Mayflower Descendent*, XI, 222)

18. Rogers, *Journals*, 79-83.

19. Ibid., 83-84.

20. Pouchot, *Memoirs*, 130; Hamilton, *Bougainville Journal*, 197-198; *NY Col. Doc.*, X, 837-838; Pouchot lists the strength of Durantaye's arriving detachment as two hundred native warriors and forty Canadians.

21. Casgrain, *Lettres de Bourlamaque*, 213; *NY Col. Doc*, X, 838; Rogers, *Journals*, 84.

22. Rogers, *Journals*, 84-85; "Relation of M Poularies," 78.

23. *NY Col. Doc*, X, 838; Rogers, *Journals*, 85-87.

24. Ibid., 64, 87, 91-92.

25. Loescher, *The History of Rogers Rangers*, I, 257-258. In the appendix to this volume Loescher gives a number of accounts concerning Rogers' escape down the face of Rogers Rock.

26. Rogers, *Journals*, 88; "Fitch Diary," *Mayflower Descendent*, XIII, 160-161.

27. Boutoun, *A History of Concord*, 200; Rogers, *Journals*, 87-102; *NY Col. Doc.* X, 693. Loescher, *The History of Rogers Rangers*, I, gives a complete breakdown of Rogers' losses, (369-371).

28. *NY Col. Doc.* X, 693, 697, 924; Casgrain, *Lettres de Bourlamaque*, 213-214. A reasonable assessment would seem to be that the French suffered at least as many casualties as Rogers.

CHAPTER 4: "AN IRRUPTION INTO CANADA BY WAY OF CROWN POINT"

1. Kimball, *Pitt Correspondence*, I, 134-140, 143-150, 151-153; Distribution of forces in North America for the Campaign of 1758, C.O. 5/50.

2. Kimball, *Pitt Correspondence*, I, 136-140, 143-150, 159. At the same time Pitt promoted all regular army lieutenant colonels to the rank of colonel in America only.

3. Ibid., I, 145, 151-153.

4. *Fitch Papers*, I, 328-330; Kimball, *Pitt Correspondence*, I, 192-194; Pargellis, *Military Affairs in North America*, 429-432.

5. Ibid.

6. Pargellis, *Military Affairs in North America*, 235.

7. *Dictionary of American Biography*, Vol. I, 28-29.

8. Parkman, *Montcalm and Wolfe*, II, 89-90; *Dict. American Biography*, IX, 287-288.

9. Grant, *Memiors of an American Lady*, 66-68.

10. *Dict. American Biography*, VII, 87-88; "Factors behind the Raising of the 80th Foot in America," *Military Collector & Historian*, (Winter 1959) 97-103.

11. John Bradstreet, *DCB*, Vol IV. For more on Bradstreet's background and future endevours the reader is directed to William Godfrey's, *Pursuit of Profit and Preferement in Colonial North America: John Bradstreet's Quest*, (1982).

12. Kimball, *Pitt Correspondence*, I, 203-204, 216, 221-222, 225-227, 234-235; *N.H. Provincial Papers*, VI, 659-660; *Journal of the Legislative Council of New York*, 1332-1333.

13. Kimball, *Pitt Correspondence*, I, 225-228; "The Disaster of Fort Ticonderoga: The Shortage of Muskets during the Mobilization of 1758," *Huntington Library Quarterly*, #3, 1951, 309.

14. *Collections of the New-York Historical Society for 1891*, 514-516; "The Disaster of Fort Ticonderoga. . .," 308; Kimball, *Pitt Correspondence*, I, 228.

15. "The Disaster of Fort Ticonderoga. . .," 311-312; Kimball, *Pitt Correspondence*, I, 261.

16. Ibid., 261-262. De Lancy was not alone. Fitch, Pownall, and Wentworth raised the question of impressing arms, but in each case their respective assemblies quickly laid the touchy matter aside. (Minutes of a council held in Boston, May 9, 1758, C.O.5/50; *Public Records of Connecticut*, XI, 123; *N.H. Provincial Papers VI*, 676).
"Mismanagement: The 1758 British Expedition Against Carillon," *FTMB*, #4 (1992), 261-262; Kimball, *Pitt Correspondence*, I, 261, 263; "The Disaster of Fort Ticonderoga. . .," 312-313.

17. Kimball, *Pitt Correspondence*, I, 248-256. The various governors reported the colonial arms available as of June 1 as, Massachusetts 3,000 to 4,000, New York 5,310, New Jersey 100, Connecticut 2000, Rhode Island 500. (Kimball, *Pitt Correspondence I*, 261, 264); Pownall to Abercromby 1 June, 1758 W.O. 34/25; *Records of the Colony of Rhode Island, VI*, 151; *Public Records of Connecticut, XI*, 123). If New Hampshire, which complained of a shortage of arms, procured 400 arms (half of the 800 required) and 3,500 is used for the reported Massachusetts portion then the total arms available comes to 11,810. The majority of Stanwix numbers are certainly included in those reported by the governors, yielding an approximate total of 12,000 arms available for the colonial forces.

18. Kimball, *Pitt Correspondence*, I, 145, 194, 231, 252-255; Godfrey, *Pursuit of Profit and Preferement in Colonial North America: John Bradstreet's Quest*, 116-118; "Diary of Benjamin Glasier," *EIHC*, 86 (1950) 71, 75.

19. Kimball, *Pitt Correspondence*, I, 253-254.

20. Pargellis, *Lord Loudoun in North America*, 298-299; "Mismanagement: The 1758 British Expedition Against Carillon," *FTMB*, #4 (1992), 254; Perry, *Recollections of an Old Soldier*, 9.

21. Thompson, *Diary*, 6; "A Journal of the Rev. Daniel Shute," 134; "Sweat's Diary," 39-40; Seth Tinkham's "Diary," in *The History of Plymouth County, Massachusetts*, 996.

22. Appy to Wood, 2 July, 1758, and Abercromby to Pitt, 29 June, 1758," C.O.5/50; "Ensign Aaron Guild Journal," in Plimpton, *The Dedication of a Monument...*, 16-17.

23. Abercromby to Pitt, 29 June, 1758, C.O.5/50. The regular and provincial returns dated June 29 are included in Abercromby's letter to Pitt. From these it appears that Abercomby was stating his regulars as effectives, given that the numbers from these returns yield a total of 7,050. It should also be pointed out that Abercromby left 200 provincials at Half Moon, 200 at Stillwater, 200 at Saratoga, and 200 at Fort Miller. In addition to this a company of the 60th was left at Albany, and two companies of the 42nd and 400 provincials were left to garrison Fort Edward.

24. JP, II, 843-854, 866.

25. Kimball, *Pitt Correspondence*, I, 259-260; *JP*, II, 845-854.

CHAPTER 5: MONTCALM AND VAUDREUIL

1. Hamilton, *Bougainville Journals*, 185, 187; Casgrain, *Levis Journal*, 118-119.

2. Ibid.,112-114; Casgrain, *Lettres du Marquis de Montcalm*, 88-89.

3. *NY Col. Doc.*, X, 686; Hamilton, *Bougainville Journals*, 188, 195, 201-202.

4. *NY Col. Doc.*, X, 704.

5. "Agriculture and War in Canada, 1740-1760," *CHR*, XVI, (June 1935), 123-130.

6. Casgrain, *Lettres and Pieces Militaires*, 25-28; *NY Col. Doc.*, X, 719. Levis' detachment was to consist of eight hundred Canadians, four hundred regulars, and four hundred troops of the Marine.

7. Casgrain, *Lettres and Pieces Militaires*, 29-32.

8. Casgrain, *Montcalm Journal*, 376.

9. Casgrain, *Lettres and Pieces Militaires*, 32-43.

10. Hamilton, *Bougainville Journals*, 206-207, 211-213, 219-221.

11. Rogers, *Journals*, 105-108; Hamilton, *Bougainville Journals*, 204, 208; *New American Magazine, May 1758*; Loescher, *The History of Rogers Rangers*, III, 26.

12. Hamilton, *Bougainville Journals*, 205, 209-210; *NY Col. Doc*, X, 710, 842; Loescher, *The History of Rogers Rangers*, III, 69.

13. Rogers, *Journals*, 108-110; Abercromby to Pitt, 29 June, 1758, C.O.5/50; Hamilton, *Bougainville Journals*, 213-214; *NY Col. Doc*, X, 843; "Journal of Rev. John Cleaveland," FTMB, #3 (1959), 193. Rogers' losses were five killed, three captured, and a few wounded including the Ranger leader himself.

14. Abercromby to Pitt, 29 June, 1758, C.O.5/50.

15. Loescher, *The History of Rogers Rangers*, II, 205-206, Appendix II; *NY Col. Doc.*, X, 892.

16. Casgrain, *Montcalm Journal*, 384-385; *NY Col. Doc.*, 732. The marquis was in desperate need of native detachments to conduct scouts and keep him abreast of the enemy's movements.

17. Hamilton, *Bougainville Journals*, 222-223; *NY Col. Doc.*, X, 721, 737, 844; "Relation of M Poularies," 80.

18. *NY Col. Doc*, X, 737-738; Hamilton, *Bougainville Journals*, 222-225.

19. Ibid., 225-226; "Relation of M Poularies," 80; *NY Col. Doc*, X, 722, 844-845.

20. Hamilton, *Bougainville Journals*, 226; *NY Col. Doc.*, X, 722, 738, 845, 894; "Relation of M Poularies," 81.

CHAPTER 6: LORD HOWE

1. Loring to —-, 19 Aug, 1758, Chatham Fonds MG23-A2, vol 8.

2. "Alexander Moneypenny's Orderly Book," *FTMB*, #5 (1969), 348-357, #6 (1970), 434-438; "Amos Richardson's Journal," *FTMB*, #4 (1968), 273-274; "The Journal of Captain Samuel Cobb," *FTMB*, #1 (1981), 17-18; "The Journal of Dr. Caleb Rea," *EIHC*, XVIII (1881), 101; "Journal of Lemuel Lyon," *The Military Journals of two Private Soldiers, 1758-1775*, 17-20; "Diary of Abel Spicer," *Spicer Genealogy*, 393. The organization of Abercromby's army was; *Regulars*: 1st Brigade (Haviland)—27th, 1st Batt 60th, 4th Batt 60th; 2nd Brigade (Grant)—42nd, 46th; 3rd Brigade (Donaldson)—55th, 44th; Eng Brigade (Clerk); Artillery (Ord) *Provincials*: Left Wing (Lyman)—1st Brig: Lyman, Fitch, 2nd Brig: Whiting, Wooster, 3rd Brig: Johnston, Babcock. Right Wing (Preble)—1st Brig: Preble, Williams, 2nd Brig: Ruggles, Bagley, 3rd Brig: Glazier, Woolsey *Rangers & Boatmen*: 80th, Rogers, Partridge, Doughty, Bradstreet, Johnson's Mohawks.

3. Abercromby to Pitt, 29 June, 1758, C.O.5/50; "Alexander Moneypenny's Orderly Book," *FTMB*, #5 (1969), 354; *NY Col. Doc.*, X, 892; *Pennsylvania Gazette, 27 July, 1758.*

4. Alexander Monneypenny's Orderly Book," #6 (1970), 439; "Journal of Lemuel Lyon," 20; "The Journal of Captain Samuel Cobb," 18.

5. "Alexander Moneypenny's Orderly Book," *FTMB*, #6 (1970), 438-439; Knox, *Journal*, I, 190; Order of March on Lake George, WO34/76; Abercromby to Pitt, 12 July, 1758, C.O.5/50; *Diary of Lt. Samuel Thompson*, 8-9; Samuel Fisher's Diary, LOC. Abercromby stated that the army embarked consisted of 6,367 regulars and 9,024 provincials, but given the late influx of colonial troops and their inconsistent returns, it is likely that this last number was a best estimate. (Abercromby to Pitt, 12 July, 1758, C.O.5/50).

6. *NY Col. Doc.*, X, 734; "Arnot Journal," in Westbrook's "Like Roaring Lions...," *FTMB*, XVI, (1998), 35; "Journal of Rev. John Cleveland," FTMB, X, (1959), 197; "Seth Tinkham's Diary," 996; *Memoir and Official Correspondence of Gen. John Stark*, 25.

7. Rogers, *Journals*, 111-112; "Arnot Journal," 36.

8. *Scot's Magazine, Aug 1758* and *Scot's Magazine, Appendix 1758*; Loring to —-, Aug 19, 1758, Chatham Fonds MG23-A2, vol 8.

9. Rogers, *Journals*, 112-113; "Arnot Journal," 36-37; Abercromby to Pitt, 12 July, 1758, C.O.5/50. The order of march was: leftmost column—Connecticut and Rhode Island regiments; left center column—44th, 55th, 46th, 42nd; right center column—27th, 4/60th, 1/60th; rightmost column—Massachusetts, New York, and New Jersey regiments, with one of the New York battalions having been left at the landing site. "Arnot's Journal," 37; "Monypenny Map," FTMB, #2, (1930); Order of March on Lake George, W.O.34/76; "Alexander Moneypenny's Orderly Book," #6 (1970), 436). In "Like Roaring Lions...," note 69, Westbrook cites a Connecticut provincial who states that the Massachusetts regiments march with the leftmost column. Based on the landing arrangements, the provincial brigading, and the firsthand accounts of the upcoming skirmish in predominantly Massachusetts journals it seems likely that this is mistaken.

10. Loring to —-, Aug 19, 1758, Chatham Fonds MG23-A2, vol 8; *NY Col. Doc.*, X, 747; "Major Moneypenny to John Calcraft, July 11, 1758," printed in Pell, *Fort Ticonderoga*, 27-29.

11. See *Gentleman's Magazine, September 1758*; *Hervey Journal*, 49; Abercromby to Pitt, 12

July, 1758, C.O.5/50 and Oliver Patridge to Wife, 12 July, 1758, *Isreal Williams Papers* MHS, to name but a few.

12. "Relation of M Poularies," 81; Hamilton, *Bougainville Journals*, 228; *NY Col. Doc.*, X, 722, 845. It seems far more likely that Langy, had he wished to return to Fort Carillon, would have followed the north bank of Trout Brook back to the La Chute River. Not only would this route have made it next to impossible to get lost but it would have afforded an excellent defensive position. By placing the Trout Brook between Langy and the English it would have forced the English to descend into the valley created by the stream if they wished to attack the detachment, giving the French the significant advantage of higher ground.

13. *NY Col. Doc.*, X, 747, 845. In the "LaPause Papers," (*RAPQ*, 1933-1934, 88) it states that Trepezac's orders were to observe the march of the enemy and ambush in the valley those elements left in the rear.

14. "The Journal of Dr. Caleb Rea,"103; "Journal of Colonel Archelaus Fuller. . .," *EIHC*, XLVI, (1910) 213.

15. Rogers, *Journals*, 113-114.

16. "Montcalm's Victory," *FTMB*, #2 (1936), 44, 47.

17. Perry, *Recollections of an Old Soldier*, 10.

18. *NY Col. Doc.*, X, 735.

19. Pargellis, *Military Affairs in North America*, 418-419.

20. "Arnot Journal," 36; *NY Col. Doc.*, X, 747. An anonymous French journal gives the French casualties as 4 officers and 184 soldiers killed or taken prisoner (*Relations et Journaux*, 164) while Montcalm in a letter to his wife a few days later claimed that he lost 8 officers and 183 men in the engagement ("Montcalm Correspondence," 73). One British account lists the casualties among the regulars as Howe, Lt. Cumberfort of the 80th, and eight men killed and another six wounded (*NY Col. Doc.*, X, 735). Provincial casualties are difficult to gauge, primarily because many of the missing eventually regained their units. A reasonable assessment would place provincial losses on the same order as those suffered by the regulars.

21. Samuel Fisher's Diary, LOC. Fisher concluded his journal entry on the skirmish with "Giving a true account of this fight is impossible." An anonymous account, seemingly from a member of the New York contingent, printed in *Gentlemen's Magazine* (*Sept 1758*) was more succinct. "The whole engagement was attended with the utmost confusion; where ever any firing was heard, thither all those who were not already engaged immediately rushed, and by that means brought the whole into disorder." The actual location of the skirmish is still in debate. Local tradition has it taking place near the present site of St. Mary's Cemetery in the western portion of the modern-day town of Ticonderoga. After reviewing the written evidence including Moneypenny's map and a map from John Almon's *Remembracer* printed in Gipson, *The Victorious Years*, 228, the author agrees with the general location. Another location, west, near the northeast corner of Bear Mountain and south of Trout Brook has been proposed by Bearor in his text *French and Indian War Battlesites: A Controversy*. A contemporary map in the Thomas Gage Papers at the William L. Clements Library supports this claim, showing the skirmish taking place near the one proposed by Bearor. Placing the engagement this far west, however, calls into question a good number, if not all, of the documents and eyewitnesses accounts surrounding this event.

22. Pargellis, *Military Affairs in North America*, 419; "James Abercrombie to Harry Erskine, 10 July, 1758," in Westbrook's "Like Roaring Lions. . .," *FTMB*, XVI, (1998), 68; "Mont-

calm's Victory," *FTMB*, #2 (1936), 44-45; *Hervey Journal*, 49; Oliver Patridge to Wife, 12 July, 1758, *Isreal Williams Papers* MHS; Abercromby to Pitt, 12 July, 1758, C.O.5/50; *The Lee Papers, NYHS Collections*, (1871), 10-11.

23. "Experiences in Early Wars in America," *Journal of American History*, (1907), 91; "Montcalm's Victory," *FTMB*, #2 (1936), 45; Pargellis, *Military Affairs in North America*, 419. A British officer in the 60th Regiment concurred with Eyre's assessment, saying, "I am certain had the enemy had 3 or 400 Indians with them at the beginning of this encounter, they would have beaten us and driven us to our bateaux. 'Tis a singular case that 350 men drove back and threw into considerable confusion about 11,000." (*NY Col. Doc.*, X, 735.)

24. *The Lee Papers*, 10; "Major Moneypenny to John Calcraft, 11 July, 1758," printed in Pell, *Fort Ticonderoga* (1935), 29.

CHAPTER 7: THE HEIGHTS OF CARILLON

1. Hamilton, *Bougainville Journals*, 226-228; Pouchot, *Memoirs*, 141-142; *NY Col. Doc.*, X, 722, 738, 845; "Relation of M Poularies," 81; Both Pouchot and Poularies speak to Bourlamaque's desire to resist the English landings.

2. Pouchot, *Memoirs*, 142; Hamilton, *Bougainville Journals*, 229; *NY Col. Doc.*, X, 738, 845.

3. Hamilton, *Bougainville Journals*, 231; *NY Col. Doc.*, X, 702.

4. *NY Col. Doc.*, X, 720. Like other regular French engineers such as Desandrouins and Pouchot, Pontleroy's opinions of works constructed by colonial engineers smacked of the professional rivalry that existed between the Department of War and the Department of the Marine. Added to this, one should consider the political rift that had occurred between Montcalm and his supporters, and the governor and his supporters. As we have seen, similar criticism of other engineers' works was prevalent among the English as well. In almost every case, be it French or English, the architect of the criticism never explores the background behind the works, that is, the circumstances, resources, and motivations under which the fortifications were formulated are never addressed. As for the actual state of the English on the evening of July 6, entries in *Montcalm's Journal* (394) and several other French sources for this date imply that the French command knew of Howe's death, but questions remain as to whether or not these journal entries were actually made on the stated date. A French deserter by the name of Jonas Mathie claimed during his interrogation that a pair of English deserters were taken by the French near the sawmills on the evening of the sixth, making it possible that Montcalm and his staff knew of Howe's death. However, one should consider a letter Montcalm wrote Vaudreuil on July 9 stating that he had just learned from three deserters and a letter found on a slain English officer that Lord Howe had been killed during the skirmish with Trepezac's detachment on the sixth. (Examination of Jonas Mathie, W.O. 34/75; *NY Col. Doc.*, X, 749.)

5. Hamilton, *Bougainville Journals*, 237; "The Strategy of Montcalm," *FTMB*, #3, (1953), 189-191.

6. "The Strategy of Montcalm," *FTMB*, #3, (1953), 183-197.

7. *NY Col. Doc.*, X, 706-710. D'Hugues, who had spent more time studying Fort Carillon than most French officers, had a better appreciation for the nature of forts in North America. Forts were purposely built small in the past he noted for two reasons. First, because the train of artillery necessary to take them had never been seen in the field before, and second because there were not enough men to garrison a large fort. Hence, such forts only needed to be secure enough to prevent being taken by surprise. (Note that 1 toise = 2.13 yards.)

8. "Relation of M Poularies," 81; Hamilton, *Bougainville Journals*, 229-230; *NY Col. Doc.*, X, 742; Gabriel, *Desandrouins*, 168.

9. Abercromby to Pitt, 12 July, 1758, C.O.5/50; Loring to —-, Aug 19, 1758. Chatham Fonds MG23-A2, vol 8; "The Journal of Dr. Caleb Rea," 103; "Col. Babcock Letter, July 10, 1758," in Chaplin, *A List of Rhode Island Soldiers and Sailors in the Old French and Indian War, 1755-1762*, 13; "Journal of the Rev. Daniel Shute," *EIHC*, (1874) 137.

10. Oliver Patridge to Wife, 12 July, 1758, *Isreal Williams Papers* MHS; Loring to —-, Aug 19, 1758, Chatham Fonds MG23-A2, vol 8; Abercromby to Pitt, 12 July, 1758, C.O.5/50; Pargellis, *Military Affairs in North America*, 419-420; *Hervey Journal*, 49-50.

11. Hamilton, *Bougainville Journals*, 230.

12. Gabriel, *Desandrouins*, 165-167; Pouchot, *Memoirs*, 137-138. "Flanked en Cremaillere" is how Desandrouins described the saw-toothed nature of the lines. (Gabriel, *Desandrouins*, 165.)

13. Pouchot, *Memiors*, 138. An interesting question is whether or not Montcalm consulted Lotinbiere on his plans. The latter wrote a letter to the Minister of War claiming that he spoke with the marquis on the merits of defending the heights of Carillon, convincing him to pursue this course of action. The letter, however, printed in *NY Col. Doc.*, X, 889-897, has remarks by the minister in the left-hand column claiming that it is filled with falsehoods and deceptions. A level of animosity existed between Montcalm and his supporters and Lotinbiere, who was a relative of Governor Vaudreuil, which was certainly communicated to the minister, but this in and of itself does not invalidate Lotinbiere's statements. Although it seems unlikely that Montcalm's plan to defend the heights of Carillon originated with Lotinbiere, the engineer, who had laid out and worked on the fort for the last three years, was a logical person to consult with regardless of whatever feelings the marquis held toward him. In the same vein it would seem an incredibly brazen act on the part of Lotinbiere, an officer of the Marine Department, to write the Minister of War of a fictitious conversation that he knew could be easily contradicted by a high-ranking regular officer, particularly one that was a protégé and old friend of the minister. What seems likely is that Montcalm did indeed speak with Lotinbiere on the matter, either to verify his own thoughts or as a courtesy to the colonial troops, and that Lotinbiere took it for more than it was. The conversation was then later denied by Montcalm as part of the ongoing fued between himself and Vaudreuil, leaving the engineer's letter to be viewed as yet another attempt by the governor to undermine the marquis' position and credability.

14. Quoted in Sautai, *Montcalm at the Battle of Carillon*, 66.

15. Parkman, *Montcalm and Wolfe*, II, 433-435; Bascom, "The Legend of Duncan Campbell," 36-37.

CHAPTER 8: SCARLET AND WOOD

1. "Spicer Journal," 406-407; Rogers, *Journals*, 114.

2. *Hervey Journal*, 50; *Scot's Magazine, Appendix 1758*; Abercromby to Pitt, 12 July, 1758, C.O.5/50. The foreign engineer Abercromby dispatched reported, "I saw completely clearly in front of me, and if there is an entrenchment there, it must be under the guns of the fort." (*Hervey Journal*, 50). Legend has it that when the detachment returned and met with Abercromby, Stark objected to Clerk and Abercrombie's assessment of the strength of the French lines. Although this may well have been Stark's opinion it is doubtful that he was ever given

a chance to express it before Abercromby or the council of war that followed shortly there-after. (*Memoir and Official Correspondence of Gen. John Stark, 26.*)

3. Abercromby to Pitt, 12 July, 1758, C.O.5/50; General Abercromby to Mr. Abercromby, 19 Aug, 1758, Chatham Fonds MG23-A2, vol 6. The conventional wisdom of the day called for at least a three-to-one numerical superiority when conducting a siege.

4. Loring to ——-, 19 Aug, 1758, Chatham Fonds MG23-A2, vol 8; Knox, *Journal*, I, 191; Abercromby to Pitt, 12 July, 1758, C.O.5/50; "J.B. Letter, 25 Aug, 1758," in "Like Roaring Lions. . .," *FTMB*, #1 (1998), 84-87; Pargellis, *Military Affairs in North America*, 420.

5. Such multitasking was nothing new for Major Eyre. One will recall in Johnson's Crown Point campaign that Eyre acted as chief engineer, head of the artillery, and quartermaster for the provincial army.

6. Pargellis, *Military Affairs in North America*, 420.

7. Abercromby to Pitt, 12 July, 1758, C.O.5/50; General Abercromby to Mr. Abercromby, 19 Aug, 1758, Chatham Fonds MG23-A2, vol 6; Pargellis, *Military Affairs in North America*, 420; Oliver Patridge to Wife, 12 July, 1758, *Isreal Williams Papers* MHS; "Arnot Journal," 40.

8. Hamilton, *Bougainville Journals*, 230-232; Pouchot, *Memoirs*, 145.

9. *NY Col. Doc.*, X, 739-740. Apparently the distance was not too great for one musket, as a French lieutenant by the name of d'Arenes is reported to have had his arm broken by a musket ball during this incident. (*NY Col. Doc.*, X, 723.)

10. Rogers, *Journals*, 114-115; Pouchot, *Memoirs*, 146.

11. "Joshua Goodnough's Old Letter," 886.

12. Oliver Patridge to Wife, 12 July, 1758, *Isreal Williams Papers* MHS; *Gentleman's Magazine, Sept 1758.*

13. "Relation of M Poularies," 81-82; "LaPause Papers," *RAPQ, 1931-32*, 353-354; Hamilton, *Bougainville Journals*, 231-232.

14. "Relation of M Poularies," 81-82; Gabriel, *Desandrouins*, 167.

15. "Joshua Goodnough's Old Letter," 886; "Montcalm's Victory," *FTMB*, #2 (1936), 45.

16. Pargellis, *Military Affairs in North America*, 420; "Alexander Moneypenny's Orderly Book," *FTMB*, #6, 460-461; Abercromby to Pitt, 12 July, 1758, C.O.5/50. Note part of Moneypenny's entry for August 7 is out of order and pertains to the attack on July 8.

17. Pargellis, *Military Affairs in North America*, 420; "James Abercrombie to Harry Erskine, 10 July, 1758," in Westbrook's "Like Roaring Lions. . .," *FTMB*, #1 (1998), 68-69.

18. *NY Col. Doc.*, X, 736; Pargellis, *Military Affairs in North America*, 420-421; "Like Roaring Lions. . .," *FTMB*, #1 (1998), 85.

19. Hamilton, *Bougainville Journals*, 232; Pouchot, *Memoirs*, 146; Gabriel, *Desandrouins*, 175; "LaPause Papers," *RAPQ, 1931-32*, 353-354.

20. *NY Col. Doc.*, X, 846; "LaPause Papers," *RAPQ, 1931-32*, 353-354; "Montcalm's Orders of Battle," *FTMB*, #2 (1930), 67-69.

21. Knox, *Journal*, I, 192.

22. *Pennsylvania Gazette, 27 July, 1758*; Rogers, *Journals*, 115-116; *NY Col. Doc*, X, 723, 735-736, 740, 749, 846, 896; Dr. James Searing, "The Battle of Ticonderoga, 1758," *New York Historical Society Proceedings*, (Oct 1847), 116; Hamilton, *Bougainville Journals*, 233; "French and Indian War Diary of Benjamin Glasier of Ipswich, 1758-1760." *EIHC*, Vol 86 (1950), 76. The French claim to have sunk or swamped two barges while the English make

no mention of any loss in this incident. It seems likely that the French did succeed in sinking or at least damaging the artillery rafts, for the English did not make a second attempt to land their artillery even though news of the aborted attempt must have reached Clerk before the engineer was fatally wounded.

23. *Scot's Magazine, Aug 1758* and *Appendix for 1758*. Grant was an extremely popular officer among men. When the lieutenant colonelcy of the regiment became open his men collected a sum of money to purchase the position for Major Grant. The money, however, was not required as the promotion was issued without purchase. (Stewart, *Sketches of the Highlanders of Scotland*, I, 295.)

24. "Arnot Journal," 41; *CHR*, II, (1921), 361; Stewart, *Sketches. . .of the Highlanders of Scotland*, I, 301-302; *Pennsylvania Gazette, 27 Aug 3, 1758*; "Cleveland Journal," 198; "Spicer Journal," 305.

25. "Cleveland Journal," 199; *Pennsylvania Gazette, 3 Aug, 1758*; "Col. Babcock Letter, July 10, 1758," in Chaplin, *A List of Rhode Island Soldiers and Saliors in the Old French and Indian War, 1755-1762*, 13.

26. "Montcalm's Victory," *FTMB*, #2 (1936), 45; "Joseph Nichols Journal," MS. HM 89, Huntington Library; "Captain James Murray Letter, July 19, 1758," in Richards, *The Black Watch at Ticonderoga*, 24.

27. "Montcalm's Victory," *FTMB*, #2 (1936), 46; Perry, *Recollections of an Old Soldier*, 11-12.

28. "Eyewitnesses' Accounts of the British Repulse at Ticonderoga," *CHR*, vol. 2 (Dec. 1921), 362; "Goodnough's Old Letter," 887-888; Pouchot, *Memiors*, 147; "Fuller Journal," 214.

29. Pouchot, *Memiors*, 147-148; "Relation of M Poularies," 82; Gabriel, *Desandrouins*, 180. "I began to get suspicious and ordered the troops to fire on them having done so myself," Poularies wrote of the incident. English accounts of this incident can be found in *Scot's Magazine, August 1758, Pennsylvania Gazette, 3 Aug, 1758*, and "The Journal of Dr. Caleb Rea," 105, among others.

30. *NY Col. Doc.*, X, 740, 743; "Relation of M Poularies," 82; Gabriel, *Desandrouins*, 181.

31. Hamilton, *Bougainville Journals*, 238, 254; *NY Col. Doc.*, X, 749, 754.

32. Gabriel, *Desandrouins*, 176.

33. Samuel Fisher Diary, LOC.

34. *NY Col. Doc.*, X, 740, 796; *Lee Papers*, I, 12.

35. Rogers, *Journals*, 116; *Lee Papers*, I, 13; "James Abercrombie to Harry Erskine, 10 July, 1758," in Westbrook's "Like Roaring Lions. . .," *FTMB*, #1 (1998), 69; Loring to —-, 19 Aug, 1758, Chatham Fonds MG23-A2, vol 8; Perry, *Recollections of an Old Soldier*, 13.

CHAPTER 9: "VERY FINE LIMBS, BUT NO HEAD"

1. Loring to —-, 19 Aug, 1758, Chatham Fonds MG23-A2, vol 8; *Lee Papers*, I, 13; "Col. Babcock Letter, 10 July, 1758," in Chaplin, *A List of Rhode Island Soldiers. . . 1755-1762*, 13; Col. William Williams Letter, 11 July, 1758, *Isreal Williams Papers*, MHS.

2. *Hervey Journal*, 50; "James Abercrombie to Harry Erskine, 10 July, 1758," 69; General Abercromby to James Abercromby, 19 Aug, 1758, Chatham Fonds MG23-A2, vol 6; "Spicer Journal," 395, 407-408.

3. Oliver Patridge to Wife, 12 July, 1758, *Isreal Williams Papers* MHS; "Fuller Journal," 214;

Loring to —-, 19 Aug, 1758, Chatham Fonds MG23-A2, vol 8; "The Journal of Henry Champion," in Trowbridge, *Champion Genealogy*, 419; "Journal of Lemuel Lyon," 23.

4. "Experiences in Early Wars in America," *Journal of American History*, (1907), 92; Samuel Fisher's Diary, LOC; "Spicer Journal," 395, 408; Loring to —-, 19 Aug, 1758, Chatham Fonds MG23-A2, vol 8; *Gentleman's Magazine, September 1758*; "Journal of Lemuel Lyon," 23; *Lee Papers*, I, 14; *Hervey Journals*, 50. Both Captain Charles Lee and Captain William Hervey claimed that Abercromby was among the first to set sail.

5. *NY Col. Doc.*, X, 724-725; Casgrain, *Levis Journal*, 138-139.

6. "Relation of M Poularies," 84; Casgrain, *Levis Journal*, 138-140; Pouchot, *Memiors*, 150; *NY Col. Doc.*, X, 724-725, 740-741, 847-848.

7. Gabriel, *Desandrouins*, 187.

8. Captain Lee held that Clerk was "a stripling, who had never seen the least service and of scarcely any rank on the establishment." (*Lee Papers*, I, 12.) General James Wolf, however, was among those who thought otherwise, saying, "young Clarke (Clerk) under my Lord Howe. . .will make a good figure as an engineer for the field." (Heinermann, *The Life and Letters of James Wolf*, 369.)

9. Loring to —-, 19 Aug, 1758, Chatham Fonds MG23-A2, vol 8; "James Abercrombie to Harry Erskine, 10 July, 1758," 69.

10. "James Abercrombie to Harry Erskine, 10 July, 1758," 69; General Abercromby to James Abercromby, 19 Aug, 1758, Chatham Fonds MG23-A2, vol 6; Hamilton, *Bougainville Journals*, 255; "A Journal of the Rev. Daniel Shute," 137-138. An officer of the 44th by the name of Elver supported Captain Abercrombie's claim. He informed Rev. Cleveland on July 27 that "his solid opinion was that the reason why the general ordered the retreat from Ticonderoga was his harkening to boys who never saw a fight and neglecting to ask counsel of knowing officers." ("Cleveland Journal," 205.)

11. "Spicer Journal," 394, 407; "Journal of Lemuel Lyon," 22-23; "The Journal of Captain Samuel Cobb," *FTMB*, #1 (1981), 19; Samuel Fisher's Diary, LOC. Eyre noted in a letter to a friend regarding the battle that "we had part of our artillery not far from the rear of the attack, but no use was made of them either before or after," (Pargellis, *Military Affairs in North America*, 422), and Colonel Williams, confounded by the lack of organization complained in a letter to his uncle a few days later, "I know not of one single order given from 5 o'clock in the morning to 5 at night." (Col. William Williams Letter, 11 July, 1758," *Isreal Williams Papers*, MHS.)

12. Loring to —-, 19 Aug, 1758, Chatham Fonds MG23-A2, vol 8; Col. William Williams Letter, 11 July, 1758, *Isreal Williams Papers*, MHS; *Lee Papers*, I, 7-8, 14. See Appendix B for French and British casualty returns.

13. "The Journal of Dr. Caleb Rea," 106; "Captian William Sweat's Personal Diary of the Expedition against Ticonderoga May 2—Nov 7, 1758." *EIHC* , (1957) 44.

14. Abercromby to Pitt, 12 July, 1758, C.O.5/50; General Abercromby to James Abercromby, 19 Aug , 1758, Chatham Fonds MG23-A2, vol 6. Among the field officers killed were Brigadier General Lord Augustus Howe, Colonel John Donaldson commander of the 55th, Colonel Samuel Beaver commander of the 46th, Major John Rutherford of the 4th batt/60th, Major Thomas Proby of the 55th, and Major Duncan Campbell of the 42nd (died of wounds July 17). Wounded were Major William Eyre of the 44th, Major William Browning of the 46th, and Major John Tullikins of the 1st Batt/60th. Added to this, but

not listed in the returns, were Colonel Francis Grant commander of the 42nd, and Colonel Frederick Haldimand commander of the 1st Batt/60th both of whom were slightly wounded. (*NY Col. Doc.*, X, 728-732.)

15. Council of War at Lake George, 13 July, 1758, and Abercromby to Bradstreet, 13 July,1758 in Preston, *Royal Fort Frontenac*, 256-258.

16. Rogers, *Journals*, 117-118; Abercromby to Pitt, 19 Aug, 1758, C.O.5/50; "Cleveland Journal," 209; "Spicer Journal," 400; Loescher, *The History of Rogers Rangers*, II, 17, 211.

17. Hamilton, *Bougainville Journals*, 258, 260; *NY Col. Doc.*, X, 818, 851.

18. Rogers, *Journals*, 117-119; Abercromby to Pitt, 19 Aug, 1758, C.O.5/50; *New American Magazine, Aug 1758*; "Cleveland Journal," 209-211; "Spicer Journal," 400-401; Loescher, The *History of Rogers Rangers*, II, 17-18, 211; Hamilton, *Bougainville Journals*, 261-262; "Relation of M Poularies," 85; *NY Col. Doc.*, X, 818-819, 851. Rogers gave his losses at thirty-three killed or missing and forty wounded. In his official report, Marin listed ten killed and twelve wounded. This is at odds with Rogers' report of the battlefield and the general nature of the engagement. Unofficially, Marin was probably not anxious to quantify his casualties for fear of appearing bested after preparing an ambush, or perhaps he simply never had a clear account of how many troops he actually had with him at the time and thus could never give a true account of his losses.

19. "Alexander Moneypenny's Orderly Book," *FTMB*, #1 (1970), 96; "Cleveland Journal," 215-216; Kimball, *Pitt Correspondence*, I, 343-345.

20. *An Impartial Account of Lt. Col Bradstreet's Expedition to Fort Frontenac*, 1-31; "The Journal of Benjamin Bass," *NY History Magazine*, (Oct 1935), 449-452; "Colonel Charles Clinton's Journal," *FTMB*, #4 (1992), 293-315; Bradstreet to Abercromby, 31 Aug, 8 Sept, 13 Sept, 1758, C.O.5/50; MacAulay to Gates, 30 Aug, C.O.5/50.

21. *Pennsylvania Gazette, 14 Sept, 1758*.

10. VICTORY, DIVISION, AND RECALL

1. *NY Col. Doc.*, X, 749, 753-754.

2. Ibid., 753-754.

3. Ibid., 780-782, 788-798. One point of contention became the actual number of Marine and Canadian troops present during the battle. On July 28 Vaudreuil wrote the Minister of the Marine informing him that 326 Marines, 844 Canadians, and 40 Indians were present with Montcalm's troops while another 80 Marines and 273 Canadians arrived at the start of the action. ("Vaudreuil to Minister, July 28, 1758," Collection Moreau St. Mery.) In his journal Bougainville counters such claims with a tally of the forces under Montcalm's command for July 6 through July 8 showing a total of 591 Marines and Canadians present, with another 338 arriving the afternoon of the battle. (Hamilton, *Bougainville Journals*, 254.)

4. *NY Col. Doc.*, X, 757.

5. Ibid., 757-758.

6. Ibid., 770, 779-783.

7. "Montcalm's Correspondence," 73; *NY Col. Doc.*, X, 733, 778-779, 783.

8. Ibid., 778-779, 810, 812-813, 831-832; Hamilton, *Bougainville Journals*, 260.

9. *NY Col. Doc.*, X, 812-813. "I should live on the best terms with them," Bigot informed the Minister of the Marine, "but I doubt if they will do the same; their hauteur is too much opposed the one to the other."

10. "Alexander Moneypenny's Orderly Book," *FTMB*, #1 (1970), 97-109; "The Journal of Henry Champion," 428-431; "The Journal of Captain Samuel Cobb," *FTMB*, #1 (1981), 25-28; "Spicer Journal," 404; *By Wind and Iron*, 194-196; *Fitch Papers*, I, 352-353.

11. "Cleveland Journal," 221, 229; Kimball, *Pitt Correspondence*, I, 365, 399; Webster, *The Journal of Jeffery Amherst*, 89-92.

12. "Alexander Moneypenny's Orderly Book," *FTMB*, #1 (1970), 114-116, #2 (1971), 151-152; Kimball, *Pitt Correspondence*, I, 401-402; "Experiences in Early Wars in America," 92.

APPENDIX C: EYEWITNESS ACCOUNTS

1. "Diary of Abel Spicer," *Spicer Genealogy*, 71-73.

2. Ibid., 394-395, 406-408.

3. W.A.B. Douglas, "Joshua Loring," *Dictionary Canadian Biography*, IV; Knox, *Journal*, II, 140-143, 409-413.

4. Chatham Fonds MG23-A2, vol 8.

5. Laramie, "Where Duty Leads: Lt. Col. William Eyre," *Journal of America's Military Past*, XLVII, No. 1 (Winter 2022), 5-30.

6. Pargellis, *Military Affairs in North America*, 418-422.

7. Taillemite, "Gabriel de Maurès de Malartic," *DCB*, IV; Malartic, Gabriel de Maurès de. *Journal des campagnes au Canada de 1755 à 1760 par le comte de Maurès de Malartic*, Ed. Paul Gaffarel Paris: Libairie Plon, 1890.

8. *NY Col. Doc., X*, 722-725.

BIBLIOGRAPHY

MANUSCRIPT SOURCES

France, Archives Nationales. (Paris)
    Sèrie C11A, Canada et Dépendances (Lettres des Gouverneurs,
    Intendants, officers et autres)
    Sèrie F3 Collection Moreau de Saint-Méry
Canada. National Archives. (Ottawa)
    Manuscript Division
    MG1: Fonds des Colonies
    C11A—Correspondance générale
    MG7: Bibliothèque nationale
    IA2—Département des manuscrits, Fonds français
    MG18: Pre-Conquest Papers
    K9—Bourlamaque Papers
    N21—Williamson Papers
    MG23: Late Eighteenth Century Papers
    A2—Chatham Papers
Great Britain, Public Record Office (London)
    Colonial Office
    C.O.5, America and West Indies, Correspondence, originals on
    microfilm
    War Office
    W.O.34, Amherst Papers, originals on microfilm
United States, Library of Congress (Washington D.C.)
    Fisher, Samuel. Diary, 1758. Manuscript Division
Massachusetts Historical Society (Boston)
    Isreal Williams Papers.

PRINTED SOURCES

Albertson, Garrett. "Montcalm's Victory." *The Bulletin of the Fort Ticonderoga Museum,* IV, #2 (1936), 43-47.

Ambler, Charles. *George Washington and the West.* New York: Russell & Russell, 1936 (1971).

Amherst, Jeffery. Jeffery Amherst Papers. Great Britain, Public Records Office, W.O. 34.

Anderson, Fred W. "Why did Colonial New Englanders Make Bad Soldiers?" *William and Mary Quarterly,* 38 (1981), 395-417.

Anderson, Fred W. *A People's Army: Massachusetts Soldiers and Society in the Seven Years' War.* Chapel Hill: University of North Carolina Press, 1984.

Anon. *La Campagne de 1755.* Montreal: C.A, Marchand, 1900.

Anon. "Attack and Repulse at Ticonderoga, July 1758." *The Bulletin of the Fort Ticonderoga Museum,* VII, #1 (1945), 15-18.

Anon. "The Building of the Fort," *Fort Ticonderoga Museum Bulletin,* II, #3 (1931), 88-97.

Bartlett, John Russell, ed. *Records of the Colony of Rhode Island and Providence Plantations in New England.* 10 vols.; Providence: A. C. Greene, 1856-65.

Bascom, Robert. "The Legend of Duncan Campbell." *Proceedings of the New York State Historical Association,* 1902, vol. 2 (1902), pp. 32-38.

Bass, Benjamin. "The Journal of Benjamin Bass," *New York. History,* XVI, (1935), 449-452.

Beatson, Robert. *Naval and Military Memoirs of Great Britain from 1727 to 1783.* 6 vols.; Aberdeen: J. Chalmers & Co., 1804.

Blodget, Samuel. *The Battle near Lake George in 1755: A prospective Plan with an Explanation Thereof.* London: 1756. London: Henry Stevens, Son & Stiles, 1911.

Boston News-Letter, Boston.

Boston Post Boy, Boston.

Bougainville, Louis Antoine. *Adventure in the Wilderness: The American Journals of Louis Antoine de Bougainville, 1756-1760.* (Trans. and ed.) Edward P. Hamilton. Norman: University of Oklahoma Press, 1964.

Bouton, Nathaniel. *Provincial Papers, Documents and Records Relating to the Province of New Hampshire from 1738 to 1749, Vol. V.* Nashua: Orren C. Moore, 1871.

Bouton, Nathaniel. *Provincial Papers, Dicuments and Records Relating to the Province of New Hampshire from 1749 to 1763, Vol. VI.* Manchester: James Campbell, 1872.

Bouton, Nathaniel. *A History of Concord, (N.H.)*. Concord: B.W. Sanborn, 1856.

Bradstreet, John. *An Impartial Account of Lt. Col Bradstreet's Expedition to Fort Frontenac*. London: T. Wilcox, 1759.

Buell, Rowena, ed. *The Memoirs of Rufus Putnam*. Boston: Houghton, Mifflin & Co., 1903.

Bulter, Lewis. *The Annals of the King's Royal Rifle Corps*. 7 vols.; London: Smith, Elder & Co., 1913.

Cardwell, John M. "Mismanagement: The 1758 Expedition Against Carillon." *The Bulletin of the Fort Ticonderoga Museum*, XV, #4 (1992), 236-291.

Casgrain, H.R., ed. *Collection des Manuscrits du Maréchal de Lévis*. 12 vols.; Montreal and Quebec: C.O. Beauchemin & Fils and Demers & Frère, 1889-1895. The individual volumes in this collection are:

    Vol 1: Journal du Chevalier de Levis.

    Vol 2: Lettres du Chevalier de Levis.

    Vol 3: Lettres de la Cour de Versailles.

    Vol 4: Pièces Militaires.

    Vol 5: Lettres du M. de Bourlamaque.

    Vol 6: Lettres du Marquis de Montcalm.

    Vol 7: Journal du Marquis de Montcalm.

    Vol 8: Lettres du Marquis de Vaudreuil.

    Vol 9: Lettres de L'Intendant Bigot.

    Vol 10: Lettres de Divers Particuliers.

    Vol 11: Relations et Journaux de différentes expeditions faites Durant les années 1755, 1756, 1757, 1758, 1759, 1760.

    Vol 12: Table Analytique.

Chapin, Howard M. *A List of Rhode Island Soldiers & Sailors in the Old French and Indian War, 1755-1762*. Providence: Rhode Island Historical Society, 1918.

Chapais, Thomas. *The Marquis de Montcalm*. Quebec: J.P. Garneau, 1911.

Clayton, T.R. "The Duke of Newcastle, the Earl of Halifax, and the American Origins of the Seven Years' War." *Historical Journal*, vol. 24, no. 3, (1981), 571-603.

Cleaveland, John. "Journal of Rev. John Cleaveland," *Fort Ticonderoga Musuem Bulletin*, X, #3 (1959), 192-236.

Cobb, Samuel. "The Journal of Captain Samuel Cobb, 21 May—29 October, 1758." *The Bulletin of the Fort Ticonderoga Museum*, XIV, #1 (1981), 12-31.

Collections of the New-York Historical Society for the Year 1921: Cadwaller Colden Papers, V, 1755-1760. New York: The New York Historical Society, 1923.

Collections of the New-York Historical Society for the Year 1881: Montresor Journals. New York: The New York Historical Society, 1882.

Collections of the Connecticut Historical Society, XVII: Fitch Papers, Vol I. Hartford: Connecticut Historical Society, 1918.

Collections of the Connecticut Historical Society, XVIII: Fitch Papers, Vol II. Hartford: Connecticut Historical Society, 1918.

Collections of the New-York Historical Society for the Year 1891: Muster Rolls of New York Provincial Troops, 1755-1764. New York: The New York Historical Society, 1892.

Collections of the New-York Historical Society for the Year 1871: Charles Lee Papers. New York: The New York Historical Society, 1872.

"Colonel Charles Clinton's Journal," *FTMB*, #4 (1992), 293-315.

Corbett, Julian S. *England in the Seven Years War: A Study in Combined Strategy.* 2 vols.; Longman, Green, & Co., 1907.

Craig, Neville B. *Olden Times*, 2 vols.: Pittsburgh: J.W. Cook, 1846-1847.

Cunes, John R. "Factors Behind the Raising of the 80th Foot in America." *Military Collector and Historian*, #11 (Winter 1959), 97-103.

Cutter, Benjamin. *A History of the Cutter Family of New England.* Boston: David Clapp & Son, 1871.

Dictionary of Canadian Biography. 12 vols. and index; Toronto: 1966-1991.

"Eyewitnesses' Accounts of the British Repulse at Ticonderoga," *Canadian Historical Review*, vol. 2 (Dec 1921), 360-363.

Fauteux, Aegidus. "Officiers de Montcalm," *Revue d'Histoire de l'Amérique Française*, III, #3 (December 1949), 367-382.

Fauteux, Aegidus. "Quelques officiers de Montcalm," *Revue d'Histoire de l'Amérique Française*, V, #3 (December 1951), 404-415.

Fisher, Samuel. Diary, 1758. Manuscript, Library of Congress.

Fitch, Jabez. "The Diary of Jabez Fitch, Jr." *Mayflower Descendent*, vols. 1–13, (1899-1911), various.

Ford, Worthington. *British Officers Serving in North America, 1754-1774.* Boston: David Clapp & Son, 1894.

Fowler, William Chauncey. *The History of Durham, Connecticut.* Hartford: Wiley, Waterman & Eaton, 1866.

Fuller, Archelaus. "Journal of Colonel Archelaus Fuller of Middleton, Mass., in the expedition against Ticonderoga in 1758." *Essex Institute Historical Collections*, vol. 46 (1910), 209-220.

Furcron, Thomas B. "The Building of Fort Ticonderoga, 1755-1758." *Fort Ticonderoga Musuem Bulletin,* (1955), 13-67.

Gabriel, Abbé Charles-Nicolas. *Le Maréchal de camp Desandrouins, 1729-1972.* 2 vols.; Verdun: Renvé-Lallement, 1887.

Gentleman's Magazine, London.

Gipson, Lawrence Henry. *The British Empire Before the American Revolution, Volume VI: The Great War for the Empire, The Years of Defeat, 1754-1757.* New York: Alfred A. Knopf, 1949.

Gipson, Lawrence Henry. *The British Empire Before the American Revolution, Volume VII: The Great War for the Empire, The Victorious Years, 1758-1760.* New York: Alfred A. Knopf, 1946.

Glasier, Benjamin. "French and Indian War Diary of Benjamin Glasier of Ipswich, 1758-1760." *Essex Institute Historical Collections,* vol. 86 (1950), 65-92.

Godfrey, William G. *Pursuit of Profit and Preferement in Colonial North America: John Bradstreet's Quest.* Waterloo, Ont.: Wilfrid Laurier University Press, 1982.

Grant, Anne MacVicar. *Memiors of an American Lady.* New York: S. Campbell, 1809.

Hervey, William. *Journals of the Hon. William Hervey.* Bury St. Edwards, England: Paul & Mathew, 1906.

Higonnet, Patrice Louis-René. "The Origins of the Seven Years' War," *Journal of Modern History,* no. 40 (March 1968), 57-90.

Hotblack, Kate. *Chatham's Colonial Policy.* London: George Rutledge & Sons, 1917.

Hunt, George T. *The Wars of the Iroquois: A Study in Intertribal Relations.* Madison: The University of Wisconsin Press, 1967.

Hurd, D. Hamilton. *The History of Plymouth County, Massachusetts.* 2 vols.; Philadelphia: J.W. Lewis & Co., 1884.

Johnson, Allen and Malone, Dumas. *Dictionary of American Biography,* 22 vols. New York: Charles Scribner's Sons, 1943.

Journal of the Legislative Council of the Colony of New York, Begun the 8th day of December 1743 and ended the 3rd of April 1775. Albany: Weed, Parsons & Co., 1861.

Kimball, Gertrude Selwyn, ed. *The Correspondence of the Colonial Governors of Rhode Island, 1723-1775.* 2 vols.; New York: Houghton, Mifflin & Co., 1902-1903.

Kimball, Gertrude Selwyn, ed. *The Correspondence of William Pitt.* 2 vols.; New York: The Macmillan Co., 1906.

Knox, John. *An Historical Journal of the Campaigns in North America for the Years 1757, 1758, 1759, and 1760.* 2 vols.; London: 1764. Edited by Arthur G. Doughty and reprinted in 3 vols., Freeport, New York: Libraries Press, 1970.

Kopperman, Paul. *Braddock at the Monongahela.* Pittsburgh: University of Pittsburgh, 1977.

Lanctot, Gustave. *A History of Canada, 1600-1763.* 3 vols.; Trans. Josephine Hambleton and Margaret Cameron. Cambridge: Harvard University Press, 1963-65.

Laramie, Michael G. *By Wind and Iron.* Yardley, PA: Westholme, 2015.

Laramie, Michael G. "Where Duty Leads: Lt. Col. William Eyre," *Journal of America's Military Past*, XLVII, no. 1 (Winter 2022), 5-30.

Lecky, William Edward Hartpole. *A History of England in the Eighteenth Century.* 8 vols.; New York: D. Appleton and Co., 1878-1917.

Lincoln, Charles H., ed. *The Correspondence of William Shirley, Governor of Massachusetts and Military Commander in America, 1731-1760.* 2 vols.; New York: The Macmillan Co., 1912.

Loescher, Burt Garfield. *The History of Rogers Rangers.* 2 vols.; San Franciso, 1946 and San Mateo, CA, 1969.

Loudoun, Earl of Loudoun Papers, Huntington Library, San Marino, CA.

Lunn, Jean Elizabeth. "Agriculture and War in Canada, 1740-1760." *Canadian Historical Review,* 16 (1935), 123-136.

Malartic, Gabriel de Maurès de. *Journal des campagnes au Canada de 1755 à 1760 par le comte de Maurès de Malartic.* Ed. Paul Gaffarel Paris: Libairie Plon, 1890.

Mante, Thomas. *The History of the Late War in North America.* London: 1772. New York: Research Reprints Inc., 1970.

Meech, Susan Spicer, and Meech, Susan Billings. *History of the Descendants of Peter Spicer, a landholder in New London, Connecticut, as early as 1666.* Boston: Gilson, 1911.

McCulloch, Lt. Col. Ian. "Men of the 27th Foot: Lt. Col. Archibald Gordon." *Fort Ticonderoga Musuem Bulletin,* XVI, #2, (1999), 128-151.

McCulloch, Lt. Col. Ian. "Men of the 27th Foot: Thomas Busby, Grenadier." *Fort Ticonderoga Musuem Bulletin,* XVI, #2, (1999), 119-127.

McDonald, de Lery A. "Michel Chartier de Lotbiniere the Engineer of Carillon." *New York History,* XV (1934), 31-38.

Montcalm, Marquis de."Montcalm's Orders of Battle," *The Bulletin of the Fort Ticonderoga Museum,* II, #2 (1930), 67-69.

Moneypenny, Alexander. "Moneypenny Orderly Book." *The Bulletin of the Fort Ticonderoga Museum,* II, #2 (1930), 56-67; XII, #5 (1969), 328-357;

XII, #6 (1970), 434-461; XIII, #1 (1970), 89-116; XIII, #2 (1971), 151-184.

New American Magazine, Philadelphia.

O'Callaghan, E.B., ed. *Documents Relative to the Colonial History of the State of New York.* 15 vols.; Albany: Weed, Parsons & Co., 1856-1877.

O'Callaghan, E.B., ed. *Documentary History of New York.* 4 vols.; Albany: Weed, Parsons & Co., 1849-1851.

Pargellis, Stanley M. *Lord Loudoun in North America.* New Haven: Yale Historical Publications, 1933.

Pargellis, Stanley M., ed. *Military Affairs in North America, 1748-1765.* New York: D. Appleton-Century Co., Inc., 1936.

Parkman, Francis. *Montcalm and Wolfe.* 2 vols. Boston: Little, Brown, and Co., 1885.

Pease, Theodore Calvin, ed. *Anglo-French Boundary Disputes in the West, 1749-1763.* Springfield: Collections of the Illinois State Historical Library, 1936.

Pell, Robert, T. "Montcalm: Origins and First Steps." *The Bulletin of the Fort Ticonderoga Museum*, VIII, #4 (1949), 131-159.

Pell, S.H.P. *Fort Ticonderoga: A Short History.* Ticonderoga, NY: Fort Ticonderoga Museum, 1966.

Pell, Robert, T. "The Strategy of Montcalm." *The Bulletin of the Fort Ticonderoga Museum*, IX, #3 (1953), 175-201.

Pennsylvania Gazette, Philadelphia.

Perry, Arthur Latham. *Origins in Williamstown.* New York: Charles Scribner's Sons, 1894.

Perry, David. *Recollections of an Old Soldier.* Windsor, VT: 1822. Cottonport, La.: Polyanthos Press, 1971.

Plimpton, George. The Dedication of a Monument to the Men of Walpole. Walpole, Mass.: Private Publish, 1902.

Pomeroy, Seth. *The Journals and Papers of Seth Pomeroy.* Ed. Louis Effingham de Forest. New Haven: Tuttle, Morehouse & Taylor Co., 1926.

Pond, Peter. "Experiences in Early Wars in America: Journal of Peter Pond, Born in 1740," *The Journal of American History*, I, #1 (1907), 89-93.

Porter, Whitworth. *History of the Corps of Royal Engineers*, vol. I. London: Longmans, Green, and Co., 1889.

Pouchot, Pierre. *Memoirs on the Late War in North America between France and England.* 3 Vols.; Yverdon: 1781. Trans. Michael Cardy and Ed. Brian Leigh Dunnigan. Youngstown, New York: Old Fort Niagara Association, 1994.

Preston, Richard and Lamontagne, Leopold. *Royal Fort Frontenac.* Toronto: University of Toronto Press, 1958.

Public Records of the Colony of Connecticut, 1636-1776. 15 vols.; Hartford: Brown & Parsons Co., 1850-1890.

Rapport de l'Archiviste de la Quebec pour 1931-1932. Quebec: Rédempti Paradis, 1932: La Pause, "Mémoire et Observations sur mon Voyage en Canada," and Poulariès, "Relation de Poulariès Envoyé à Marquis de Montcalm," 47-125.

Rapport de l'Archiviste de la Quebec pour 1932-1933. Quebec: Rédempti Paradis, 1933: La Pause, "Les Mémoires du Chevalier de La Pause," 303-391.

Rapport de l'Archiviste de la Quebec pour 1933-1934. Quebec: Rédempti Paradis, 1933: La Pause, "Les Papiers La Pause," 65-231.

Ray, F.M., ed. "The Journal of Dr. Caleb Rea written during the expedition against Ticonderoga in 1758." *Essex Institute Historical Collections,* Vol. 18 (1881), 81-120.

Remington, Fredric, ed. "Joshua Goodnough's Old Letter." *Harper's Magazine,* (Nov. 1897), 878-889.

Report on the Public Archives for 1929. Ottawa: F.A. Acland, 1930. "Montcalm's Correspondence," 31-108.

Richards, Fredrick B. *The Black Watch at Ticonderoga.* Ticonderoga, NY: Ft. Ticonderoga Museum, 1929.

Richardson, Amos. "Amos Richardson's Journal," *The Bulletin of the Fort Ticonderoga Museum,* XII, #4 (1968), 267-291.

Ricord, Frederick W. *Archives of the State of New Jersey: Documents Relating to the Colonial History of the State of New Jersey,* 1st series, vol. 13-18. Trenton: John L. Murray Publishing Co., 1890-1893.

Riker, Thad. "The Politics behind Braddock's Expedition," *American Historical Review,* vol. 13, no. 4 (Jul 1908), 742-752.

Rocque, Mary Ann. *A Set of Plans and Forts in North America, Reduced from Actual Surveys.* London: M.A. Rocque, 1763.

Rogers, Robert. *The Journals of Major Robert Rogers.* London: 1765. Ann Arbor, MI: University Microfilms, Inc., 1966.

Rogers, H.C.B. *The British Army of the 18th Century.* London: George Allen & Unwin, 1977.

Rouville, Albert. *William Pitt, Earl of Chatham,* 3 vols. New York: G.P. Putnam's Sons, 1907.

Sargent, Winthrop. *The History of an Expedition Against Fort Du Quesne.* Lewisburg, PA: Wennawoods Pub., 1997.

Sautai, Maurice. *Montcalm at the Battle of Carillon.* Paris: 1909. Trans. John S. Watts. Ticonderoga, NY: Fort Ticonderoga Museum, 1941.

Schutz, John A. "The Disaster of Fort Ticonderoga: The Shortage of Muskets during the Mobilization of 1758." *Huntington Library Quarterly,* 24 (1951), 307-315.

Scot's Magazine, Edinburgh.

Searing, Dr. James. "The Battle of Ticonderoga, 1758," *New-York Historical Society Proceedings,* vol. V (Oct 1847), 112-117.

Shute, Daniel. "Journal of the Rev. Daniel Shute," *EIHC,* (1874), 132-151.

Stanley, George F.G. *New France: The Last Phase, 1744-1760.* Toronto: McCelland and Stewart Ltd., 1968.

Stark, Caleb. *Memoir and Official Correspondence of Gen. John Stark.* Concord: Edson C. Eastman, 1877.

Steele, Ian K. *Betrayals: Fort William Henry & the "Massacre."* New York: Oxford University Press, 1990.

Stewart, David. *Sketches of the Character, Manners, and Present State of the Highlanders of Scotland.* 2 vols.; London: 1822; Edinburgh: John Donald Publishers Ltd., 1977.

Sullivan, James and Hamilton, Milton W., eds. *The Papers of Sir William Johnson.* 14 vols.; Albany: University of the State of New York, 1921-65.

Sweat, William. "Captian William Sweat's Personal Diary of the Expedition against Ticonderoga May 2—Nov 7, 1758." *Essex Institute Historical Collections,* vol. 93 (1957), 36-57.

Thompson, Samuel. *Diary of Lieut. Samuel Thompson of Woburn, Massachusetts while serving in the French War, 1758.* Ed. William Cutter. Boston: David Clapp & Son, 1896.

Tomlinson, Abraham (ed.) *The Military Journals of Two Private Soldiers, 1758-1775.* Poughkeepsie: A. Tomlinson, 1855.

Trowbridge, Francis Bacon. *The Champion Genealogy.* New Haven: Private Printing, 1891.

Vaudreuil, Marquis de. "Marquis Vaudreuil to Sieur de Lotbiniere, 20 September 1755." *Fort Ticonderoga Museum Bulletin,* I, no. 3 (1928), 2-3.

Westbrook, Nicholas, ed. "Like roaring lions breaking from their chains." *The Bulletin of the Fort Ticonderoga Museum,* XVI, no. 1 (1998), 16-91.

Williams, Basil. *The Life of William Pitt, Earl of Chatham,* I. London: Longmans, Green, & Co., 1915.

Williams, Thomas. "The Correspondence of Dr. Thomas Williams of Deerfield, Massachusetts." *The Historical Magazine,* 2nd series, no. 7 (1870), 209-216.

ACKNOWLEDGMENTS

First and foremost, thank you Lord. Secondly, I must thank my wife Pam and my children for their support, which included a few trips to the fort. To my friends and colleagues, those at the various institutions and libraries who have helped me in this, and the people at Folgers, you have my thanks as well. I would also like to thank a number of authors from the past and present: Francis Parkman, Lawrence Gipson, and Ian Steele whose works I have found influential; with beacons such as these it becomes much easier to illuminate this period of the past.

Lastly, I would like to thank all those who preserve the monuments of the past in the Champlain Valley, and in particular Fort Ticonderoga, and the role they played in the shaping of the United States of America.

INDEX

Abenaki, 43, 64

Abercrombie, James, xii, 49-52, 55, 135-136, 145, 160, 162, 184, 201

Abercromby, James
army's landing near Fort Carillon and, 112
army in state of confusion and, 120
arrival at Howe's camp and, 89-90
as field commander and, 75, 128-133, 149-150, 154-156
being replaced after the battle and, xii, 179
captured officers and, 102, 183
changes in staff and, 80
countering French movements and, 24
holding council of war and, 135-140
Joshua Loring as advisor to, 188-189
letter from William Pitt and, 71-73
meeting with Robert Rogers and, 54-57
questioning Eyre's ability to command, 193
questions after the battle and, 159-169
recruitment efforts and, 82-84, 88, 108-109
returns of action report, 182-183
securing winter quarters for army and, 177-178
strengths as an organizer and, 75-77
taking command and, 19-20
transportation problems and, 85-86, 107

Albany, 18-21, 32, 37-38, 54, 58-59, 71, 74, 78, 82, 84, 86-89, 164-165, 177-178, 196

Albertson, Garret, 117, 120-121, 151

Alcide, 7, 18

Amherst, Jeffrey, 73, 88-89, 109, 164, 166, 169-170, 177-179, 188, 193

Angel, Samuel, 37

Anson, George, 7

Artillery Cove, 31

Auxerrois Regiment, 15

Bald Mountain (Rogers Slide), 62, 67-68, 106, 115, 198, 202

Bartman, George, 32-34, 37-41

Bassignac, Jean, 152

Bear Mountain, 62, 64-65, 69

Bearn, 2, 46, 103, 105, 141-142, 146, 152, 197-200

Bergen op Zoom, 193

Bernard, Antoine, 103, 105, 122, 124, 142, 144, 148, 158, 199-201

Berry Regiment, 27, 99, 103, 128-129, 141-147, 153-154